The Psychology Major's Handbook

Fifth Edition

To my best friend, FHM.

—TKM

Sara Miller McCune founded SAGE Publishing in 1965 to support the dissemination of usable knowledge and educate a global community. SAGE publishes more than 1000 journals and over 800 new books each year, spanning a wide range of subject areas. Our growing selection of library products includes archives, data, case studies and video. SAGE remains majority owned by our founder and after her lifetime will become owned by a charitable trust that secures the company's continued independence.

Los Angeles | London | New Delhi | Singapore | Washington DC | Melbourne

The Psychology Major's Handbook
Fifth Edition

Tara L. Kuther
Western Connecticut State University

Los Angeles | London | New Delhi
Singapore | Washington DC | Melbourne

FOR INFORMATION:

SAGE Publications, Inc.
2455 Teller Road
Thousand Oaks, California 91320
E-mail: order@sagepub.com

SAGE Publications Ltd.
1 Oliver's Yard
55 City Road
London EC1Y 1SP
United Kingdom

SAGE Publications India Pvt. Ltd.
B 1/I 1 Mohan Cooperative Industrial Area
Mathura Road, New Delhi 110 044
India

SAGE Publications Asia-Pacific Pte. Ltd.
18 Cross Street #10-10/11/12
China Square Central
Singapore 048423

Acquisitions Editor: Lara Para
Editorial Assistant: Drew Fabricius
Production Editor: Bennie Clark Allen
Copy Editor: Christina West
Typesetter: C&M Digitals (P) Ltd.
Proofreader: Eleni Maria Georgiou
Indexer: Jean Casalegno
Cover Designer: Karine Hovsepian
Marketing Manager: Katherine Hepburn

Printed in the United States of America

Library of Congress Cataloging-in-Publication Data

Names: Kuther, Tara L., author.

Title: The psychology major's handbook / Tara L. Kuther, Western Connecticut State University.

Description: Fifth edition. | Los Angeles : SAGE, [2020] | Includes bibliographical references and index.

Identifiers: LCCN 2018042202 | ISBN 9781544359465 (pbk. : alk. paper)

Subjects: LCSH: Psychology—Study and teaching (Higher) | Psychology—Vocational guidance. | Psychology, Applied—Vocational guidance.

Classification: LCC BF77 .K855 2020 | DDC 150.71/1—dc23
LC record available at https://lccn.loc.gov/2018042202

This book is printed on acid-free paper.

19 20 21 22 23 10 9 8 7 6 5 4 3 2 1

• Brief Contents •

• Detailed Contents •

Chapter 5 • Self-Management Skills 97

Chapter 6 • Study Tips: Tools for Academic Success 113

• Preface •

More people go to college than ever before. Psychology is consistently among the most popular majors, with about 117,000 baccalaureate degrees awarded in 2016 (up from about 94,000 in 2000). Nearly 2 decades ago I began writing the first edition of *The Psychology Major's Handbook*. I envisioned it as a source of practical information for students who are considering majoring in psychology and as an informal mentor to guide psychology majors as they complete their degree. Choosing a major is one of the most stressful decisions that college students make. *The Psychology Major's Handbook* examines how to choose a major, the competencies acquired by psychology majors, as well as career options at the undergraduate and graduate level.

As in prior editions, the fifth edition of *The Psychology Major's Handbook* covers topics relevant to all students, such as how to succeed in college, develop an active learning style, hone study skills, and become more self-aware. New college students are often surprised by the autonomy required of students. Perhaps the biggest difference between high school and college is that college requires students to take an active role in their education. *The Psychology Major's Handbook* is intended to help students recognize their role in steering their own education. No book can replace the guidance of a faculty advisor, but *The Psychology Major's Handbook* is a helpful resource for students who seek general assistance and it may serve as a springboard for student-advisor discussions.

The Psychology Major's Handbook is also tailored to the specific needs of psychology students. Chapters take a close look at the process of writing psychology term papers, how to read psychology articles, and how to write an APA-style empirical report. Psychology students learn how to gain valuable academic and applied experiences, search for a job after graduation, and apply to graduate school in psychology.

Overview of *The Psychology Major's Handbook*

The Psychology Major's Handbook is organized to accompany students on their journey from Introductory Psychology through graduation. Chapter 1 introduces students to the scope of psychology, including subspecialties, the wide range of places where psychologists work, and academic degrees. Chapter 2 aids students facing the challenge of choosing a college major by discussing self-assessment as a tool for learning about oneself and providing a series of exercises to help students discover their interests and abilities in order to determine whether psychology is the right choice. Chapter 3 examines careers for psychology majors. Readers learn about what employers look for, jobs that emphasize the research and interpersonal skills that psychology students acquire, and how to match training with career goals.

Chapters 4 through 8 are intended to accompany students through the college years, serving as a resource to periodically review. Chapter 4 examines how students can take an active role in their education and seek opportunities for personal and professional development, including developing relationships with faculty and obtaining research and applied experiences. Chapter 5, a new chapter, examines the role of self-management in academic success, including information about motivation, mindset, time management, and managing distractions. Reading, note-taking, test-taking, and study skills are covered in Chapter 6. Chapter 7 examines the psychology term paper or literature review: how to choose a topic, narrow it, locate information, understand the format of research articles, take notes, avoid plagiarism, write the first draft, and revise it. In Chapter 8, the empirical paper is demystified. Readers learn about the structure of the empirical paper, what to include in each section, and APA style; a template describing and illustrating APA style is provided at the end of the chapter.

Chapters 9 through 11 encourage students to think ahead, after graduation. Chapter 9 provides advice on how to obtain a job after graduation, including finding positions, completing applications, writing résumés and cover letters, and preparing for interviews. Chapter 10 examines careers that require a graduate degree, takes a close look at the master's degree with specialties in psychology and related fields, and discusses careers for master's and doctoral degree holders. The final chapter, Chapter 11, provides application advice for students who are interested in attending graduate school. Readers are encouraged to examine their reasons for applying to graduate school. Specific advice is provided on gathering program information, evaluating programs, preparing for the GRE, completing admissions essays, acquiring recommendation letters, and succeeding in interviews.

As in prior editions, the fifth edition of *The Psychology Major's Handbook* emphasizes active learning. Exercises and writing prompts help readers consider how the material applies to them and what actions they might take to shape their own professional development. It is my hope that *The Psychology Major's Handbook* will help students determine the path that is right for them and aid them on their journey. I hope to aid faculty in encouraging students to make informed decisions about their major and to help faculty support and guide students through the college years.

New to the Fifth Edition of *The Psychology Major's Handbook*

Each chapter has been reviewed and updated. I've paid particular attention to the role of technology in students' lives. Where relevant, students' everyday use of technology is acknowledged and information about technology and social media is included. Some of the specific changes are as follows.

Chapter 1

- Added coverage of Community Psychology and a new "Myths About Psychology" section

- Updated Table 1.1 ("Subfields in Psychology")

- Retitled "Real Tips for Real Students" as "Practical Tips" throughout

- Updated and expanded Exercise 1.2 ("Psychology in the Media")

Chapter 2

- Revised the "College Majors and Careers" section and the "Become Informed of Your Options" and "Skills and Knowledge You'll Develop as a Psychology Major" subsections

- Added new Exercises 2.1 ("Learning About Majors: Questions to Consider"), 2.2 ("Learning About Majors: What to Ask Recent Graduates"), and 2.3 ("Learning About Majors: What to Ask Professors"), and 2.6 ("Identify Your Holland Personality Type")

- Updated and expanded Exercise 2.4 ("Learning About Majors: Summing Up What You've Learned"), and revised Exercises 2.5 ("Assess Your Personal Traits") and 2.7 ("Assess Your Skills")

- Added new coverage in the "Reduce Stress and Gain Insight Into Yourself" subsection and a new "Psychological Literacy" subsection

- Reorganized the "How to Learn About Yourself" section

- Revised the reflection prompts (replaced "My Questions" with "Why Psychology?")

Chapter 3

- Moved from Chapter 7 to Chapter 3

- Updated the career statistics and a new "Salaries in Psychology" section

- Updated Tables 3.1 ("Top 15 Attributes Employers Seek in Prospective Employees") and 3.2 ("Positions Obtained by Psychology Majors")

- Updated the "Skills and Attributes Sought by Employers" section

- Reorganized the "Jobs for Psychology Majors" section and "Research and Applied Experience" subsection

- Retitled the "Administrative Assistant" (now "Office Management") subsection and the Human Service Skills (now "Job Settings That Emphasize Interpersonal Skills") section

- Updated coverage of O*NET

- Revised the "Match Your Training to Your Goals" section

- Added new Exercise 3.4 ("Assess and Improve Your Fit")

- Added a new Practical Tip ("Consider a Minor")

Chapter 4

- Added a new section ("Take an Active Role: Academic Advising") and revised additional sections ("Get to Know Professors" and "Get Applied Experience") and a subsection ("Why Do Professors Seek Student Research Assistants?")

- Moved Table 4.1 ("Academic Advising Checklist")

- Updated Exercises 4.1 ("Do You Display Appropriate In- and Out-of-Class Behavior?") and 4.2 ("What Not to Do: 15 Behaviors That Turn Off Faculty") and expanded Exercise 4.6 ("Academic and Professional Organizations")

- Added a new Table 4.2 ("Characteristics of Effective Mentors")

- Updated and reorganized Table 4.4 ("Undergraduate Psychology Journals")

Chapter 5

- Added this new chapter on self-management skills

Chapter 6

- Updated Exercise 6.1 ("Study Skills Assessment")

- Updated and revised the "Reading Textbooks With the SQ3R Method" subsection

- Provided a new Practical Tip ("Rereading Is Not an Effective Study Strategy")

- Added a new reflection prompt ("My Last Exam")

Chapter 7

- Updated Tables 7.2 ("Psychology Dictionaries and Resources") and 7.3 ("Conducting a Literature Search With PsycINFO")

- Revised and updated the "Reference Librarian," "Psychology Journals," "Don't Rely on Google," and "Take Notes" subsections

- Updated the Practical Tip ("Supplement Your Search With Google Scholar")

Chapter 8

- Edited the material throughout
- Updated Table 8.2 ("APA Style Checklist")

Chapter 9

- Added a new Practical Tip ("Characteristics of an Effective LinkedIn Photo")
- Added a new Table 9.1 ("Social Media and Hiring Decisions: When Social Media Harms")
- Updated Exercises 9.2 ("Become Aware of Your Digital Footprint"), 9.6 ("Construct a LinkedIn Profile"), 9.7 ("Common Interview Questions"), and 9.8 ("Questions to Ask During an Interview")
- Updated the "Parts of the Résumé" subsection
- Reorganized and updated Table 9.2 ("Action Verbs for Your Résumé") and provided new examples in Tables 9.3 ("Chronological Résumé") and 9.4 ("Functional Résumé")

Chapter 10

- Updated the career statistics and the "Financial Opportunities and Considerations" and "What Can You Do With a Doctoral Degree?" subsections
- Updated Table 10.2 ("Master's Degrees in Other Helping Fields")

Chapter 11

- Added new Exercise 11.1 ("Is Graduate School for You?")
- Expanded the "Can You Afford Graduate School?" subsection
- Reorganized the "Are You Prepared for the Academic Demands of Graduate Study?" and "Are You Prepared for the Personal Demands of Graduate Study?" subsections
- Updated the "Professional Psychologist-Practitioner Model (PsyD)" subsection
- Updated the GRE statistics and revised the "GRE Psychology Test" subsection to the new 2017 format
- Updated Table 11.4 ("Sample Curriculum Vitae")
- Reorganized the "What Do Graduate Admissions Committees Look For?" section
- Added the new "Wait-List" subsection

• Acknowledgments •

The Psychology Major's Handbook has benefited from the input of many. All of what appears in these pages has been inspired by over 20 years of interaction with my students and colleagues at Western Connecticut State University, whom I thank for sharing their experiences, questions, ideas, and enthusiasm. I am appreciative of the constructive comments and helpful suggestions offered by colleagues, instructors, students, and readers over the last one and one-half decades. I thank Vicki Knight, editor of the first and second editions, for her support in my early years as an author. I appreciate the oversight provided by Jon-David Hague and Tim Matray on the third and fourth editions, respectively.

Most notably, I am ecstatic that *The Psychology Major's Handbook* has found a new home at SAGE. I am humbled by the support I've received from my SAGE family, and I thank Reid Hester and Michele Sordi. I am especially fortunate to work with my talented editor, Lara Parra, who is responsible for this seamless transition.

Finally, I thank my family, both Kuther and Martell, especially my parents Philip and Irene Kuther, who have provided unwavering support and guidance. My very patient husband, Fred Martell, provided emotional and logistical support to make this book—and my career—happen. And of course, I thank D and D.

SAGE Publishing would also like to gratefully acknowledge the reviewers who generously provided feedback for this edition.

• About the Author •

Tara L. Kuther is professor of psychology at Western Connecticut State University, where she has taught courses in child, adolescent, and adult development for over 20 years. She earned her BA in psychology from Western Connecticut State University and her MA and PhD in developmental psychology from Fordham University. Dr. Kuther is a Fellow of the Society for the Teaching of Psychology (American Psychological Association, Division 2), has served in various capacities in the Society for the Teaching of Psychology and the Society for Research on Adolescence, and is the former chair of the Teaching Committee for the Society for Research in Child Development. She is author of the award-winning *Lifespan Development: Lives in Context* and *Lifespan Development in Context: A Topical Approach*. Dr. Kuther is coauthor of *Careers in Psychology: Opportunities in a Changing World* (with Robert Morgan). Her research interests include social cognition and risky activity in adolescence and adulthood.

1

What Is Psychology?

Chapter Outline	

What Is Psychology?
Psychology's Breadth
    Behavioral Neuroscience
    Clinical Psychology
    Cognitive Psychology
    Community Psychology
    Counseling Psychology
    Developmental Psychology
    Educational Psychology
    Experimental Psychology
    Forensic Psychology
    Health Psychology
    Human Factors Psychology
    Industrial-Organizational
        Psychology
    Quantitative Psychology and
        Psychometrics
    School Psychology
    Social Psychology
	Exercise 1.1: Subfields of Psychology

Myths About Psychology
    Myth: Psychology Is Just
        Common Sense
    Myth: Psychology Is Not a
        Real Science
    Myth: Psychologists Can Read
        Your Mind
    Myth: Majoring in Psychology
        Will Make You a Psychologist
	Exercise 1.2: Psychology in the Media

(Continued)

(Continued)

Chapter Outline	

Degrees in Psychology
   Bachelor's Degree in
      Psychology
   Master's Degree in
      Psychology
   Doctoral Degree in
      Psychology
   Why Major in Psychology?
	Exercise 1.3: Internet Scavenger Hunt

Overview of *The Psychology Major's Handbook*	

Close your eyes and envision a psychologist at work. What do you see? What is he or she doing? Does your image include any of the following?

- Conducting research with monkeys
- Monitoring a magnetic resonance imaging (MRI) machine to understand what parts of the brain are active when people view pictures of various items and situations
- Creating and administering a survey on employee perceptions of their work environments
- Developing and evaluating an intervention for families with a history of domestic violence
- Helping educators learn about how the mind works and how to teach most effectively
- Counseling a client who suffers from depression
- Teaching physicians how to understand the emotions that accompany illness in order to communicate more effectively with patients
- Developing and implementing training programs for employees
- Helping police departments by providing information about criminal behavior, assisting officers in managing stress, or explaining the limitations of eyewitness testimony

If you answered yes to any of these examples, you would be right because psychologists engage in each of these activities and more. Are you surprised? Although psychologists are most often portrayed in the media as therapists in private practice settings, psychologists do much more than provide therapy. In this chapter we discuss the broad range of activities and responsibilities that fall under the umbrella of psychological science.

What Is Psychology?

Broadly speaking, psychology is defined as *the scientific study of behavior.* Behavior refers to anything an animal or a person does, feels, or thinks. Many students are surprised to learn that some psychologists work with animals. Psychologists often study animal physiology and behavior to extend what they learn to humans. As scientists, psychologists apply precise methods of observation, data collection, analysis, and interpretation to learn about what makes people and animals behave like they do. Psychologists generate hypotheses, or educated guesses, about what might cause a particular behavior or phenomenon, and they conduct careful scientific research to test those hypotheses. The field of psychology examines interactions among the brain, the environment, psychological functioning, and behavior. For example, topics of psychological study include social relationships, the brain and the chemicals that influence it, visual and auditory perception, human development, the causes of normative and atypical behavior, and much more. Psychologists conduct a variety of activities in many settings. Of course, we cannot forget that psychologists also work directly with people, applying psychological science to help improve their lives.

Most people are most familiar with psychologists' roles as service providers, providing psychological therapy and treatment to clients. However, less than half of psychologists work in service provider roles (Lin, Christidis, & Stamm, 2017a, 2017b). What do the rest do? Some psychologists are employed as professors at universities, community colleges, and high schools. Others work as researchers in university, hospital, corporate, and government settings. Psychologists work as administrators, managing hospitals, mental health clinics, nonprofit organizations, government agencies, businesses, schools, and more. Most psychologists perform in more than one of these roles. For example, a psychologist who works as a college professor might also have a private practice or conduct research with a social service agency.

Psychology's Breadth

Psychology is a diverse discipline. A wide range of topics fall under the umbrella of psychology and each topic is its own specialized field of study. The following sections present the most common specialties within psychology. In each of these areas, some psychologists spend most of their time conducting research to expand the knowledge base, some practice or apply research findings to help people and communities, and some do both, as scientist-practitioners. In addition, over one-third of psychologists teach and conduct research at colleges and universities. The following sections briefly examine the subfields of psychology.

PRACTICAL TIP
INTRODUCTORY PSYCHOLOGY OFFERS JUST THE BRIEFEST TASTE OF PSYCHOLOGY

It's not uncommon for students to find the Introductory or General Psychology course challenging. There's a good reason for that: Introductory Psychology presents the entire field of psychology at a whirlwind and dizzying pace. As you learn, try to remember that each chapter of your Introductory Psychology text presents an overview of an entire subfield of psychology—an area in which psychologists specialize and spend their entire lives working. If you find a particular chapter interesting, note that your college offers at least one and often more than one course in that area. If you find a chapter (and thus subfield) uninteresting, the good part about the Introductory Psychology course is that you'll move on to a different chapter and different subfield in just a week or two.

Behavioral Neuroscience

Behavioral neuroscience refers to the psychological and physiological study of the brain and behavior. How do neurotransmitters influence our behavior? What part of the brain is responsible for motivation, language, or emotion? Behavioral neuroscientists conduct research to answer questions about how the brain influences our emotions and behavior. They teach and conduct scientific research in academic settings, as well as train medical doctors, clinical psychologists, and other health professionals. Some behavioral neuroscientists conduct applied work as part of a health care team assessing and treating persons with brain injuries in clinics and within neurology, psychiatric, and pediatric units of hospitals.

Clinical Psychology

Clinical psychologists study, diagnose, and treat persons who experience emotional, behavioral, and psychological problems or disorders. Most people are familiar with the practitioner role of a clinical psychologist as it is commonly depicted on television. Clinical psychologists may treat people with problems ranging from normative life changes, like helping someone deal with grief or a crisis, to more serious and chronic disorders such as anxiety and mood disorders. Some clinical psychologists work with specific age groups, such as children or older adults. Others specialize in particular problems, such as depression or anxiety. Some psychologists are generalists and treat people of all ages and with all types of problems. Not all clinical psychologists conduct therapy. Many conduct scientific research. For example, clinical psychologists may research risk factors for mental disorders, such as how genetic and environmental factors contribute to mental health. Others study treatments, such as the effectiveness of a given medication, therapy, or intervention. Finally, clinical psychologists work in universities as professors and researchers.

Cognitive Psychology

Cognitive psychology is the scientific study of the mind and mental processes. It examines the nature of thought, known as *cognition*. Cognitive psychologists study how we think—specifically, how we take in information, store it, learn, and use it to make decisions. Topics of study include attention, memory, learning, and decision-making. Some cognitive psychologists study these processes in animals and apply what they learn to humans. Some specialize in particular age groups, such as studying attention in infants or memory in older adults. Cognitive psychology is part of a larger interdisciplinary field of *cognitive science*, which includes findings from other research disciplines such as neuroscience, anthropology, and linguistics. Cognitive psychologists and scientists are found in academic settings as professors and researchers. They are also found in applied settings where they might assist companies in applying cognitive research to improve their products or to better advertise them. For example, Internet companies may turn to cognitive psychologists to provide information about how people scan webpages and make decisions online.

Community Psychology

Individuals are embedded in groups, including families, communities, and society. Community psychologists seek to understand how individuals and their communities interact—that is, how communities influence individuals as well as how individuals influence their communities. Community psychologists who conduct applied work may examine how neighborhood resources promote well-being in community members and may create prevention and intervention programs to address emerging problems. Community psychologists work in government settings, such as for city councils, where they might study community functioning and needs to anticipate and address problems before they escalate. Others work in human service settings, for school districts, and as researchers in policy settings. In academic settings, community psychologists teach and conduct research.

Counseling Psychology

Counseling psychologists engage in many of the same activities as clinical psychologists but focus their activities on normative functioning, rather than psychological disorders. As researchers, counseling psychologists study how to help people manage everyday life issues, such as divorce, remarriage, career changes, and transitions to and from college. Practicing counseling psychologists help people adjust to life changes and provide vocational assessment and career guidance. Like clinical psychologists, counseling psychologists work in academic settings as professors and researchers and in community settings such as mental health clinics, halfway houses, college counseling centers, criminal justice settings, and social service agencies.

Developmental Psychology

Developmental psychologists study human development across the life span. In academic settings, developmental psychologists teach and conduct scientific research on the emotional, intellectual, and physical development of children, adolescents, and adults. Research topics include a diverse array of issues such as whether most adults experience a midlife crisis, how babies learn to crawl, or what factors influence adolescent drug use. Developmental psychologists also work as researchers, consultants, and program evaluators in applied settings, such as pediatric hospitals, geriatric centers, and nonprofit organizations. A developmental psychologist might provide advice on how to design a nursing home that meets the needs of older adults or develop and evaluate early childhood education programs. Some developmental psychologists engage in applied activities, such as conducting developmental assessments of children to ensure that they are timely in meeting developmental milestones.

Educational Psychology

Educational psychologists study how people learn and apply that knowledge to educational settings. They develop methods and materials to increase the efficiency and effectiveness of educational programs and curricula designed for people of all ages. Educational psychologists work in academic settings and conduct research on learning and instruction. Some study how people learn to read or complete math problems. Others train teachers and develop methods of instruction to enhance the educational setting.

Experimental Psychology

Experimental psychologists specialize in conducting scientific research. While all psychologists are trained in scientific research, experimental psychologists' education emphasizes methodology and statistics skills. They are experts in conducting research. Experimental psychologists usually focus their research on one topical area within psychology such as cognition, perception, human performance, or social psychology. Some experimental psychologists study animals to apply what they learn to humans, or simply because animal behavior is interesting. Most experimental psychologists are employed in academic settings, teaching and conducting research. Others work as researchers for businesses, corporations, and the government.

Forensic Psychology

Forensic psychologists study legal issues from a psychological perspective. They conduct scientific research on topics such as the reliability of eyewitness testimony, juror selection, and how to interview eyewitnesses without contaminating their testimony. Forensic psychologists apply research findings by providing expert testimony on cases in criminal, civil, and family courts. They may evaluate prisoners, assist in making parole decisions, and assess defendants to determine whether they are competent to provide testimony. Forensic psychologists work not only with lawyers and judges but also with police departments to select, train, and evaluate police officers. Forensic psychologists are found in academic settings as well as applied settings, such a law firms, government agencies, and policy settings.

Health Psychology

Health psychologists study how psychological, biological, and social factors influence health and illness. They conduct scientific research on health-related topics, such as whether relaxation techniques and social support can help people overcome illness more quickly, or how to change people's attitudes about smoking. Health psychologists design, assess, and modify programs to promote health and wellness (e.g., stress management, smoking cessation, and weight loss). They work in academic and research settings such as universities and medical schools, as well as in applied settings such as hospitals and clinics.

Human Factors Psychology

Human factors or engineering psychologists study how people interact with machines, environments, and products. They conduct research on how people understand and use machines to increase people's safety, efficiency, and productivity. Human factors psychologists might work on designing a computer monitor to prevent user fatigue and eyestrain, or they might arrange the instruments on a car's dashboard to enhance access and safety. Human factors psychologists design, evaluate, and modify military equipment, airplanes, computer terminals, and consumer products. Most human factors psychologists work in industry and government; some work in academic settings.

Industrial-Organizational Psychology

Industrial and organizational psychologists apply psychological principles and scientific research findings to the workplace. They are concerned with the relation between people and work. Industrial and organizational psychologists often work for companies, corporations, and the government, studying how to recruit, select, train, and evaluate employees. They conduct applied research on questions like what personality factors make a good employee, how to improve worker productivity, and characteristics of effective leaders. Industrial and organizational psychologists develop programs to improve employee morale and make the workplace more efficient and pleasant. Others teach and conduct research as members of academic departments in psychology and business.

Quantitative Psychology and Psychometrics

Quantitative psychologists study and develop new scientific methods and techniques for acquiring, analyzing, and applying information. Quantitative psychologists help other researchers in designing, conducting, and interpreting experiments. Psychometricians, a type of quantitative psychologist, specialize in testing. They create and revise psychological tests, intelligence tests, and aptitude tests. Quantitative psychologists and psychometricians work as researchers in academic, business, and government settings.

School Psychology

School psychologists work to foster the intellectual, emotional, educational, and social development of children. They apply the science of psychology to the school environment. School psychologists conduct research on educational topics such as how the classroom climate influences student learning, or how to promote appropriate behavior in the classroom. They work in schools to assess and counsel students, work with parents and teachers, and develop behavioral interventions.

Social Psychology

Social psychologists study how people interact with each other and how they are influenced by the social environment. They conduct research on personality theories, attitude formation and change, persuasion and conformity, and how people relate to one another, including attraction, prejudice, group dynamics, teamwork, and aggression. Social psychologists work in academic settings as teachers and researchers, but they also work for corporations and advertising agencies, conducting marketing research and studying how consumers view products.

Clearly, psychology is diverse and entails much more than conducting therapy with patients relaxing on leather sofas. Instead, the field of psychology offers a variety of careers in direct service, academics, government, and business. That is, not all psychologists conduct therapy or even study people. What all of the subfields of psychology have in common, however, is a concern with understanding the causes of behavior (Table 1.1 and Exercise 1.1).

PRACTICAL TIP
START YOUR OWN PSYCHOLOGY DATABASE

One of the first things psychology students often learn is that the field is constantly evolving and changing. Keep up with the ever-changing field by creating your own database of resources. Cultivate a list of bookmarks, subscribe to newsletters, and follow researchers, psychologists, and organizations on

Twitter and/or Facebook. Save articles and ideas in a folder or note on your computer, phone, or app. Cloud services, like Evernote, Google Keep, DropBox, and OneNote, are also great options for saving material and enabling quick effective searches later. Organize your sources as well as what you learn and you'll not only expand your knowledge of psychology, but you'll also gather ideas for future papers and projects. Before long you will have cultivated a small library of sources and findings that can help you learn more about the topics that interest you. Students who keep track of interesting findings and ideas find it easier to come up with topics for class papers and assignments.

TABLE 1.1 ● Subfields in Psychology

Subfield	Emphasis
Behavioral Neuroscience	Brain and behavior
Clinical Psychology	Emotional, behavioral, and psychological problems or disorders
Cognitive Psychology	Mind and mental processes
Community Psychology	Interactions between individuals and their communities
Counseling Psychology	Normative function and healthy adaptation
Developmental Psychology	Optimizing human development across the life span
Educational Psychology	Understanding how people learn and modifying educational settings accordingly
Experimental Psychology	Scientific methodology and research
Forensic Psychology	Applying psychology to inform and study legal issues
Health Psychology	Psychological, biological, and social influences on health and wellness
Human Factors or Engineering Psychology	People's interactions with machines, environments, and products
Industrial-Organizational Psychology	Optimizing the workplace
Quantitative Psychology and Psychometrics	Devising techniques for acquiring, measuring, and analyzing behavior
School Psychology	Fostering children's development in the school setting
Social Psychology	People's interactions with each other and the social environment

EXERCISE 1.1
SUBFIELDS OF PSYCHOLOGY

Choose three subfields of psychology, and do the following for each:

1. Explain the subfield in more detail than provided here.

2. Identify at least one psychologist in the subfield and discuss his or her work.

3. Describe two other topics of research conducted by psychologists in the subfield.

Myths About Psychology

Try this experiment. As you go about your day at home, work, or school, ask the people you meet a simple question: "What's psychology?" Or, for more interesting answers, ask "What do you think of psychology?" You'll find that everyone knows a little something about psychology, but knowledge is often intermingled with misconceptions. Some of the common myths or misconceptions about psychology are as follows.

Myth: Psychology Is Just Common Sense

Common sense refers to the knowledge that anyone with sound reasoning capacities should know. Many people believe that psychology research simply confirms what "everyone knows." Yet some psychology findings are counterintuitive. For example, promoting children's self-esteem does not improve their school performance, some people are not "right brained" or "left brained," and students do not learn better when teachers match their learning style (Baumeister, Campbell, Krueger, & Vohs, 2003; Corballis, Lalueza-Fox, Orlando, Enard, & Green, 2014; Gazzaniga, 1998). Just become something seems that it should be true doesn't mean that it is. That's why we test our hypotheses—and we often find that folk beliefs are false. As you study psychology you'll encounter many research findings that will make you think twice about what you believe is "common sense."

Myth: Psychology Is Not a Real Science

Let's consider the nature of science. *Science* refers to the process of building and acquiring knowledge about natural phenomena though the use of systematic observation and experimentation. Scientists collect empirical evidence (data) to develop and test explanations for phenomena. They create theories to explain observations and generate hypotheses to systematically test their theories. Through the application of the scientific method, scientists systematically test and revise hypotheses in light of their data. Psychologists use this very process—the scientific method—in conducting research in which they test hypotheses about human and animal behavior.

Myth: Psychologists Can Read Your Mind

If you choose to major in psychology, don't be surprised if someone, such as a friend or family member, jokes or even seriously asks about your emerging ability to read minds. A psychology education does not impart the ability to read other people's minds (if only!). You will, however, gain insight into people's behavior and that knowledge may make it seem to others as if you have a portal into their minds.

Myth: Majoring in Psychology Will Make You a Psychologist

One of the most important things that psychology majors must understand is that the bachelor's degree in psychology *does not* prepare graduates to be psychologists. It typically takes another 5 to 8 years of study after the bachelor's degree to become a psychologist. So how does one become a psychologist? We consider this question next.

EXERCISE 1.2
PSYCHOLOGY IN THE MEDIA

Locate a magazine article or website describing a research finding having to do with psychology.

1. Provide a brief summary of the findings as described in the article.

2. Explain what subfield of psychology the research represents.

3. Consider the findings described in the article. What further questions do you have? What questions should be addressed next? If you were the researcher whose work was mentioned in article, what would you try to learn next?

4. Locate the research study cited in the article (if a link isn't provided, try searching for the researchers' names).

5. Read the abstract and provide a one-sentence explanation of the authors' findings.

6. Compare the description provided in the abstract with the magazine or web article. How accurately are the research findings portrayed? Why do you think there are (or are not) discrepancies?

Degrees in Psychology

Before we begin our discussion about education in psychology, it is important to note that a bachelor's degree prepares students for a wide range of careers. Graduate study entails more specialized training, as discussed in the following sections, but is not needed to have a successful career.

Bachelor's Degree in Psychology

The bachelor's degree, a BA (bachelor of arts) or BS (bachelor of science) degree, typically is the culmination of 4 years of undergraduate study. Whether the bachelor's degree is labeled a BA or BS often depends on the university rather than the program's rigor. Psychology students are awarded BA degrees in some universities and BS degrees in others, yet their education usually is identical. Most students who earn bachelor's degrees enter the work world after graduation, working in business and human service settings (see Chapter 3). Some enter graduate school to earn a master's degree or doctorate.

Master's Degree in Psychology

The master's degree is a graduate degree that typically requires 2 years of study beyond the bachelor's degree. There are many different types of master's degrees, most commonly the MA (master of arts) and MS (master of science). Requirements for service-oriented fields such as clinical, counseling, and school psychology usually include practical experience in an applied setting, which may span longer than the 2 years of coursework.

What can you do with a master's degree? Depending on the program and curriculum, a master's degree enables graduates to do the following: (a) teach psychology in high school (other certification may be needed), (b) become more competitive for jobs in government and industry, (c) practice industrial/organizational psychology in business settings, (d) obtain certification to practice school psychology (depending on the state), and (e) obtain certification as a counselor or marriage and family therapist and practice counseling. Students who are interested in graduate study for the sole purpose of becoming a therapist should carefully consider a master's degree, as it is a quicker, more cost-effective alternative to a doctoral degree and can fulfill certification requirements to practice. Can master's trained individuals provide effective therapy? Studies have shown that there are no convincing differences in therapeutic outcomes as a function of the practitioner's level of training (Atkins & Christensen, 2001; Seligman, 1995). A far greater number of students pursue master's degrees than doctoral degrees in psychology.

Doctoral Degree in Psychology

A doctoral degree provides a greater range of flexibility and autonomy than the master's degree, but it requires a greater commitment of time and money. A doctoral degree usually requires 5 to 7 years of graduate work to complete (and as many as 8 or 9 years for some individuals). In clinical, counseling, and school psychology, the requirement for the doctoral degree generally includes a year or more of internship or supervised experience.

Why do students seek doctoral degrees? Generally, students pursue doctoral degrees for any of the following reasons: (a) to teach college, (b) to conduct research in a university or private organization in industry or business, (c) to practice clinical psychology without supervision, or (d) to engage in a variety of consulting roles allowing autonomy. There are two types of doctoral degrees in psychology, and each provides training that prepares students for specific professional activities. The PhD refers to the doctor of philosophy. Like the master's degree, the PhD is awarded in many fields. It is a research degree that culminates in a dissertation based on original research. PhD graduates may work as researchers and as practitioners in a variety of settings. The PsyD refers to the doctor of psychology. It is offered only in clinical and counseling psychology and is considered a professional degree, much like a JD (doctor of jurisprudence, a lawyer's degree). The PsyD emphasizes practice; students become expert practitioners but do not become researchers. The EdD (doctor of education), a third doctoral option for psychology students, is not as popular as the PhD and PsyD. The EdD is offered in departments of education, rather than psychology. Typically, EdD graduates work in the field of education and educational psychology as researchers, administrators, and professors. We discuss graduate degrees in more depth in Chapter 11.

In short, there are many levels of education in psychology and many educational paths that will prepare you to work with people. Not all psychology majors will become psychologists. In fact, the vast majority will not.

Why Major in Psychology?

If a bachelor's degree in psychology doesn't make you a psychologist, why major in psychology? As many majors explain: Because it is interesting. More importantly, because you will learn how to adopt a scientific perspective and way of thinking that may influence all areas of your life. A background in psychology will change how you see your world. As you learn more about psychology you will become able to see the world through the lens of psychological science, offering a unique perspective and understanding of people. Although you will not be a psychologist with a bachelor's degree, you will learn about psychological principles you can apply in your day-to-day life. A psychological perspective can shape much of what you do and how you view your world.

●

EXERCISE 1.3
INTERNET SCAVENGER HUNT

Use the Internet to answer each of the following questions about specialties in psychology. Provide the search terms used, the website, and your response.

(Continued)

(Continued)

1. In what states can psychologists prescribe medication?

2. How is forensic psychology different from psychology and the law?

3. Identify three applied psychology subfields.

4. During World War II, psychologists used their skills in new ways to help the war effort. In what ways did psychologists contribute? What field of psychology developed from these contributions?

5. What is Principle A of the American Psychological Association Ethics Code?

6. What subfield(s) is (are) concerned with a biopsychosocial model? What is a biopsychosocial model?

7. When was the PsyD born?

8. Discuss two subfields of experimental psychology.

9. Identify three ways in which psychologists can contribute to businesses and corporations.

10. What is *Eye on Psi Chi*? What did it replace?

Overview of *The Psychology Major's Handbook*

Now that you have had an introduction to the field of psychology, let's talk about what you can expect from this book. Your first step in choosing a major and preparing for a career is to get to know yourself. Chapter 2 will introduce you to new ways of understanding yourself that will help you choose a major. Part of choosing a major is considering career possibilities. Chapter 3 examines career opportunities for psychology majors.

A major theme of this book is that *you* play a major role in determining your success in college and beyond. Chapter 4 will show you how to take an active role in your education and shape your own future. Chapter 5 offers an introduction to self-management, a set of cognitive and organizational skills that are helpful for all students. Regardless of your major, you'll need to learn how to study and how to write papers. Chapters 6, 7, and 8 will introduce you to study tips as well as specific information about how to write college papers—specifically, psychology papers.

The remaining chapters of this book encourage you to look ahead. In Chapter 9, we discuss how to search for a job with a bachelor's degree in psychology. In Chapter 10, you'll learn what careers are available with a graduate degree in psychology. Chapter 11 provides an overview of how to apply to graduate school. The college years offer opportunities and challenges. *The Psychology Major's Handbook* will help you navigate these years and keep the big picture—your future—in mind.

2

Choosing a Major

Is Psychology for You?

(Continued)

(Continued)

Chapter Outline	

Choosing Psychology
    Skills and Knowledge You'll
        Develop as a Psychology Major
            Knowledge of Human
                Behavior
            Information Acquisition
                and Synthesis Skills
            Research Methods and
                Statistical Skills
            Critical Thinking and
                Problem-Solving Skills
            Reading, Writing, and
                Speaking Skills
            Interpersonal and
                Intrapersonal Skills
            Adaptability
        Psychological Literacy
    What to Expect as a
        Psychology Major
            Introductory Psychology/
                General Psychology
            Methodology and
                Statistics
            Breadth Courses
            Elective Courses
            Capstone Course	

"**W**hat's your major?" As a new college student, this is likely one of the most common questions you'll encounter from your friends and relatives. If you haven't yet chosen a major, this may also be a particularly frustrating question. Don't fret. You're not alone in your frustration. Choosing a major is one of the most difficult decisions you'll face in college. After all, how do you decide what to do with your life? Fortunately, you don't need to have your life plan laid out in order to choose a college major that fits you. A common misconception about college is that one's choice of major determines one's career. It's no wonder that students who buy into this myth find selecting a major daunting. Luckily, this common belief is not true. In this chapter we'll examine the process of choosing a major and what skills you can expect to develop as a psychology major.

College Majors and Careers

Choosing a major is not the same as choosing a lifelong career. For example, many people assume that students who major in humanities, sciences, and social science fields, including English, history, biology, sociology, and psychology, are qualified only for careers in those specific areas. This isn't true. A history major does not have to become a historian, a biology major does not have to become a biologist, and a psychology major does not have to become a psychologist in order to be gainfully employed. This is especially fortuitous because each of these professions requires years of graduate study beyond the baccalaureate degree. Students who earn undergraduate degrees with these majors find jobs in business, research, human services, education, and a variety of other fields (see Chapter 3 for more information about careers with a bachelor's degree in psychology). Although the question of what major to pursue may feel pressing, your choice of majors does not limit your opportunities.

Within 10 years after graduation, most people work in careers that are not directly connected to their undergraduate majors—and that's not a bad thing. As people acquire experiences their interests often change. A solid skill set will help you adapt to your changing interests and circumstances and will help you build a flexible career. In addition, new types of jobs are emerging each year, and most of us have no way of knowing what those jobs will be or what type of education will be needed in order to qualify for them. For example, 15 years ago, most people had never heard of a patient advocate or a web developer, and social media managers and app developers didn't exist! Without a doubt, other careers will evolve over the coming years. Consequently, career counselors recommend that college students focus on developing general transferable skills that employers want, such as competence in writing, speaking, problem solving, technology use, and team building. These are skills that you can develop with any major. Therefore, choose a major that reflects *your* interests and abilities and provides you with opportunities to develop these generalizable skills as well as those that are unique to your chosen field. The exercises in this chapter will help you learn more about yourself; assess your interests, skills, and abilities; and determine which major is right for you.

How to Choose a Major

As you begin the process of selecting a major, remember that there is no bad choice. Every college major offers opportunities to develop competence in communication, information management, and critical thinking skills. However, majors differ in the specific set of competencies emphasized. For example, the emphasis on scientific reasoning and problem solving, coupled with a focus on understanding how people think and behave, is what makes psychology unique among majors. Carefully consider your options, your skill set, and your interests when selecting a college major. At the end of this process, you may find that psychology is the major for you or you may make another choice. Listen to yourself and make the decision that is right for you, but also recognize that many students change their major sometime during their college years. It is not set in stone. Follow these steps to ensure that you're true to yourself in choosing the college major that is right for you and one that you'll stick with throughout your college years.

Become Informed of Your Options

The first step in making any decision is to become informed of your options. What majors does your college offer? Some majors, such as psychology, English, and economics, are available at all colleges and universities. Other majors, such as engineering, can be found only at some institutions. What options does your college offer? How do you find out what majors are offered? Every college has a student handbook. Check the "students" area of your school's homepage or use the search function. The handbook will likely list the available majors at your school.

Another way to learn about your options is to examine each academic department online (my preferred option—it's thorough!). Your school's homepage likely has a link to a webpage listing academic departments, or you can use the search function to find this page. Scroll through and click on each department, one by one. You'll probably want to do this in more than one sitting because you'll scan a lot of webpages. Take a moment to review each department's program, even if at first glance you think it isn't interesting or right for you.

You might spend just a few minutes studying most programs, but some will likely strike your interest and cause you to probe further. It is important to review a wide range of programs, even those that you think you might not like. Sometimes we have preconceived biases and incorrect information about a discipline or major. For each major, ask yourself the following questions and quickly note your responses so that you can easily revisit your work and compare majors later.

- What are some of the required classes?
- Are any clubs or activities listed?
- Who are the faculty? What are their research interests? Does it look like students are involved in their research?
- Is any information available about graduates' employment?

After you've scanned each academic department and major, list all of the majors that sound interesting to you, without making judgments. Then, for each potential major, gather additional information to complete the checklist of questions in Exercise 2.1. If you are unable to answer a question, it's time to move beyond Internet research and seek advice from others.

Seek Information From Students, Graduates, and Professionals

Internet research can get you only so far. In order to learn about majors and career options, it's essential to gather information from knowledgeable people. Current students, graduates, career counselors, and professors can offer invaluable information and perspectives.

Current Students

Ask other students how they chose their major and why they think it's a good choice. What do they think about their courses, the topic, professors, and

EXERCISE 2.1
LEARNING ABOUT MAJORS: QUESTIONS TO CONSIDER

- What is this field? What does it study?
- How interested am I in this topic? Is it a new interest or a long-standing one? Do I enjoy the subject?
- Do I have any experience in this area?
- Have I taken a class in this subject? If so, what did it cover? What was the class like?
- How motivated am I to study this subject? Is it inherently interesting or fun? Do I dread classes or homework in this area?
- What classes can I expect to take as a major?
- What other experiences do majors typically obtain (for example, internships and/or research experiences)?
- What jobs have recent graduates obtained?

Prompt

After considering the above questions, respond to the following in a short essay: What do you know about the field? What are your experiences? What can you expect as a major during college and after graduation?

PRACTICAL TIP
DON'T LET PROFS (NEGATIVELY) COLOR YOUR PERSPECTIVE

As you go about the process of considering majors and your experiences in various fields, remember that sometimes an experience with a professor can color your view of a discipline. For example, an introductory course taught by a professor who you find unappealing may make a subject that you'd otherwise find interesting seem boring. When you evaluate a field negatively, take a moment to consider what experiences have led to this evaluation. If it's the result of a single classroom experience, consider giving the discipline another shot before you rule it out.

opportunities after graduation? What are the required courses like? Every major has its most challenging set of courses: What are those courses? Why are they considered challenging? What about the professors? Do students have out-of-class interactions with faculty? What kind? What out-of-class experiences are available? Is there a student club?

Recent Graduates

Ask recent graduates about their experiences. Ask them some or all of the questions you asked current students. Also ask about their experiences after graduating (Exercise 2.2). If you don't know any recent graduates, visit the department and/or your college's career center. Most college career centers maintain records of recent graduates and may be able to put you in contact with a few graduates to help you learn more about their work and career experiences.

Career Professionals

Visit your college's career center to seek advice. Tell the career counselor what you've learned about yourself in completing the exercises in this chapter (consider sharing your responses). Career counseling professionals can help you narrow your choice of majors and provide additional opportunities to learn about yourself by completing additional personality and interest assessments. Take advantage of this important (and free!) resource.

Professors

Don't forget to talk with professors to learn more about majors. Visit the office hours of a professor who teaches a class in which you are enrolled,

EXERCISE 2.2

LEARNING ABOUT MAJORS: WHAT TO ASK RECENT GRADUATES

- What did they like most about their major? Least?
- What was the job search like?
- What kinds of jobs did they seek?
- How were they received by potential employers?
- Where were they hired?
- How well does their job match their expectations?
- What are the positive and negative features of their work?
- What role, if any, did their major play in their job search and career?
- Do they feel that their major prepared them for their jobs?
- If they could do it again, what major would they choose? Why?

Prompt

Address the following topics in a short essay: What jobs do recent graduates hold? What was their job search like? How do recent graduates view their college major as preparation for their current job?

seems approachable, or works in a field of interest to you. Ask questions about the undergraduate major and what kinds of jobs recent graduates hold (Exercise 2.3). Do some homework beforehand to ensure that your questions are informed. For example, read the department website to learn a little bit about the major, basic course requirements, and, if possible, what courses the professor teaches. Visit the professor's website to learn about his or her courses and research. It will be easier to know what to ask if you know a little bit about the program and professor. You might begin by explaining that you're thinking about becoming a major and would like to know more about the field. Students sometimes feel uncomfortable approaching a professor, but remember that office hours are times specifically allocated to interacting with students. Take advantage of this time to ask the questions that will help you determine if a given major is for you.

EXERCISE 2.3
LEARNING ABOUT MAJORS:
WHAT TO ASK PROFESSORS

- What are some of the major requirements in the major? Specifically, what is the recommended timetable for completing specific courses or experiences?
- Are there formal opportunities to work closely with faculty, such as courses with small enrollments, research classes, or independent study courses?
- Do many students interact with faculty outside of the classroom (for example, assisting with research)?
- Do students tend to participate in clubs and outside activities, such as group trips to conferences?
- What do graduates do?
- Are there opportunities to participate in off-campus applied activities, such as internships?
- How did the professor choose his or her major?
- Does the professor have any advice on choosing a major?
- What are important attributes for a successful student?
- What advice would the professor give for a new student in the major?

Prompt

Address the following topics in a short essay: What are some of the opportunities and recommended experiences for majors? What jobs do recent graduates hold? What advice or experiences did the professor share about choosing a major?

As you can see, there are multiple sources of information about any given major. Approach the task of choosing a major as if you were solving a puzzle. Each source provides a unique bit of information and perspective. Sources may disagree about particular qualities or characteristics of a major. Compile all of the information and weigh it based on the person's perspective (as a student, graduate, or faculty member, for example), perceived accuracy (Does the information seem accurate? What is the source's perspective?), and perceived similarity (How similar are your and the source's views?) (Exercise 2.4). Once you have gathered information and decided on several majors that may be a good fit for you, it's time to shift your attention inward and learn about yourself.

●

EXERCISE 2.4

LEARNING ABOUT MAJORS:
SUMMING UP WHAT YOU'VE LEARNED

After evaluating one or more majors and speaking with degree-seekers, degree-holders, and professionals, what have you learned?

1. What majors did you evaluate?

2. What are some of the opportunities for students and graduates in this major, according to students?

3. What are some of the opportunities for students and graduates in this major, according to professors and other professionals?

4. Do students and professors share the same views on the challenges of this major? If not, where do they diverge? Why do you think they disagree?

5. What are the most important commonly mentioned positive and negative features of this major?

6. How well do you think you could overcome the challenges?

7. What do you think is the most positive aspect of this major?

How to Learn About Yourself

An essential part of choosing a major that will provide the preparation that you desire is knowing your own interests and aspirations. Specifying them, however, is challenging. How do you know what you want? How can you anticipate your interests over the next few years? How do you tackle such an amorphous topic as choosing an area of study? I won't lie: Learning about yourself and uncovering your interests and aspirations isn't easy and can even feel uncomfortable. This is especially true if you view it as one burning task that has a strict deadline. Don't force it. You have time to explore and find what's right for you.

Learn About Yourself Through Reflective Writing

After completing the exercises earlier in this chapter and book, you may have noticed that writing is a useful way of organizing your ideas and recording what you learn about various majors. Writing is also useful for learning and organizing what you know about yourself. Always good advice, understanding yourself is critical to choosing a major that will satisfy your intellectual curiosity and fulfill your career goals. Consider keeping a log of your thoughts and experiences, a record of reflective writing. Some might call this record a log, journal, or diary. Whatever you call it, reflective writing—capturing your thoughts and perspective in writing—can help you learn about yourself. Your log is a collection of your creative activity and can be saved in a simple notebook, computer file, or even your phone. It is a private learning space where you can reflect on yourself and your experiences, goals, dreams, and anxieties and learn more about who you are. Recording your thoughts can serve many purposes and aid you throughout college and your career. As you proceed through college, you may find it useful to use your log to record ideas for papers and, if your program requires it, thesis topics. There is a benefit to being mindful, and your log can help you become more aware of yourself and the world around you. If you are still wondering what writing and maintaining a log of your thoughts can do, let's consider some of the uses of reflective writing.

Uses of Reflective Writing

Sometimes we're not aware of our thoughts and feelings until we capture them with the written word. Expressing your ideas in words forces you to focus your thoughts, identify your opinions and values, and clarify your sense of identity. Here are four ways that you can use regular self-reflective writing.

Record your experience. A reflective log provides a record of your life and your thoughts. Days, weeks, and months pass all too quickly. Memory is fallible. Most people look back on their college years fondly and view those years as critical in shaping their identity. Return to your writing to help you to remember events, experiences, feelings, and intentions. Your log is a place to record accomplishments, hopes, and dreams as well as to retain details that you would probably otherwise forget.

Reduce stress and gain insight into yourself. Do you find yourself fuming after an argument or conflict? Do you repeatedly think about what you should have said in a conversation or in class hours or days later? Writing can help you process your experiences and move past ruminating over what has already happened and what you cannot change. Write your inner dialogue rather than rehearse it in your head. Review what you have written. Is it complete? There's no need to keep recycling negative thoughts; you've recorded them, so there is no need to keep them in mind. Letting go gives you space to move on. Therefore, after a long day or a difficult experience, reflective writing can give you a private opportunity to consider your feelings and release stress. From a therapeutic perspective, looking back over your writing weeks, months, or years later permits the opportunity to reflect on patterns of experience, interaction, and emotion, providing insight into yourself and your perspective on life. How have you changed and grown?

Use reflective writing as an organizational tool. Your writing does not have to be particularly deep. Some people use their reflection logs for creating lists and plans, sometimes referring to their log as a "bullet journal." Perhaps the easiest way to begin keeping a log is to use it as a place to record lists of immediate tasks to be accomplished. With regular use, writing becomes a habit and can grow beyond making lists to include reflection, planning, and goal setting. You can write about your goals and document the steps needed to achieve them, as well as note your progress. In this way, your log can help to organize your daily life and plan for the future.

Try reflective writing as a problem-solving tool. Writing is an effective tool for problem solving because writing is thinking. The next time you find yourself confronted with a problem or a big decision, try writing about it. Explain the problem. What do you know about it? Discuss your feelings about the problem and analyze it. Writing may lead you to brainstorm potential solutions. Then your writing might shift toward analyzing each solution. Expressing ideas in written form requires a different thought process than thinking. We think in new ways when we write. This allows us to conceptualize problems differently and come to solutions more quickly.

Tips for Beginning a Reflection Log

Your log can take many forms. It might be a plain notebook, text or word processing file on your computer or synced in a cloud service, or an app on your phone. The form your log takes doesn't matter, as long as it is readily and easily accessible to you. The cardinal rule of reflective writing is to remember that your log is for your eyes only. Don't let spelling, handwriting, and grammar be major concerns. Get your feelings and experiences down in writing, any way that you can. No one else will review or grade it. To get started, consider the following tips.

Don't overthink it: Just write. There are no rules. You can write about anything that comes to mind, like ideas for papers and projects, everyday items such as lists of accomplishments and tasks to be completed, and even creative writing ideas such as story or poetry ideas, if that's your thing. Write about your problems or everyday frustrations. Observe your life. If you're having difficulty writing, you might even write about the trouble that you're experiencing. You can write your thoughts as they come, even if you're writing that you don't know what to write.

Try a third-person perspective. If you are having trouble getting started, try writing about events that are happening to you or around you from a third-person perspective, using pronouns such as *he* and *she*, as if you are observing someone else. For example, begin writing with the phrase, "It was a time when . . . ," and then describe the situation in detail, using as many of your senses as possible. What are the sounds, smells, sights, and feelings present? This exercise can help you to put things into perspective; it is especially effective when writing about life changes (like the transition to college), relationships (like that argument with your boyfriend or girlfriend), and events that you found upsetting (like finding out that you didn't do so well on that test).

Write for brief periods, often. The goal of keeping a reflective log is to catch your thoughts. The more often you write, the more you'll learn about yourself. Keep your log close at hand. If you have 15 minutes between classes, write. You might write about what you've learned in your prior class and how it relates to your experience, which will make it more likely that you learn and retain the material. Or you might simply write about what you're thinking or feeling, such as whether you are hungry, tired, or antsy. Get into the habit of writing each day, even for just a few minutes. Try writing at bedtime or right after you wake up. It doesn't take much time. You'll be surprised at how much you can capture in just a few minutes if you don't censor yourself. Also try to write some longer entries, because they will give you the opportunity to flesh out your thoughts and make insights about yourself.

Avoid expectations. Your log is whatever you choose to create. It does not have to be filled with descriptions of monumental experiences. Entries don't have to be well written or scholarly. Don't let these beliefs rob you of the chance to benefit from reflective writing. Also note that reading is not required. Some people reread their logs as chronicles of their lives. Others rarely read their logs but instead use writing to process their thoughts. Remember that the information is always there should you choose to read it, but you don't have to read it.

Try reflective writing. It can help you explore who you are and discover who you hope to become. Through writing and reflecting, the mundane can become profound. Throughout this book, you'll find plenty of topics and ideas to write about, which will help you learn about yourself and make plans for your future. Take a chance and explore yourself through writing.

Learn About Yourself Through Self-Assessment

By now you likely realize that understanding yourself is critical to choosing a major that keeps your interest over the college years. Reflective writing is an important tool, but choosing a major requires a thorough self-assessment. It sounds technical, but *self-assessment* is simply the process of examining your skills, abilities, motivations, interests, values, experience, and accomplishments. In other words, it's how you learn about yourself, which will help you make decisions about your major. The following exercises will help you to better understand yourself, but remember that a useful self-assessment is not generated instantaneously. It takes time, hard work, and honesty.

Assess Your Traits

Who are you? What characteristics best describe you? Understanding your unique personality traits will help you to choose a major that is right for you and, later, a job that complements your characteristics and is rewarding. Exercise 2.5 will help you to get a better understanding of your personality, which is essential to choosing a major that you'll be happy with.

EXERCISE 2.5
ASSESS YOUR PERSONAL TRAITS

Check off those traits that describe you. Brainstorm additional traits if needed. Take your time to evaluate each and be honest with yourself.

❑ Academic	❑ Extroverted	❑ Practical
❑ Accurate	❑ Fair-minded	❑ Private
❑ Active	❑ Farsighted	❑ Productive
❑ Adaptable	❑ Feeling	❑ Progressive
❑ Adept	❑ Firm	❑ Protective
❑ Adventurous	❑ Flexible	❑ Prudent
❑ Affectionate	❑ Forceful	❑ Punctual
❑ Aggressive	❑ Formal	❑ Quick
❑ Alert	❑ Frank	❑ Quiet
❑ Ambitious	❑ Frugal	❑ Rational
❑ Analytical	❑ Future-oriented	❑ Realistic
❑ Appreciative	❑ Generous	❑ Receptive
❑ Articulate	❑ Gentle	❑ Reflective
❑ Artistic	❑ Good natured	❑ Relaxed
❑ Assertive	❑ Gregarious	❑ Reliable
❑ Astute	❑ Hardy	❑ Reserved

❑ Athletic	❑ Helpful	❑ Resourceful
❑ Attentive	❑ Honest	❑ Responsible
❑ Balanced	❑ Hopeful	❑ Reverent
❑ Brave	❑ Humorous	❑ Risk-taker
❑ Broad-minded	❑ Idealistic	❑ Sedentary
❑ Businesslike	❑ Imaginative	❑ Self-confident
❑ Calm	❑ Impersonal	❑ Self-controlled
❑ Candid	❑ Independent	❑ Self-disciplined
❑ Capable	❑ Individualistic	❑ Self-starter
❑ Caring	❑ Industrious	❑ Sensible
❑ Cautious	❑ Informal	❑ Sensitive
❑ Charitable	❑ Initiator	❑ Serious
❑ Cheerful	❑ Innovative	❑ Sincere
❑ Clean	❑ Intellectual	❑ Sociable
❑ Clear	❑ Intelligent	❑ Sophisticated
❑ Competent	❑ Introverted	❑ Stable
❑ Competitive	❑ Intuitive	❑ Strong
❑ Congenial	❑ Inventive	❑ Strong-minded
❑ Conscientious	❑ Jovial	❑ Structured
❑ Conservative	❑ Judicious	❑ Subjective
❑ Considerate	❑ Just	❑ Successful
❑ Consistent	❑ Kind	❑ Tactful
❑ Conventional	❑ Liberal	❑ Talented
❑ Cooperative	❑ Likable	❑ Tenacious
❑ Courageous	❑ Literary	❑ Thorough
❑ Creative	❑ Logical	❑ Thoughtful
❑ Critical	❑ Loyal	❑ Tolerant
❑ Curious	❑ Mature	❑ Trusting
❑ Daring	❑ Methodical	❑ Trustworthy
❑ Decisive	❑ Meticulous	❑ Truthful
❑ Deliberate	❑ Mistrustful	❑ Understanding

(Continued)

(Continued)

❑ Delicate	❑ Modest	❑ Unexcitable
❑ Democratic	❑ Motivated	❑ Uninhibited
❑ Dependable	❑ Nurturing	❑ Verbal
❑ Detail-oriented	❑ Objective	❑ Versatile
❑ Diligent	❑ Observant	❑ Vigorous
❑ Discreet	❑ Open-minded	❑ Warm
❑ Distinctive	❑ Opportunistic	❑ Wholesome
❑ Dominant	❑ Optimistic	❑ Wise
❑ Dynamic	❑ Orderly	
❑ Eager	❑ Organized	
❑ Easygoing	❑ Original	
❑ Effective	❑ Outgoing	
❑ Efficient	❑ Patient	
❑ Eloquent	❑ Peaceable	
❑ Emotional	❑ Perceptive	
❑ Empathetic	❑ Persistent	

Prompt

Examine the list of personality descriptors that you have selected. Carefully consider each. How well does each adjective describe you? Choose three to five adjectives that you find most relevant.

1. Why did you choose those descriptors? Provide examples from your experience that illustrate how each word describes you.

2. Think back to your childhood dreams. Do you remember being asked by friends and family "What do you want to be when you grow up?" How did you typically respond? What careers did you select as a child? Why?

3. Consider your childhood career goal. What traits are needed to succeed in that career?

4. Do you still have the same career-related dreams? How have your interests changed?

5. Consider your characteristics listed in question 1. How do these traits compare with those needed for the career of your childhood dreams? How do they fit with your revised adult view?

Identify Your Occupational Interests

Another way to use what you know about yourself to choose a major is to identify your occupational interests. Pay attention to your interests to determine the work environment that you'll find most appealing. Holland (1959, 1997) proposed that people's interests and the matching work environments can be loosely categorized into six themes or codes: realistic, investigative, artistic, social, enterprising, and conventional. Although they were created half a century ago, the Holland Occupational Codes remain the most commonly used assessment of career interests (Ruff, Reardon, & Bertoch, 2007). Complete Exercise 2.6 for a brief insight into your career interests. Another option is the O*NET Interest Profiler, a self-assessment inventory that applies Holland codes to help individuals identify their work-related interests (Lewis & Rivkin, 1999). The O*NET Interest Profiler is a free computer program sponsored by the U.S. Department of Labor/Employment and Training Administration and the American Job Center Network (http://www.onetcenter.org/CIP.html). A short version of the O*NET Interest Profiler is also available (http://www.onetcenter .org/IPSF.html). These tools are a good start, but an accurate Holland career assessment is conducted by a career professional using specialized tools. The career development center at your college can help you determine and interpret your Holland Code.

EXERCISE 2.6
IDENTIFY YOUR HOLLAND PERSONALITY TYPE

Realistic

- ❏ I am mechanically inclined
- ❏ I am athletically inclined
- ❏ I like working outside with tools, plants, or animals
- ❏ I like creating things with my hands
- ❏ I am practical
- ❏ I like to see direct results of my work
- ❏ I am a nature lover
- ❏ I am systematic
- ❏ I am persistent
- ❏ I am calm and reserved
- ❏ I am independent
- ❏ I dislike vagueness and ambiguity

(Continued)

(Continued)

Investigative

- ❏   I like learning, observing, problem solving, and working with information
- ❏   I like solving abstract, vague problems
- ❏   I am curious
- ❏   I am logical
- ❏   I am reserved
- ❏   I am introspective
- ❏   I am independent
- ❏   I am observant
- ❏   I am interested in understanding the physical world
- ❏   I like working alone or in small groups
- ❏   I like to be original and creative in solving problems
- ❏   I enjoy intellectual challenges

Artistic

- ❏   I am imaginative and creative
- ❏   I like to express myself by designing and producing
- ❏   I prefer unstructured activities
- ❏   I am spontaneous
- ❏   I am idealistic
- ❏   I am unique
- ❏   I am independent
- ❏   I am expressive
- ❏   I am unconventional
- ❏   I am compassionate
- ❏   I am bold
- ❏   I prefer to work alone

Social

- ❏   I am compassionate
- ❏   I like helping and training others
- ❏   I am patient

- ❏ I am dependable
- ❏ I am supportive
- ❏ I am understanding
- ❏ I am perceptive
- ❏ I am generous
- ❏ I am idealistic
- ❏ I am cheerful, well liked
- ❏ I am people-oriented and friendly
- ❏ I am concerned with the welfare of others
- ❏ I am good at expressing myself and getting along well with others

Enterprising

- ❏ I like to work with people
- ❏ I like persuading people
- ❏ I like managing situations
- ❏ I like achieving organizational or economic goals
- ❏ I am a leader
- ❏ I am talkative
- ❏ I am extroverted
- ❏ I am optimistic
- ❏ I am spontaneous and daring
- ❏ I am assertive
- ❏ I am energetic
- ❏ I am good at communicating
- ❏ I am good at selling and persuading
- ❏ I prefer tasks that require quick action

Conventional

- ❏ I am good with numbers
- ❏ I like to work with data and carry out tasks in detail
- ❏ I am persistent
- ❏ I am practical
- ❏ I am conforming
- ❏ I am precise

(Continued)

(Continued)

- ❑ I am conscientious
- ❑ I am meticulous
- ❑ I am adept
- ❑ I am practical
- ❑ I am frugal
- ❑ I am stable and dependable
- ❑ I am well controlled
- ❑ I prefer tasks that are structured
- ❑ I prefer to know what's expected
- ❑ I prefer a well-defined chain of command

Prompt

Count your checkmarks to determine which sets of descriptors best match your characteristics.

Most students find that two or more sets of qualities fit them. Which set(s) of descriptors best described you? Provide an example of an experience or ability that illustrates this set of descriptors.

Source: Adapted from Holland (1966, 1997).

Understanding your career interests may make it easier to choose a major because some majors are better suited to particular constellations of interests than are others. Table 2.1 lists college majors, organized by Holland Code. Remember that this is simply a guide. Not all possible careers are listed, and the categories are much more fluid than they appear. Notice that many college majors fit more than one Holland Code. College majors tap multiple interests and abilities—and foster similar skills in students, such as critical thinking and communication skills.

Assess Your Skills

In addition to understanding your interests, your choice of major should reflect your skills and abilities. What are your skills? What activities do you do best? If you're unsure, use your log to write an experiential diary to get a better grip on your skills. An experiential diary lists all the jobs, leadership positions, and extracurricular activities that you've engaged in, and then all the tasks comprising each of these activities and jobs. Once you've created a master list, write down the skills required to perform the tasks on your list. For example, if the task was answering the phone, it probably entailed the

TABLE 2.1 ● Careers by Holland Personality Type

Realistic	Investigative	Artistic
Agriculture/Forestry	Animal Science	Advertising
Architecture	Anthropology	Architecture
Criminal Justice	Astronomy	Art Education
Engineering	Biochemistry	Art History
Environmental Studies	Biological Sciences	Communications
Exercise Science	Chemistry	English
Geology	Computer Science	Foreign Language
Health and Physical Education	Engineering	Graphic Design
Medical Technology	Geography	History
Plant and Soil Sciences	Geology	Interior Design
Recreation and Tourism Management	Mathematics	Journalism
Sport Management	Medical Technology	Music
	Medicine	Music Education
	Nursing	Speech/Drama
	Nutrition	
	Pharmacy	
	Philosophy	
	Physical Therapy	
	Physics	
	Psychology	
	Sociology	
	Statistics	

Social	Enterprising	Conventional
Audiology	Advertising	Accounting
Counseling	Broadcasting	Business
Criminal Justice	Communications	Computer Science
Elementary Education	Economics	Economics
History	Finance	Finance
Human Development	Industrial Relations	Mathematics
Library Sciences	Journalism	Statistics
Nursing	Management	

(Continued)

TABLE 2.1 ● (Continued)		
Social	**Enterprising**	**Conventional**
Nutrition	Marketing	
Occupational therapy	Law	
Philosophy	Political Science	
Physical Education	Public Administration	
Political Science	Speech	
Psychology		
Religious Studies		
Social Work		
Sociology		
Special Education		
Urban Planning		

Source: Adapted from Holland (1966, 1997).

following skills: communication (the effective use of language), problem solving, and the ability to direct inquiries. Also identify specific skills that you've learned, like the ability to use computer programming languages or speak a non-native language. Even with an experiential diary, it is sometimes difficult to list and remember all of your skills and abilities. Exercise 2.7 will help you to better understand your skills.

EXERCISE 2.7
ASSESS YOUR SKILLS

Check off all of the skills that apply to you, then complete the activity below.

❑ Acting or performing   ❑ Leading

❑ Administering   ❑ Listening to others

❑ Advising   ❑ Managing

❑ Analyzing data   ❑ Measuring

❑ Applying   ❑ Mediating

❑ Arranging social functions   ❑ Motivating

❑ Budgeting   ❑ Navigating

❏ Calculating

❏ Checking for accuracy

❏ Coaching

❏ Collecting money

❏ Communicating

❏ Compiling statistics

❏ Conceptualizing

❏ Controlling

❏ Coordinating events

❏ Counseling

❏ Creating new ideas

❏ Decision-making

❏ Designing

❏ Dispensing information

❏ Dramatizing ideas or problems

❏ Editing

❏ Entertaining people

❏ Evaluating

❏ Expressing feelings

❏ Finding information

❏ Fund raising

❏ Generalizing

❏ Goal setting

❏ Handling complaints

❏ Identifying problems

❏ Illustrating

❏ Implementing

❏ Improving

❏ Initiating with strangers

❏ Innovating

❏ Interpreting

❏ Interviewing

❏ Investigating problems

❏ Judging

❏ Negotiating

❏ Observing

❏ Organizing

❏ Painting

❏ Persuading

❏ Photographing

❏ Planning

❏ Problem solving

❏ Programming

❏ Promoting

❏ Proofreading

❏ Questioning

❏ Reading

❏ Reasoning

❏ Record keeping

❏ Recording

❏ Recruiting

❏ Researching

❏ Scheduling

❏ Selling

❏ Singing

❏ Sketching

❏ Speaking

❏ Supervising

❏ Synthesizing information

❏ Teaching or training

❏ Team building

❏ Thinking logically

❏ Tolerating ambiguity

❏ Translating

❏ Troubleshooting

❏ Visualizing

❏ Writing

(Continued)

(Continued)

Prompt

1. What skills did you check?

2. Can you think of examples of how each skill has developed or how you've used it to achieve a goal?

3. Based on your consideration, choose your top three to five skills and explain your choices. These skills are your strengths.

4. Now look at all of the skills that you checked:

    a. Do any of these skills need further development?

    b. Which of these skills do you prefer using? Why?

    c. Which are you interested in using in the future? Why?

    d. Do you dislike engaging in any of your skills? Why?

5. Are there any skills that you don't currently have but would like to develop? Explain.

By now it should be apparent that you already have an array of skills. Are you interested in using and pursuing them? We tend to like and be interested in things that we are good at. Is that true for you? You may not be skilled in a particular area, but if you find it interesting, you can seek the education and training to become skilled. Don't let your current competence levels dictate your choices. If you are willing to work, you can make great strides and learn many skills that can help you meet your career goals.

Use Career Assessment Tools

While you can learn a lot about yourself through reflection and surveying your own interests, a visit to the career center at your college can provide you with an objective and detailed profile of your interests. A career counselor can administer several inventories to help determine what career path is right for you. The two most commonly administered inventories are the Strong Interest Inventory (Strong, Donnay, Morris, Schaubhut, & Thompson, 2004) and the Myers-Briggs Type Indicator (MBTI) (Myers, McCaulley, Quenk, & Hammer, 1998).

The Strong Interest Inventory is administered at your college's career center, and it contains 291 items that survey your occupational interests and values. It takes about 40 minutes to complete and yields a detailed report that includes your Holland Code, a list of your top interests and what you find most motivating and rewarding, and comparisons of your interests with those of people working in 122 occupations. The Strong Interest Inventory also lists occupations in which people whose interests most closely match yours work. Finally, your values (that is, preferences regarding work style, learning environment, leadership style, risk taking, and team orientation) are listed. A summary provides a graphic representation of your results. The career counselor will discuss your results with you. Remember that although a number of compatible careers are listed, you are free to pursue whatever career appeals to you. The Strong Interest Inventory provides a more detailed look at the aspects of career assessment than we have discussed in this chapter. It's especially useful is you have tried the activities in this book and still find yourself puzzled about what really interests you.

Another assessment option available in your college's career center is the MBTI. With over 100 items, the MBTI assesses individuals' perceptions, preferences, and judgments in interacting with the world (Myers et al., 1998). Created by mother and daughter, Katharine Cook Briggs and Isabel Briggs Myers, the MTBI is based in Carl Jung's theory that there are 16 personality types in which people may be categorized based on their preferences along four dimensions or subscales. The MBTI contains several subscales. The extraversion/introversion subscale refers to the degree to which you turn outward or inward—that is, the degree to which you are oriented toward people and actions or the internal world of thoughts and ideas. The sensation/intuition subscale examines how you prefer to understand information: do you focus on the facts or do you prefer to interpret and add meaning? Do you focus on logic and reasoning when making decisions or do you first look at circumstances and people (thinking/feeling)? Your preference for structure is assessed by the judging/perceiving scale, which examines whether you prefer to make decisions or remain open to new ideas and options. Finally, the measure categorizes takers into a "personality type," suggesting their own set of preferences. If you choose to take the MBTI, remember that it is simply a tool to help you learn about yourself. In fact, some psychologists argue that despite its popularity, there is insufficient research to conclude that the MBTI is an effective measure of personality (Pittenger, 2005). Ultimately, it's up to you to determine if the results make sense to you.

Examine Your Values

While choosing a major does not tie you to a particular career, it is useful to consider your career aspirations and life goals in order to seek the educational experiences that will prepare you for them. What do you want out of life? How do you define success? Would you rather live in a city or in a rural area? Is personal time and flexibility important to you? Would you like a family (and if so, large or small)? Is financial success important? Values are the things that are important to you, that you see as desirable in life. Spend time thinking through your priorities. Reflective writing can help you to understand and clarify your values. Consider the following collection of values, categorized by theme (Exercise 2.8). Check off the ones that appeal to you.

EXERCISE 2.8
EXAMINE YOUR VALUES

Service

❑ Active in community

❑ Help others

❑ Help society and the world

❑ Work with and help people in meaningful way

Adventure

❑ Excitement

❑ Risk taking

❑ Travel

❑ Drama

❑ Exciting tasks

❑ Good health

❑ Travel

Leadership

❑ Influence people and opinions

❑ Supervise others

❑ Power authority and control

❑ Make decisions

❑ Direct work of others

❑ Leadership

❑ Coordinate people data and stuff

❑ Hiring and firing responsibility

Creativity

❑ Aesthetic appreciation

❑ Artistic creativity

❑ Creative expression

❑ Develop and express new ideas

❑ No routine

❑ Work on own or as creative team

❑ Flexible working conditions

Relationships

❑ Organization affiliation

❑ Work friendships

❑ Family

❑ Work with others/ teamwork

❑ Public contract

❑ Friendly work atmosphere

❑ Work with people you like

Financial Reward

❑ High earnings

❑ Commission-based work

❑ Material possessions

❑ Very high salary

❑ Extra pay for extra work

❑ Long hours

Prestige

❑ Recognition

❑ Status

❑ Respect stature

❑ Professional position

Meaning and Purpose

❑ Spirituality

❑ Personal fulfillment

❑ Work related to ideals

❑ Make a difference

Variety

❑ Changing work responsibilities

❑ Diversity of tasks

❑ New projects

❑ Varied tasks

❏ Responsibility	❏ Express inner self in work	❏ Meet new people
❏ Responsibility and pay are related to education and experience	❏ Integrate belief system into work	❏ Range of settings and situations

Security	**Independence**	**Physical Activity**
❏ Stability	❏ Time freedom	❏ Outdoor work
❏ Predictably	❏ Autonomy	❏ Physical challenge
❏ Low pressure	❏ Work alone	❏ Physical fitness
❏ Job assurance	❏ Set own pace and working conditions, flexible hours	❏ Desk job
❏ Guaranteed annual salary in secure stable company	❏ Choose team or work alone	
❏ Retirement benefits		
❏ Live in familiar location		

Intellectual Challenge	**Productivity**	**Advancement**
❏ Address challenging problems	❏ Competent and proficient	❏ Promotions
❏ Pursue/obtain knowledge	❏ Fast-paced work	❏ Work under pressure
❏ Constant updating of information and ability to deal with new ideas	❏ Efficient work habits	❏ Competition
❏ Work with creative and intellectually stimulating people	❏ Hard work is rewarded	❏ Limited only by energy and initiative
❏ Acknowledged expert	❏ Quality and productivity rewarded by rapid advancement	
❏ Research and development		

(Continued)

(Continued)

Prompt

1. What values did you check? Do your selected values cluster into a few areas?

2. How have these values influenced your choices and behaviors? Consider your extracurricular activities and interests.

3. How might these values inform your career choices?

An effective way of assessing your interests and values is to write about your personal history. Exercise 2.9 helps you to identify your strengths and is a fantastic self-esteem builder because it focuses on your accomplishments—the things that make you special. By understanding which achievements you cherish, you'll have a better idea of your interests and values, which is essential to choosing a major or career that's right for you.

EXERCISE 2.9
REVIEW YOUR PERSONAL HISTORY

1. List and write about all of the times that you can think of when you have encountered a problem (regardless of its size) and have taken action to solve that problem. List as many as you can. Don't stop when it becomes difficult, but probe further.

2. Next, write about your achievements. They may be related to your list from item 1. If you're stumped, try free writing about your achievements, writing whatever comes to mind, without censoring or editing it. Keep the ideas flowing. Looking over the exercises in this chapter can help. The accomplishments that you list need not be monumental. Accomplishments can be small, and they don't have to be recognized by other people. Write about the achievements that are personally relevant to you and of which you are most proud.

3. Next examine the problems you have solved and your accomplishments. Which have brought you the most satisfaction? Which do you value most highly? Why?

Draw Conclusions

Now that you're aware of your traits, interests, skills, and values, compile this information to get a comprehensive view of yourself. Review the lists and descriptions of majors in your college handbook. Do any seem to fit your set of traits, skills, and interests? Some majors and careers will match many of the personal traits and skills that you possess, and others will not match your self-description. Review what you have learned about various majors and about yourself. If you are still puzzling over what major to choose, list the two or three front-runners. Use your college handbook and department websites to find additional information. Once you have narrowed down your choice of majors, consider the pros and cons of each major. Consider the questions listed in Table 2.2.

The happiest and most successful students choose majors that they find engaging and that match their traits, skills, interests, and values. Some students decide on a major before they understand themselves. They take courses for a semester or two and then realize that they've chosen a major in which they have minimal interest or ability. Engaging in self-assessment early in your college career can save you from changing majors and wasting time.

Choosing Psychology

After completing the exercises in this chapter, speaking with others, seeking outside information, and doing some careful thinking, you may have narrowed down your choices of majors. If that's true for you, fantastic! If not, keep working and thinking; you will find what is right for you. All majors offer important educational opportunities. In that sense, you can't choose a "wrong" major.

TABLE 2.2 ● Comparing Majors

Choose a potential major (or two or three, if you're still searching) and determine the following:

1. How interested am I in this topic? Is it a new interest or a long-standing one? Do I enjoy the subject?

2. What is the curriculum for this major? What kinds of classes do I have to take?

3. How well does the major match my personal traits, skills, and abilities? Can I perform well in this subject? Is it too easy or too challenging?

4. Which professors teach this subject? Do I know any? Have I taken courses with any?

5. How motivated am I to study this subject? Is it inherently interesting or fun? Do I dread classes or homework in this area?

6. Do I tend to seek out other students and faculty in this department for discussions and other informal interactions?

7. What kinds of jobs do graduates hold? Will the major prepare me for the kind of career I desire?

That said, there are some majors that will better fit your interests and aspirations than others. Let's take a closer look at psychology: What skills and knowledge are acquired with the psychology major?

Skills and Knowledge You'll Develop as a Psychology Major

The psychology major prepares graduates for "lifelong learning, thinking, and action" (McGovern, Furumoto, Halpern, Kimble, & McKeachie, 1991, p. 600). Like other liberal arts majors, psychology students learn valuable thinking and communication skills. Psychology education, however, is unique because it emphasizes learning and applying principles of psychology to understand human behavior. As a psychology major you will have the opportunity to develop the following competencies.

Knowledge of Human Behavior

Undergraduate education in psychology is intended to expose students to the major facts, theories, and issues in the discipline. Understanding human behavior entails learning about physiology, perception, cognition, emotion, development, and more. Consequently, psychology majors construct a broad knowledge base that serves as the conceptual framework for lifelong learning about human behavior as well as the capacity to apply their understanding in everyday situations.

Information Acquisition and Synthesis Skills

The knowledge base of psychology is constantly expanding. Successful psychology students learn how to gather and pull together, what professors often refer to as *synthesize*, information. They learn how to use a range of sources, including the library, computerized databases, and the Internet, to gather information about an area of interest. More important, psychology students learn how to weigh and integrate information into a coherent and persuasive argument. In addition, successful psychology students apply their advanced understanding of cognition and memory to enhance their own processing and recall of information.

Research Methods and Statistical Skills

Psychology students learn how to apply the scientific method to address questions about human behavior. They learn how to identify a problem, devise a hypothesis, choose and carry out scientific methods to gather information about the problem, conduct statistical analyses to evaluate a hypothesis, and interpret data summaries to devise a conclusion. In other words, psychology students become able to pose and answer questions about human behavior and experience.

Critical Thinking and Problem-Solving Skills

Exposure to the diverse perspectives within psychology trains students to think flexibly and to accept some ambiguity. Introductory psychology students often ask for the "right" answer; they soon learn that answers often aren't black or white, but many shades of gray. Psychology students acquire skills in thinking critically about complex problems. They learn to weigh multiple sources of information, determine the degree of support for each position, and make a reasoned decision about which position has more merit and how a problem is best solved.

Reading, Writing, and Speaking Skills

Psychology students develop reading, writing, and presentation skills for effective oral and written communication. They learn how to think critically about what they read, as well as comprehend and present arguments from a psychological standpoint. Moreover, their understanding of human behavior aids students in constructing arguments that are easily comprehended by others. Information derived from psychology regarding cognition, memory, listening, persuasion, and communication enhances psychology majors' ability to communicate orally and in writing.

Interpersonal and Intrapersonal Skills

Psychology students develop the ability to communicate their ideas and use their knowledge of human behavior to devise persuasive arguments. Successful students can lead, collaborate with others, and work effectively in groups. Psychology students are primed to be effective communicators because they are trained to be sensitive to issues of culture, race, class, and ethnicity. Students of psychology also develop intrapersonal awareness, or self-knowledge. They are able to monitor and manage their own behavior, which is critical in succeeding in academic and interpersonal tasks.

Adaptability

Psychology students quickly learn that the perfect experiment is an unattainable goal toward which all researchers strive. Students learn how to design the best research studies possible, given limited resources. The capacity to evaluate and adapt to changing circumstances is highly valued in a volatile economy and workplace.

An undergraduate education in psychology will provide you with the opportunity to develop these skills, which, incidentally, is not an exhaustive list. The psychology major satisfies the objectives of a liberal arts education, which include critical and analytical thinking, independent thinking, leadership skills, communication skills, understanding how to learn, being able to see all sides of an issue, and understanding human diversity (Roche, 2010). However, it is the training in research design and statistical analysis, as well as human behavior, that makes the psychology major unique among liberal arts degrees.

Psychological Literacy

By now you likely realize that if you choose to major in psychology, you will expand your knowledge of human behavior. You'll also get better at discriminating relevant from trivial information. You'll learn how to find, evaluate, and synthesize information from a variety of sources. You'll learn about psychological theories, concepts, and terms that will help you to understand and influence the world around you. In other words, you will demonstrate *psychological literacy*, which is the ability to apply psychological knowledge in everyday life to improve lives—your own and others' (Cranney, Botwood, & Morris, 2012; McGovern et al., 2010). Individuals who are psychologically literate:

- Have basic knowledge and vocabulary of psychology

- Value and apply critical thinking and creative problem solving

- Apply psychological principles to address issues at home, work, and in the community

- Act ethically

- Can gather and effectively evaluate information

- Can use technology effectively

- Can communicate effectively with different audiences

- Demonstrate sensitivity to, understand, and foster respect of diversity

- Are self-reflective

Psychological literacy develops as individuals move from learning facts about psychology to applying bodies of knowledge and modes of thinking. The undergraduate psychology curriculum is designed to provide students with opportunities to develop psychological literacy. The American Psychological Association (2013) has outlined five broad goals for psychology education. The Psychology Department at your college likely models the psychology curriculum on the APA goals.

Goal 1: Knowledge Base in Psychology

   1.1   Describe key concepts, principles, and overarching themes in psychology

   1.2   Develop a working knowledge of psychology's content domains

   1.3   Describe applications of psychology

Goal 2: Scientific Inquiry and Critical Thinking

2.1   Use scientific reasoning to interpret psychological phenomena

2.2   Demonstrate psychology information literacy

2.3   Engage in innovative and integrative thinking and problem solving

2.4   Interpret, design, and conduct basic psychological research

2.5   Incorporate sociocultural factors in scientific inquiry

Goal 3: Ethical and Social Responsibility in a Diverse World

3.1   Apply ethical standards to evaluate psychological science and practice

3.2   Build and enhance interpersonal relationships

3.3   Adopt values that build community at local, national, and global levels

Goal 4: Communication

4.1   Demonstrate effective writing for different purposes

4.2   Exhibit effective presentation skills for different purposes

4.3   Interact effectively with others

Goal 5: Professional Development

5.1   Apply psychological content and skills to career goals

5.2   Exhibit self-efficacy and self-regulation

5.3   Refine project-management skills

5.4   Enhance teamwork capacity

5.5   Develop meaningful professional direction for life after graduation

Do you notice a correspondence among the APA goals, characteristics of psychological literacy, and the competencies developed with a psychology major? Most psychology departments model their programs after the APA goals with the intention of promoting psychological literacy. Psychology students develop lifelong skills that are relevant to their personal and professional lives.

What to Expect as a Psychology Major

What, specifically, can you expect as a psychology major? Like all college students, you can expect to complete a range of courses required by the university, often referred to as General Education requirements because they're intended to provide you with a broad education covering many subjects that are essential to becoming a well-rounded and capable thinker. Whereas the General Education curriculum provides breadth of knowledge, your major is intended to provide depth of knowledge in a specific area. As a psychology major you can expect to learn about human behavior and the methods that psychologists use to study human behavior. Specific requirements may vary by university; however, you can expect to complete courses in the following areas.

Introductory Psychology/General Psychology

Your first course in psychology will provide a whirlwind and fast-paced tour of the field, including all of the subdisciplines discussed in Chapter 1.

Methodology and Statistics

It is the methodology courses that will teach you how psychologists learn about human behavior. Students learn the research methods that psychologists use to ask and answer questions about behavior. They also learn statistics and the methods psychologists use to compile and draw conclusions from the information that they collect. Finally, students gain experience in designing and carrying out research studies that give them practice in asking and answering questions about human behavior.

Breadth Courses

Just as the General Education curriculum is designed to provide students with a broad knowledge base for a well-rounded education, the psychology breadth requirement imparts psychology majors with a well-rounded education in human behavior. The particular sets of requirements vary across psychology departments, but all will include courses in the clinical, developmental, cognitive, biological, and social/personality subfields. Common courses offered by psychology departments are listed in Table 2.3.

Elective Courses

You can expect to take several elective courses in your major; these are courses that are not required but are your choice. These courses are opportunities to explore your interests or gain knowledge and skills that you think will be helpful in the future.

Capstone Course

The capstone course is intended as the crowning achievement for majors, a course that requires them to synthesize all that they have learned to demonstrate that they have mastered the material. It is an advanced course that is intended to require you to integrate your knowledge about how to study psychological phenomena: how to ask research questions, devise methods of addressing questions, and draw conclusions. You might conduct an independent research study or write a lengthy review paper or senior thesis. Ask your professors to learn more about the capstone requirement and get advice so that you can plan ahead and take the courses that you believe will best prepare you for this experience.

TABLE 2.3 ● Psychology Courses

Applied Psychology

Family Psychology

Health Psychology

Industrial Psychology

Organizational Psychology

Psychology and Law

Sport Psychology

Consumer Psychology

Biological and Neuropsychology

Physiological Psychology

Sensation and Perception

Psychopharmacology

Clinical Psychology

Clinical Psychology

Abnormal Psychology

School Psychology

Developmental

Adolescent Psychology

Adulthood and Aging

Life-Span Development

Developmental Psychopathology

Child Psychology

History, Methods, and Statistics

Research Methods

Experimental Psychology

Psychological Statistics

History of Psychology

Learning and Cognitive

Psychology of Learning

Psychology of Creativity

Educational Psychology

Behavior Modification

Cognitive Psychology

Cognitive Neuroscience

Personality, Social Processes, and Measurement

Group Dynamics

Social Psychology

Psychology of Motivation

Psychology of Personality

Psychological and Educational Testing

Psychology of Adjustment

Psychology of Gender

Psychology of Women

Cross-Cultural Psychology

The above courses may be grouped in several ways, depending on department. Some psychology courses are required for majors at nearly all schools, while others are electives found at a handful of schools.

PRACTICAL TIP
PLAN AHEAD FOR YOUR CAPSTONE COURSE

Most departments offer a handful of capstone courses in different subfields of psychology. For example, one department may offer capstone seminars

(Continued)

(Continued)

in developmental psychology, cognitive psychology, social psychology, and experimental psychology. Usually these capstones have different prerequisites. The developmental psychology capstone may require students to have completed specific courses in developmental psychology and likewise for the other capstone courses. Be aware of these requirements early to ensure that you have the time and opportunity to take the prerequisite courses to gain admittance into the capstone course you desire.

What major is right for you? Is it psychology? Only you can answer that question. Psychology offers many opportunities, but other majors offer different sets of opportunities. You are the only expert in choosing your major. No one else can do it for you, and no test provides all of the answers. While parents, friends, professors, and counselors might offer assistance and advice, ultimately this is your decision. Your major will not lock you into one career path; there are many roads, and a psychology major can be the first step toward a variety of careers.

REFLECTION PROMPTS

Why Psychology?

What are some reasons to choose a psychology major? What are the aspects or benefits that most appeal to you? What do you find less appealing? Why? Do you plan to major in psychology? Why or why not? Do other majors appeal to you? Why? In what ways are they similar to or different from psychology?

Self-Review

Once you've amassed several weeks or months' worth of entries, you might use your log to reflect on how you're changing. Read over earlier log entries. How have you changed? Do you have different ideas or views about what you wrote? Do you have new interpretations of events? Do you disagree with an earlier entry? Try to track how you think, and how your thinking is changing. Can you draw conclusions about yourself from what you've written?

Why College?

Why did you decide to attend college? What did you hope to gain? What have you learned since beginning college? Do you still have the same reasons for attending?

3

What Can I Do With a Bachelor's Degree in Psychology?

(Continued)

(Continued)

Chapter Outline	
Computer Support and Information Technology Job Settings That Emphasize Interpersonal Skills Retail and Management Human Resources Human Services Law Enforcement Salaries in Psychology	
Learning About Careers	*Exercise 3.2: Using O*NET and the Occupational Outlook Handbook to Identify Careers* *Exercise 3.3: Career Research*
Match Your Training to Your Goals Coursework Research and Applied Experience Extracurricular Activities	*Exercise 3.4: Assess and Improve Your Fit*

If you've decided to major in psychology, you're in good company because psychology is consistently among the top five most popular bachelor's degrees awarded each year. In the 2015–2016 academic year, nearly 117,000 students earned bachelor's degrees in psychology (National Center for Education Statistics, 2017c). Why are so many students attracted to psychology? Psychology courses cover a range of fascinating topics, such as how we think, learn, use our memory, feel emotions, cope with adversity, and change throughout our lives. Much of what we study in psychology is directly relevant to our everyday life. We all seek to understand human behavior and the environment around us.

Many undergraduate students choose psychology because of their desire to become psychologists. However, as we discussed in Chapter 1, a bachelor's degree in psychology will not qualify you to be a psychologist. Becoming a psychologist requires a doctoral degree, which entails several years of education, training, and supervision beyond the bachelor's degree.

So why major in psychology? Although a baccalaureate in psychology won't qualify you to formally practice psychology, you'll learn skills that are applicable to a variety of jobs, including many that entail helping other people. This chapter describes the skills that employers seek, the kinds of jobs that bachelor's degree graduates in psychology hold, and how you can cultivate useful skills and enhance your employability.

Skills and Attributes Sought by Employers

A bachelor's degree in psychology cultivates skills that are the foundation for a variety of career paths in the mental health professions, science, and business. When considering careers, evaluate and think carefully about the skills and knowledge that you've acquired—or have the opportunity to acquire—over the college years. It may help for you to reconsider your answers to the exercises about your interests and competencies in Chapter 2. A thorough understanding of your talents and proficiencies is particularly important because most jobs are not advertised by major and, therefore, it is unlikely that you will see classified ads listing "Psychology Majors Wanted." While it is rare to see classified ads explicitly recruiting psychology majors, don't be fooled. Your major has helped you to develop a host of skills that employers want. It's up to you to identify those skills and educate employers.

What do employers look for in a new hire? Table 3.1 lists the most desirable qualities in prospective employees, according to a survey of a broad sample of employers (National Association of Colleges and Employers, 2018). Carefully examine the list and you'll quickly notice that interpersonal skills (so-called "people skills"), such as the abilities to communicate, influence others, and

TABLE 3.1 ● Top 15 Attributes Employers Seek in Prospective Employees
1. Problem-solving skills
2. Ability to work in a team
3. Communication skills (written)
4. Leadership
5. Strong work ethic
6. Analytical/quantitative skills
7. Communication skills (verbal)
8. Initiative
9. Detail-oriented
10. Flexibility/adaptability
11. Technical skills
12. Interpersonal skills (relates well to others)
13. Computer skills
14. Organizational ability
15. Strategic planning skills

Source: Reprinted with permission of the National Association of Colleges and Employers, copyright holder.

work in groups, are highly valued. Psychology majors learn about the science of interpersonal interactions and have opportunities to practice interpersonal skills through coursework practica and extracurricular activities, providing an upper hand in the job market.

At first glance this list might seem overwhelming, but consider the following competencies embodied in these skills and you may feel differently.

Interpersonal and Teamwork Skills

These interpersonal skills ("ability to work in a team," "leadership," and "verbal communication skills") enable you to work effectively with others, which is critical to succeed in any job setting. Group skills, the ability to share responsibility with others, conflict management, and an appreciation of individual differences are desired by employers. Employers want to hire and promote individuals who are able to effectively lead a group to accomplish tasks. Interpersonal skills include the ability to listen and communicate, clearly, concisely, and persuasively.

Thinking and Problem-Solving Skills

Good problem-solving skills ("strategic planning skills") are essential to any job. Each task your employer assigns you is a problem to be solved. Any problem can be solved in a number of ways. Knowing how to approach a problem and solve it efficiently is an important skill. Effective problem solvers are skilled in *information acquisition*. They know how to gather information about the problem. Strong reading skills and the ability to extract ideas from information are essential. Effective problem solvers also have analysis skills. They are able to apply knowledge and personal experience to determine causes and solutions to problems. Psychology students are trained to think critically and to employ the scientific method in considering research problems. Research is problem solving—identifying an issue to study, devising a hypothesis, and constructing a study to test it. Employers value good judgment and analytical and decision-making skills because many of today's jobs require higher levels of complex, critical thinking than ever before.

Written Communication Skills

Strong writing skills, such as the ability to write reports, proposals, and summaries, are desirable. Reading skills are connected to writing skills. The abilities to extract important ideas from reading and to document them are valued by employers.

Data Analysis Skills

Employers seek prospective employees with analytical/quantitative skills, the ability to reason numerically, and the ability to identify and solve problems in data. Graduates who can collect, record, and report statistical information will find success.

Computer Literacy

Knowledge of computer applications, including word processing, spreadsheet, and database software, and familiarity with the Internet and e-mail are essential. The ability to learn new technology is highly desirable.

Self-Management and Adaptability

Peruse the list of desirable attributes ("strong work ethic," "initiative," "detail-oriented," "flexibility/adaptability, and "organizational ability") and you may notice that one-third of the items employers seek most reflect self-management skills. The ability to maintain motivation to pursue long-term goals, tolerate stress, control one's emotions, and engage in appropriate behavior are helpful to employees in any field. Employers seek employees who are adaptable, flexible, and capable of handling multiple tasks. Time management and the ability to apply resources in order to effectively complete tasks (e.g., creating a schedule, writing a budget, assigning space, and managing others) is essential. Employers also value the ability to tolerate ambiguity—the fact that there often is no clear right or wrong answer or approach to a problem. Instead, successful employees adapt to the situation and carefully evaluate options to determine the best approach for a given situation.

Do these competencies sound familiar? Turn back to our Chapter 2 discussion of the skills and knowledge you'll develop as a psychology major. The goals of undergraduate education in psychology, imparting psychological literacy, match employers' expectations well. Psychology students have the opportunity to acquire these desirable skills as well as specific, useful, knowledge about psychology, such as how attitudes are formed and changed or how people think, solve problems, and process information.

In addition to these competencies, employers rate *career-related work experience* as very important in a new hire. Successful job applicants have obtained hands-on, practical experience through cooperative education, internships, practica, part-time jobs, or summer work experience. They can apply their school-based knowledge in practical settings. The importance of experience means that you should think ahead to where you'd like to be after graduation and work toward obtaining related experience. Internships, part-time jobs, or volunteer work in a related setting are sources of valuable experience. Any setting in which you develop and demonstrate problem-solving, leadership, and communication skills will aid your professional development (Exercise 3.1).

●

EXERCISE 3.1
DEVELOPING SKILLS

Consider how psychology majors can develop the following competencies desired by employers:

- Interpersonal and teamwork skills

- Thinking and problem-solving skills

- Written communication skills

- Data analysis skills

- Computer literacy

- Self-management and adaptability

Prompt

For each competency, discuss at least two courses or experiences that can aid its development.

Jobs for Psychology Majors

The majority of students who graduate with a bachelor's degree in psychology do not go to graduate school. It is estimated that about one-quarter of psychology undergraduate degree recipients attend graduate school immediately after graduation (Goldstein, 2010). Instead, psychology baccalaureates head into the job market and find success. A recent study of bachelor's degree recipients found that about 2.9% of psychology bachelor's degree recipients age 25 to 29 were unemployed in 2016, compared with the national average of 3.1% (National Center for Education Statistics, 2018). Unemployment rates ranged from about 1% in nursing to about 5% in fine arts. Moreover, between 2010 and 2016, the unemployment rate of psychology majors dropped 3% (from 5.9% in 2010).

The skills that employers seek can be categorized into two sets of competencies: *research skills* and *interpersonal skills* (human service skills, commonly referred to as "people skills"). Employers seek research skills such as the ability to identify problems and locate, analyze, and apply information to solve problems, carry out research, conduct statistical analyses, and write reports. Interpersonal skills include the relational, communication, and self-management skills we have discussed, such as understanding of psychological principles, group dynamics, and persuasion. The psychology curriculum provides opportunities for students to develop and integrate both sets of skills, setting psychology majors apart from other graduates. All jobs entail both types of skills but to differing degrees. Your career options are varied if you think creatively and focus on these sets of skills.

Psychology degree recipients work in a variety of settings. Surveys of working adults age 24 to 54 with bachelor's degrees suggest that about one-third work in human service settings (Julian, 2012). Nearly 40% work in business, management, and human resource positions (including advertising, marketing, finance, and public relations). About 20% work in sales, and the remaining 10% to 15% work in education. Table 3.2 lists common job titles psychology majors have obtained after graduation, by setting. It is not a complete list; many other opportunities are out there waiting for you. Next we examine some of the fields in which psychology majors are employed. Although the jobs are grouped by the degree to which they emphasize research and interpersonal skills, remember that both sets of skills, in differing ratios, are needed for all jobs.

TABLE 3.2 ● Positions Obtained by Psychology Majors	
Business and Academic Settings	**Social and Human Service Settings**
Administrative assistant	Activities coordinator
Admissions evaluator	Administrator
Advertising sales representative	Animal trainer
Advertising trainee	Army mental health specialist
Affirmative action officer	Behavioral specialist
Alumni director	Career counselor
Benefits manager	Case worker
Claims specialist	Child care provider/worker/supervisor
Community relations officer	Child protection worker
Computer programmer	Clinical coordinator
Customer relations	Coach
Data management specialist	Community outreach worker
Department manager	Conservation officer
Disability case manager	Correctional treatment specialist
Disability policy worker	Corrections officer
Employee counselor	Counselor assistant
Employee recruitment	Crisis intervention counselor
Employee relations specialist	Data management specialist
Financial aid counselor	Dietician

(Continued)

TABLE 3.2 ● (Continued)	
Business and Academic Settings	**Social and Human Service Settings**
Fund raiser	Employee health maintenance program specialist
Health care facility administrator	Employment counselor
Host/hostess	Group home attendant
Human resources coordinator/manager/specialist	Mental health assistant
Information specialist	Mental retardation aide
Job analyst	Occupational therapist
Lab coordinator	Parent/family education
Labor relations manager/specialist	Patient resources and reimbursement agent
Laboratory assistant	Police officer
Loan officer	Preschool teacher
Management analyst	Probation officer
Management trainee	Program manager
Marketing	Psychiatric aide/attendant
News writer	Psychiatric technician
Occupational analyst	Recreation leader
Personal recruiter	Recreation supervisor
Personnel manager/officer	Recreational therapist
Polygraph examiner	Rehabilitation counselor
Product and services research	Residence counselor
Programs/events coordination	Social service assistant
Public opinion surveyor	Social worker
Public relations specialist	Social worker assistant
Purchasing agent	Substance abuse counselor
Real estate agent	Veterans contact representative
Research assistant	Veterans counselor
Retail sales management	Victims' advocate
Sales representative	Vocational training teacher
Special features writing/reporting	Volunteer coordinator
Staff training and development	Youth counselor
Systems analyst	
Teaching assistant	
Technical writer	
Trainer/training officer	
Writer	

Sources: American Psychological Association (2013) and Appleby (2016).

Job Settings That Emphasize Research and Information Skills

The particular research-oriented skills valued by employers vary by setting, employer, and experience level. Research and information-related tasks include administrative work, data collection, data entry, data analysis, and interpretation and dissemination. Conceptualize the term *data* broadly, as it includes more than the quantitative data you might enter into a statistics program like SPSS. Data refers to information. Employers look for employees who can manipulate, interpret, and apply information. The following are just a small sample of the types of research and information-oriented positions psychology majors might hold.

Public Relations

Public relations professionals work in businesses, government, universities, hospitals, schools, and other organizations to build and maintain positive relationships with the public. An entry-level position usually entails assisting a public relations professional in working to improve an organization's communication with the community; with consumer, employee, and public interest groups; and with the media. Part of the job entails informing the community and media about an organization's policies, activities, and accomplishments; but public relations specialists also must keep an organization's management and administrative personnel aware of the attitudes and concerns of the public and special interest groups. Public relations work is information-laden in the sense that it entails gathering information about how a client, organization, or product is perceived, using the information to craft a message, and then gathering data to determine the effectiveness of the communication. Public relations activities include setting up speaking engagements for management, helping to prepare speeches, and assisting in planning conferences and presentations. Titles include public relations specialist, information officer, press secretary, communications specialist, public affairs specialist, and others. Entry-level titles are often labeled as *assistant*.

Advertising and Marketing

There are many different kinds of entry-level positions in advertising. Assistant account coordinators work in the account management department, which identifies and solicits new clients and ensures that clients' advertising needs are met. Assistant media planners work in the media department, which places ads; they study what people read and watch in order to determine where to place advertising, and they then attempt to place the right ad at the right time to reach the intended audience. Assistant media buyers help media buyers secure ad time and space and ensure that the advertisements appear as planned and according to the intended budget. Market research assistants work on teams to collect data about a product in order to advertise it more effectively. There are also many administrative positions within advertising and marketing firms.

Office Management

Office management positions include administrative assistants and office managers. Administrative assistants engage in office management functions and support executive staff in a variety of ways. Activities include word processing, scheduling meetings and appointments, maintaining files, and sitting in on meetings. Administrative assistants may conduct research to support a particular project, manage databases, create reports, and oversee projects. In addition to coordinating administrative and information management activities within an office, many administrative assistants train and orient new staff. The responsibilities vary with the employer, setting, and employee competencies. Larger offices may have multiple layers of office supervision, permitting employees to be promoted to managers. Employees who are capable, motivated, and take initiative are likely to be awarded greater responsibility and challenge.

Computer Support and Information Technology

Every company and organization needs personnel to provide computer support and management. A computer support specialist provides technical assistance to users of hardware, software, and computer systems, acting as a troubleshooter who interprets problems and provides technical support for hardware, software, and systems. Technical support specialists are employed by companies to help employees solve computer-related problems. They respond to inquiries from users, diagnose and solve problems, and may install, modify, clean, and repair computer hardware and software. Help-desk technicians answer telephone calls and e-mail inquiries from customers seeking technical assistance for a given hardware or software product. They help users by listening, asking questions to diagnose the problem, and walking the user through steps to solve the problem. Many companies consult help-desk technicians about customers' experiences with the product, what gives them the most trouble, and other customer concerns.

Job Settings That Emphasize Interpersonal Skills

Make no mistake, people skills are a part of every job. That said, some jobs require more contact with people and more interpersonal skills than others.

Retail and Management

The retail sector is a large and important part of the U.S. economy. Retail sales workers sell goods, provide customer service, and help buyers make informed purchases. Bachelor's degree holders are often hired as managers (often first as assistant managers). For example, many large retail stores have management training programs in which a worker learns about all aspects of the business and is then placed as an assistant manager or store manager. An understanding of consumer behavior is important in order to deliver the appropriate sale techniques to achieve success. Managers are responsible for managing the activity of part or all of a store, including managing staff, tracking inventory, marketing products, devising techniques to attract customers, and promoting sales and good customer relations.

Human Resources

Careers in human resources focus on helping employers work with their employees. Human resource positions encompass many titles (personnel administrator, employment specialist, human resources coordinator/specialist/manager, affirmative action coordinator, employee relations manager) and serve various functions: employment and placement, wage and salary administration, training and development, benefits administration, research, and information management. For example, human resources personnel work to attract the most qualified employees, match them to the jobs for which they are best suited, and help them to succeed in their jobs. Activities include recruiting and interviewing potential employees, training and development of workers to help them develop and enhance their morale and performance, organization development (helping companies and businesses deal with change), and career development (helping employees manage their careers). Human resources personnel often collect applications and résumés for jobs, assemble applicant files, perform background checks, orient new employees, educate employees about salary and benefits, and assess departmental needs for staffing. Entry-level positions often include the title *assistant* and the duties typically involve assisting a more senior human resources professional. Human resources positions involve not only working with people but also a great deal of paperwork and information management; accurate record keeping about employment salary and benefits is essential to the work of human resources personnel.

Human Services

This category of positions includes a broad range of jobs with titles such as social services worker, mental health technician, program coordinator, case management worker, social work assistant, community support worker, mental health worker, community outreach worker, child care worker, and gerontology aide. Each of these positions entails working closely with clients and providing direct and indirect services to clients. Typical duties include assessing clients' needs and eligibility for services, helping clients obtain services (such as food stamps, Medicaid, and other human services programs), and providing emotional support. Some human services workers prepare and conduct lessons and educational programs to teach about risks to health. In communities, group homes, or government-supported housing programs, human services workers assist clients in need of counseling, assist adults with daily living skills, and organize group activities. Advancement, additional opportunities, and pay raises come with experience and/or a master's degree.

Law Enforcement

Psychology majors may work in law enforcement settings in administrative roles. They also work in direct contact with law offenders. Parole officer, probation officer, juvenile correctional officer, and correctional casework specialist are examples of job titles for workers who provide services to offenders in custody or on probation or parole. Entry-level positions might carry the term *assistant*. These workers make recommendations and work with others to carry out release plans and monitor educational and employment stipulations. Police officers have lots of contact with the public, and people skills are an essential part of a successful officer's tool box. Typical activities of police officers include maintaining regular patrols, responding to calls for service, directing traffic as needed, investigating a crime scene, or providing first aid to an accident victim. As an officer is promoted through the ranks, he or she takes on more leadership responsibilities, for example, to a position as detective with a primary responsibility of investigating crime scenes. Skills in observation, attention to detail, and critical thinking are all part of the psychology major's repertoire that make for successful police officers.

Each of the careers we have discussed requires both research and interpersonal skills, to varying degrees. Plan on developing both sets of skills to support a wide range of career opportunities. Then consider your interests and tailor your education and experiences to support your chosen emphasis.

Salaries in Psychology

What can you expect to earn with your bachelor's degree? The 2016 starting salary for graduates earning bachelor's degrees in psychology was $36,548 (National Association of Colleges and Employers, 2017). In 2016, the median salary of 25- to 29-year-old bachelor's degree holders was $48,270, and the median salary in psychology was $40,100 (National Center for Education Statistics, 2018). Salaries vary by occupation, region, and experience. Generally speaking, graduates employed in business settings, including human resources, advertising, and marketing, tend to earn higher median *entry-level* salaries than do graduates employed in human service settings. According to Salary.com, the highest 2018 entry-level salaries were in retail management ($43,000), law enforcement (parole officer: $54,000; police officer: $53,000), public relations ($49,000), and human resources (assistant: $42,000; generalist: $54,000), followed by administrative assistant ($43,000), case worker ($36,000), community outreach worker ($35,000), and mental health technician ($33,000). Remember that salary is just one factor that contributes to choosing a career. Interest, ability, values, and motivation are essential components to choosing a career that will sustain you and contribute to a well-lived life.

Learning About Careers

The U.S. federal government recognizes nearly 1,000 different occupations. How many can you name? How do you learn about these opportunities? Your first stop is the *Occupational Outlook Handbook*, published by U.S. Department of Labor and available online as a searchable database (http://www.bls.gov/ooh/). The *Occupational Outlook Handbook* provides information about hundreds of careers. Details include training, job outlook, wages, related careers, as well as websites to help you explore further. The *Occupational Outlook Handbook* can help you identify job titles that you can Google to learn more about.

The U.S. Department of Labor also sponsors a search tool for career exploration and job analysis: O*NET OnLine (http://www.onetonline.org/). O*NET includes much of the information from the *Occupational Outlook Handbook* as well as information on key attributes of workers. Most notably, job seekers can search for jobs by skills, interests, knowledge, and other factors (Exercise 3.2). The U.S. Department of Labor's CareerOneStop (http://www.careeronestop.org) and California CareerZone (http://www.cacareerzone.org) are two other sources for free online tools, information, and resources on a broad variety of employment paths. Each site provides self-assessments, career videos, salary, and education requirements to help users determine their fit to specific jobs based on their skills, interests, and values. These are useful places to begin exploring careers, especially for students who are just beginning the career search process and prefer access to a very broad selection of options (Golding, Lippert, & Malik, 2018).

EXERCISE 3.2

USING O*NET AND THE *OCCUPATIONAL OUTLOOK HANDBOOK* TO IDENTIFY CAREERS

This exercise requires that you run several O*NET searches as follows, to identify jobs that match your interests and capacities.

1. Search by interest. Use the advanced tab on O*NET to search by interests. Note that the interests listed are Holland Codes (see your responses in Chapter 2 to view your specific interests). List two occupations that you find interesting.

2. Search by skills. Use the advanced tab to search by skills. List two occupations that you find interesting.

3. Search by one other means. Use another search option under the advanced tab (e.g., abilities, knowledge, work activities, and so on). Discuss the option you chose and list two resulting occupations.

4. Choose two of the six occupations that you have identified in this exercise. Look up the two occupations in the *Occupational Outlook Handbook*. For each, answer the following questions:

    a. What duties are performed in this occupation?

    b. What education or training is needed?

    c. What is the typical salary?

    d. What is the projected job outlook for this occupation?

There is a great deal of information about careers and career exploration on the Internet. Googling specific job titles can help you learn about employers who hire workers, required education or experience needed, and even information about typical salaries. Exercise 3.3 prompts you to use the Internet to locate information about a career of interest.

EXERCISE 3.3
CAREER RESEARCH

This exercise helps you to take a very close look at an occupation. Choose a career that you would like to learn more about.

1. What career did you choose?

2. Describe the nature of the work.
   a. List at least three job duties or work tasks performed in this occupation.
   b. What kind of work would someone be doing if he or she was hired as a college graduate with no prior experience in this field?
   c. What other occupations are related to this job?

3. Describe the necessary training/licensing/certification and other qualifications.
   a. What is the lowest level of education needed for entry into this occupation?
   b. What is the most desirable education level?
   c. Is special licensing or certification required? If so, please explain.
   d. Which major(s) and courses of study or training are most desirable?
   e. What kinds of skills are needed? Please be as specific as possible.
   f. Does this occupation have specific physical requirements and/ or desirable personal traits (friendliness, patience, etc.)? If so, please describe them.

4. Consider advancement opportunities and job outlook.
   a. What are the opportunities for advancement in this job?
   b. What is the turnover rate for employees in this occupation?
   c. List at least three kinds of organizations that employ people in this occupation.
   d. What is the projected employment outlook for this occupation?

5. Describe the salary and benefits.
   a. What is the potential salary range for this occupation?
   b. What other benefits are generally associated with this job?

Match Your Training to Your Goals

As you've seen, the psychology major is quite useful, with its blend of liberal arts and science, but you cannot rest on your laurels. Regardless of your major, obtaining a job and entering a career requires preparation and planning, and this is especially true in difficult economies. To enhance your marketability and help your psychology education work for you, you must plan your career goals and then match your skills to your goals. Thinking ahead can be challenging, but try to imagine your ideal self a few years from now. Assess your interests and abilities. The counseling center or career development center at your school can help you to select your goals through personality, ability, and vocational interest assessments and counseling. The career development center may also offer alumni contacts who can tell you about their experiences and offer advice. As you consider career paths, complete Exercise 3.4 to learn more about your fit to careers and to plan your education.

EXERCISE 3.4
ASSESS AND IMPROVE YOUR FIT

1. Identify one (or two) specific occupations for which you are preparing.
   a. What is the work environment of a person employed in this area (e.g., workload, hours, deadlines, travel)?
   b. Why is this occupation a good fit for you in terms of your characteristics, skills, interests, abilities, and values (refer back to Chapter 2)?
   c. How much and what kind of education will you need for this career?

2. Examine the university course catalog and the materials provided to majors. What skills can you develop that will prepare you for this occupation, if you take full advantage of the coursework available to you during your undergraduate years?

3. What electives should you choose to prepare yourself for your chosen career?

4. Identify specific opportunities for outside-of-class experience, through research, internships, or work experience. The college handbook and department website, your advisor, and the career services office at your school are useful sources for completing this task.
   a. Describe the opportunity.
   b. Who do you contact to learn more?
   c. When should you obtain this experience? How far ahead must you plan?
   d. How will this experience enhance your education? What will you learn? What skills will you gain? What are the outcomes of this experience?

Coursework

After you've considered where you'd like to be (i.e., your ultimate career goal), take a few elective courses outside of psychology that are specific to your goals. For example, if you plan to enter the business world, a course in management or accounting certainly wouldn't hurt. If you would like a job in human services, take courses in social work, communication, criminal justice, sociology, or anthropology. Regardless of your career plans, classes and experiences that enhance your communications skills (e.g., courses in writing, speech, and communications; writing for the campus newspaper) are a good investment because employers view communication skills favorably. Consider learning a language. For example, the ability to speak Spanish is useful in all settings.

Depending on your career goals, a minor or even double major can offer additional preparation. For example, students interested in human resource careers might consider a business minor, while those interested in law enforcement might consider a minor in justice and law administration. One survey of graduates with bachelor's degrees in psychology found that the happiest and most successful graduates took coursework in a field related to their career, especially a minor or double major (Landrum, 2009). However, weigh the costs and benefits of a double major or minor given your situation. If it delays your graduation, can you afford the additional time and money to complete a double major?

PRACTICAL TIP
CONSIDER A MINOR

Your electives are a way to help you develop the knowledge and skills that you will need to succeed in your chosen career. Choose your electives wisely. Many students use some of their elective credits to earn a minor in a field related to their career interests. A minor can broaden your education and provide you with experiences that can enhance your employability. A minor in business administration, management, finance, justice and law administration, social work, and communication, for example, can round out your knowledge and skill set. Put your electives to work.

Research and Applied Experience

Out-of-class experiences in research and applied activities help you build skills that support your goals. Seek research experience by assisting professors with their research or by developing an independent research project. Research experience demonstrates your ability to work independently and sharpens your analytic and critical thinking skills. It also provides employers with evidence of your motivation, initiative, and willingness to go beyond basic requirements.

Applied experiences are particularly valuable opportunities to develop competencies that match your career goals. An internship or practicum provides hands-on experience. Internships provide wonderful opportunities for learning and training that you can use later. The experience that comes with an internship can be a source of confidence and can spur personal development and maturity. Another advantage of an internship is that it lets you sample a potential career. Do you really want to work with people? Your internship experiences may surprise you. The career center at your school can place you with an internship that provides valuable hands-on experience. In addition, internships can lead to contacts in the field, a possible offer for paid employment after graduation, and someone who can provide a reference or recommendation based on your ability to apply your knowledge of psychology in a real-world setting. For example, in an annual survey, employers consistently rate internships and job-related experiences as very desirable (National Association of Colleges and Employers, 2018).

In addition to (or in place of) an internship, seek work experience. Most institutions offer work-study opportunities in which students are employed on campus for a set number of hours each week. The positions vary and students may be placed in any setting on campus. Work as an administrative assistant in an academic department or administrator's office can give you the opportunity to learn what's entailed in managing an office. Working in a high-traffic setting, such as the registrar's or cashier's office or the library can put you in contact with many people—students, faculty, and administrators—and offer opportunities to practice and improve communication and interpersonal skills. Working as a tutor can help you broaden your understanding of your field and learn how to teach and motivate others. Colleges with residential programs often offer students the opportunity to serve as a resident assistant (RA), a peer leader who supervises and offers support to students living in an on-campus residence or dormitory. RAs are often students' first stop for seeking help with a range of issues, such as resolving conflicts with peers and adjusting to college. They are involved in planning programs, disseminating information to students, and monitoring facilities. RAs develop skills in communication and interpersonal relations, planning and decision-making, and leadership.

One of the most important benefits of applied experiences—whether through internships, work-study, or part-time and summer jobs—is learning how to adapt to new settings, circumstances, and people.

Extracurricular Activities

Take advantage of the extracurricular activities available at your institution. Clubs, teams, and out-of-class activities can help you develop teamwork and leadership skills and enhance your marketability. Similar to internships and work experience, extracurricular activities can give you opportunities to test career paths, develop contacts, and work on your communication and interpersonal skills. In addition, employers value volunteer work for campus and community organizations because it shows that you're a good citizen.

Extracurricular participation gives employers evidence about your leadership skills, your ability to work effectively in a group, and your initiative and motivation.

Finally, be open to new possibilities. Flexibility is an important life skill that also is valued by employers. Keep an open mind and explore multiple possibilities to find a job that you'll love.

REFLECTION PROMPTS

Part-Time Jobs

When considering their experience, all too often students dismiss their part-time jobs. What jobs have you had? What duties did each entail? What did you do? What skills did you use to complete the job? What did you like about it? What did you dislike? What did you learn from each job?

What's Not for You?

Part of figuring out a career path is figuring out what you don't want to do. Describe one or two careers that you know are not for you. What are they? What do they do? Why aren't they for you? How do you know?

My Strengths and Weaknesses

Consider the skills that a liberal arts degree builds as well as the skills employers seek. Identify your strengths. What do you do well? What do you enjoy? What are your weaknesses? How do you feel about your weaknesses? How might you strengthen these areas?

Considering Life After College

Between taking classes, studying for exams, and writing papers, students sometimes forget to think about the big picture. By now you likely have thought about what you would like to do after graduation. Now consider how your post-graduation life will differ from your present experience. How will you spend your time? Is there anything about college that you will miss? What won't you miss? Transitions from one phase of life to another, like from college to work, are exciting but also stressful. What can you do now to prepare? What types of activities might ease your transition to work?

Take an Active Role
in Your Education

(Continued)

(Continued)

Chapter Outline		
How Do You Become a Research Assistant? Why Do Professors Seek Student Research Assistants? Conduct a Research Study		
Get Applied Experience Teaching Experience Field Experience Why Seek Field Experience? How Do You Get Field Experience?		
Get Involved in the Discipline Attend Psychology Conferences Disseminate Research Participate in Professional Organizations	*Exercise 4.5: Regional Psychological Associations* *Exercise 4.6: Academic and Professional Organizations*	

One of the biggest differences between high school and college is that college requires you to take an active role in your education. Whether you take anything of substance away from your college years, whether you learn anything, is up to you. Your own interest, motivation, and hard work will make or break your college experience. Students often are surprised by this new level of autonomy, and they often are unsure of how to take control of their education. This chapter will help you to take advantage of the resources in your department, institution, and field so that you can get the most from your college years.

Take an Active Role: Academic Advising

The first—and most important—way that you can take an active role in steering your own education is through participating meaningfully in academic advising. Every institution employs a mechanism for advising students about the coursework and experiences needed to earn a degree. In most cases, students must obtain advisement prior to registration each semester. Some departments employ "block advising," in which a faculty or staff member advises groups of students at once. Others offer one-on-one advising, where students meet with faculty on an individual basis. Frequently advisors are professors in the students' major department. Some institutions instead run advising centers staffed by advisors who meet with students of all majors for at least the first year or two of college, then students often transition to professors for advisement. Regardless of whether you meet with faculty or advising staff, on a group or one-on-one basis, it is up to *you* to ensure that you get the information and advice that you need.

Your Academic Advisor

An academic advisor is a faculty or staff member whose role is to help students select courses and other learning opportunities to provide them with a well-rounded education and preparation for their chosen career. Your advisor may assist you with academic advising, which focuses on issues such as course scheduling and availability, meeting prerequisites, fostering academic success, and graduation requirements. He or she may also assist you with career advising, which emphasizes your short- and long-term career goals and will occur during multiple discussions over your years in college.

Consult with your advisor when you are having academic difficulties or considering adding or dropping a course, changing your major, withdrawing from school, or transferring to another college. Stop by during office hours to ask a quick question, but if your questions are of a serious nature, such as whether to change your major, schedule an appointment so that you have the time to openly discuss your concerns. Your advisor has your best interests in mind and will provide you with the advice that you need to make sound decisions. When making big decisions such as whether to change your major, drop out of school, or go to graduate school, your advisor may suggest that you seek additional input and feedback from other sources such as other faculty, family, friends, and the counseling center. Your academic advisor is a source of feedback and advice; take advantage of this important resource. But always remember that your academic and career decisions are your own. Seek advice and assistance in order to make informed decisions, but the ultimate responsibility for the decisions that you make is yours.

How to Be Proactive in Academic Advising

The first, perhaps most important step in ensuring that you get the advisement you need to register on time is to begin early. Contact your advisor early, at minimum 2 weeks before your registration date. Some advisors meet with students during open office hours. Most make appointments with advisees. Expect to wait a few days for an appointment. Your advisor meets with many other students and may not have an appointment for a week or longer. How can you prepare for your meeting?

Be knowledgeable. Review the university handbook to determine the requirements of your major. Write down any questions as they arise.

Examine your record. Determine your outstanding coursework. List the courses that you have taken. Most departments have a worksheet for majors to complete that lists all general education and major requirements. Complete this sheet and keep an up-to-date copy (digital or hard copy) filed away where you can easily find it and where you won't lose it.

Examine the registration website or booklet to choose courses. Prepare a tentative schedule with several course alternatives. Be prepared to explain how the courses you have selected fulfill the curricular requirements of your major.

Prepare questions. Consider your ultimate career goals and write down any questions that you have about your plans for after graduation.

What to Do During Your Advising Meeting

Show up early for your appointment. If you're late, you'll either miss out on some of your allotted time or you'll make other students wait—effectively stealing their time. If you must cancel, notify your advisor as soon as possible, preferably well ahead of your appointment so that another student can be rescheduled in your timeslot.

Ignore your cell phone. Put it on silent. Do not look at it other than to locate information related to your meeting, such as a course schedule.

Be attentive and ready to interact. Be prepared to talk about how your semester and coursework are going. What's going well? What challenges are you experiencing?

Ask questions. Ensure that you're on track to earn your degree on time.

Share your list of preferred courses. Determine whether they meet the requirements for your major. Ask for advice about your schedule and whether the workload is feasible. Remember that advisors can help you decide between courses. Also note that advisors vary in how they approach course planning. Some advisors plan your coursework with you during the appointment. Others discuss your progress, needs, and give examples but leave planning to you. You can always follow up with your selections.

Keep the horizon in mind. That is, ask for advice on what you should consider within the next year or two. For example, are there specific courses a second-year student should enroll in? What kinds of experiences should students hope to gain (e.g., research experience, internships) and when? Is there an internship? What is the process for applying? Ask your advisor to help you think ahead.

Take notes. A lot of information will be discussed. It might seem like you'll remember your conversation, but you're better off taking notes so that you don't forget critical information.

Don't expect to cover it all in one meeting. If you're meeting about registration, you may not have time to discuss career options. Your academic advisor likely is quite busy, but advisors make time for their students. Schedule additional time to meet or make plans to visit during office hours.

Perhaps the most important take-away from this discussion is that the advisor-student relationship is a two-way street. Come prepared to discuss your interests, needs, and goals and seek advice as to how to plan to meet them. Your advisor may have dozens of other students to advise, so use your scheduled time with him or her wisely. Help your advisor to help you by being proactive. As you prepare for your advising meeting, consider the checklist in Table 4.1.

TABLE 4.1 ● Academic Advising Checklist

❑ Know who your advisor is

Advisor name: _____

Location: _____

Phone number: _____

E-mail: _____

Office hours: _____

❑ Schedule an appointment at least 2 weeks prior to your registration date.

❑ Study the university handbook to determine what courses are required of your major.

❑ Write down questions as they arise.

❑ List the courses that you have taken. Most departments have a worksheet for majors to complete that lists all general education and major requirements. Complete this sheet (digitally or on paper) and keep an up-to-date copy filed away where you can easily find it and where you won't lose it.

❑ Examine the registration website or booklet to choose potential courses.

❑ Prepare a tentative schedule with several course alternatives.

❑ Be prepared to explain how the courses you have selected fulfill the curricular requirements of your major.

❑ Consider your ultimate career goals and write down any questions that you have about your plans for after graduation.

❑ Actively discuss your career goals with your advisor and seek advice as to how to plan to meet them.

Get to Know Professors

Many students don't take advantage of their school's most valuable resource: the faculty. Sure, they attend class, take notes, and learn the content of their discipline, but learning occurs in many places outside of the classroom. When students take an active role in their education, they soon realize that there is much to learn from professors, learning that can extend beyond mere content knowledge. Perhaps one of the most important pieces of advice in this book is to get to know your professors. Establish relationships with faculty.

Faculty help your professional development in more ways than lecturing, overseeing class discussions, and bestowing grades. Professors also can help you to enrich your college years through a variety of learning experiences outside the classroom. For example, professors can involve students in their research, providing opportunities to assist them in making new discoveries and generating new knowledge. Faculty aid students' professional development in other ways too, such as by introducing students to others who can help them to meet their goals (for example, a professor in a graduate department to which you might apply). Professors also can help their students obtain special opportunities such as internships, summer positions, and teaching assistantships. Finally, job and graduate applications often require several letters of recommendation from faculty. Recommendation letters discuss more than just grades; they discuss students' abilities and aptitudes from academic, motivational, and personal perspectives. Of course, persuasive recommendation letters should not be your only reason for developing relationships with faculty members, but helpful letters are a useful motivator and reward.

Interacting With Professors in Class

If you would like to develop out-of-classroom professional relationships with faculty, note that professors want to engage with students who are bright, motivated, committed, and enthusiastic. The first step in getting to know professors is making yourself someone that your professors want to know better. All relationships are two-way streets, and relationships with faculty are no different. Who do you like to interact with? What characteristics do they show? Most people prefer to interact with others who are respectful, attentive, kind, inquisitive, and genuine. These characteristics also attract faculty.

Your behavior both in and out of class can attract or deter a professor from developing a professional relationship with you. Do you display behaviors that faculty appreciate? Take the quiz in Exercise 4.1 to assess your knowledge about appropriate in-class and out-of-class behavior. Exercise 4.2 summarizes some of the top behaviors that professors clearly *do not* want to see in class. Some of the items may appear humorous, but (believe it or not) they are regularly seen in class.

EXERCISE 4.1
DO YOU DISPLAY APPROPRIATE IN- AND OUT-OF-CLASS BEHAVIOR?

Circle yes or no for the following items. Be honest!

1.	Yes	No	I prepare before class.
2.	Yes	No	During class, I often check Instagram or text.
3.	Yes	No	I smile and say hello when I see professors.
4.	Yes	No	I take more than one make-up exam.
5.	Yes	No	I stop by during professors' office hours to discuss something from class that sparked an interest or seek assistance with class material.
6.	Yes	No	I let my phone beep during class.
7.	Yes	No	I help other students by sharing lecture notes and forming study groups.
8.	Yes	No	After missing class or arriving late, I often ask my professor to e-mail his or her notes and an explanation of what was missed.
9.	Yes	No	I sit toward the front of class.
10.	Yes	No	I often hand in assignments late.
11.	Yes	No	I rarely miss class.
12.	Yes	No	When the professor asks "Are there any questions?" I often ask "Is this going to be on the test?"
13.	Yes	No	After a particularly interesting class lecture or discussion, I often offer a compliment or thank the professor and ask additional questions.
14.	Yes	No	After each exam I often nit-pick over test questions, trying to get additional points.
15.	Yes	No	I participate in departmental events, clubs, or activities, such as Psi Chi or the psychology club.

(Continued)

(Continued)

16.	Yes	No	I often read other books or newspapers in class.
17.	Yes	No	I try to ask well-reasoned and well-formulated questions during class.
18.	Yes	No	I often leave class at break.
19.	Yes	No	I try to offer good answers to the professor's questions during class discussions.
20.	Yes	No	I use group time in class to catch up with my friends.
21.	Yes	No	I participate in class but try not to dominate class discussions (i.e., I let others speak too).
22.	Yes	No	I often arrive late to class.
23.	Yes	No	I try to show interest in the course and remain attentive during class.

Scoring

Add up the number of "yes" responses to odd items and "no" responses to even items. The higher your score, the greater number of appropriate behaviors you display and the more likely that professors view you favorably.

Prompt

1. Given your score, how favorably do you think are professors likely to view you? Why?

2. How might your in- and out-of-class behavior influence your ability to develop professional relationships with faculty?

3. How can you improve your in- and out-of-class behavior? Discuss at least three ways in which you can improve your behavior.

EXERCISE 4.2

WHAT NOT TO DO: 15 BEHAVIORS THAT TURN OFF FACULTY

1. Socialize in class, such as pass notes or chat.

2. Near the end of class, close your books firmly and jingle your car keys to help remind your instructor that time is just about up.

3. Make term papers look longer by adding blank pages after the front and back pages or using large font or big margins.

4. Be rude to classmates.

5. Roll your eyes.

6. Engage in non-class behaviors, such as reading a book, playing with a phone, checking out Facebook, or sleeping.

7. Ask "Do we have to know this?"

8. Let your phone ring, chirp, or beep during class.

9. Use technology inappropriately (that is, for non-class activities such as viewing videos or social networking).

10. Speak without being called on and/or interrupt your professor.

11. Repeatedly miss classes, arrive late, or leave early or leave and reenter the room regularly during class.

12. After missing class or arriving late, ask the professor to go over what you missed or ask, "Did I miss anything important?"

13. Visit a professor's office for the first time at the end of the semester, after receiving a poor mark, to ask for extra credit.

14. Ask for differential treatment (for example, that a late assignment policy be waived for you).

15. Quibble over the wording of test questions after each exam, emphasizing getting points more than learning.

Prompt

1. Have you noticed any of these behaviors in class? What message do you think they convey?

2. Imagine that you are giving a presentation to the class and your peers are attending to their phones as they listen. What might you feel?

3. How might poor classroom behavior interfere with your professional development in and out of the classroom?

Effective Use of E-mail to Contact Professors

One of the most common ways that students interact with professors outside of class is through e-mail. Most professors use e-mail to schedule meetings with students, answer brief questions about content, and address questions specific to the student, such as about late assignments, grades, or make-up work. Pay attention to your professor's policy about e-mail. Some professors prefer that students e-mail rather than call. Others use e-mail only to make appointments. Some don't use e-mail at all. The course syllabus usually lists the professor's preferences with regard to e-mail—when to do so, how to do so, and so on. Learn about these preferences early so that you know how to contact your professor should you need to.

The e-mail you send to faculty should look very different than the casual messages you may send to family and friends. The content of your e-mail message tells faculty about your maturity and professionalism. Addressing the professor appropriately, using proper grammar, and avoiding slang and accusatory language determines whether your message is interpreted seriously and as you'd like (Exercise 4.3). Always read your message back before sending it. Succinct messages like, "Why did you give me a C for that assignment?" can be interpreted as accusatory rather than a genuine question. Err in providing more explanation than less. Better yet, consider the advice in the Practical Tip on e-mailing professors about grades.

PRACTICAL TIP
E-MAILING PROFESSORS ABOUT GRADES

Should you e-mail your instructors to ask questions about your grades? Even professors who rely on e-mail heavily often have different policies for discussing grades. Check the course syllabus for information about a professor's e-mail policies but recognize that sensitive topics such as grades are often best discussed in person. For example, a professor is best able to answer your question about a paper grade by referring directly to the paper. Questions about grades often become learning opportunities—and that requires face-to-face contact. Likewise, questions about grades often are interpreted differently when vocalized in person compared with when questions are read in an e-mail. Asking in person requires more time and effort on your part and sends the message that you are serious about learning. Also, giving a verbal explanation to a student with a paper in hand often takes less of a professor's time than writing an e-mail, especially when writing the e-mail requires that professor to look up the student's grade and work, consider it, then reply. Bottom line: E-mail professors to set appointments to discuss grades, but consider discussing grades themselves in person.

Always remember that e-mailing faculty is a means of formal communication. Keep this in mind and the following tips are easy to anticipate.

1. **Use your institutional e-mail address.** Most institutions list it as the official method of contact. Frequently e-mails from other senders

might get caught in spam filters. Also, a silly e-mail address, like butterflygrrrl@email.com, is unprofessional.

2. **Use the subject line.** The subject line is used to identify the purpose and summarize what's in the e-mail (for example, "PSY100 Assignment Question").

3. **Be formal.** Address your professor as Professor Smith, Dr. Smith, and so on. Many professors include information on the class syllabus about how they wish to be addressed. Use it. If you are unsure whether your professor holds a doctorate and can be called Dr., err on the side of caution and refer to him or her as Professor. Moreover, note that most female faculty do not wish to be called Mrs. and often feel that it is inappropriate.

4. **Identify yourself and your course.** Remember that your professor teaches multiple courses, so stating "This is John Smith from your psychology course" is not as helpful as "This is John Smith from your Research Methods course." Professors often teach more than one section of a course, so it's more helpful to also include the course number and section, such as "I'm John Smith from your PSY201-01 Research Methods course" or "I'm John Smith from your Monday 10:00 a.m. Research Methods course."

5. **Keep your message short.** Instructors can receive dozens of e-mails each day. Make it easy for them to grasp your question and respond.

6. **Proofread.** Check spelling and grammar. Errors can be interpreted as a sign of carelessness. Do not write in all capital letters; in e-mail, it is interpreted as shouting.

7. **Do not use slang, emoticons, or abbreviations.** What is acceptable in texts and instant message communications is not appropriate for communicating with your instructor.

8. **Don't expect an immediate response.** Do not expect your instructor to reply during evenings or over weekends. Wait 24 to 48 hours for a response. Frequently professors include information on their syllabus about how long students can expect to wait for a response.

9. **Resend, if needed.** If you must resend the message, forward the original message with a quick note indicating that you're following up on your message in case it was missed.

10. **Follow up.** A simple "thank you" in response to a reply is usually appreciated.

●

EXERCISE 4.3
E-MAILING PROFESSORS

Consider the following e-mail a student sent to an instructor:

I was wondering was there anything else I can do to get a C in the course??! im workin on playin on da team for the school next term! I got sick real bad and i have a letter for u if u like. i spent 6 hours at health center and my fever was real high so they wouldn't let me go and it was hard to get up and do anything if ukno what i mean!! Im just missing a few points to earn a C- 2 points!! that better then a D+

1. What is the student attempting to communicate? Where did he or she go wrong?

2. Imagine that you are a professor reading this message from a student. What is your likely response?

3. Rewrite this e-mail message to best convey the student's concerns and get a helpful response from the faculty member.

We use technology to communicate with our friends and families each day. The informal nature of instant messages and texts helps us communicate more quickly and can convey warmth and humor in our interactions with others. However, it is critical to remember that business communication is formal, and e-mails to faculty should be formal in order to be taken seriously. Everyday communications with your professors will influence their opinions of you, which can influence the range of opportunities that come your way.

Seek a Mentor

Seek to develop a special relationship with a faculty mentor. A *mentor* is a person with expertise who takes a special interest in you; he or she may be a college professor, advisor, or job, research, or practicum supervisor. Mentors provide their protégés with opportunities to learn, be advised, and obtain moral support. Note that mentors are more than academic advisors; your academic advisor may or may not also become your mentor. While an academic advisor is assigned to you, a mentoring relationship develops more organically. A mentor facilitates your undergraduate accomplishments, provides intellectual and emotional support, and helps you on the path toward your career.

How Do You Find a Mentor?

The first step in finding a mentor is having positive interactions with a professor. Appropriate in- and out-of-class interactions and showing genuine interest in the subject can earn positive attention. Visit a professor during office hours and ask about class, the field, or his or her experience.

Seek opportunities to get involved in research. Students who are motivated and visible in their departments and who seek to get involved in faculty research will usually find it easier to meet professors who are interested in developing professional mentoring relationships. Seek opportunities and approach professors. It requires initiative and may seem scary, but the rewards are great. Tell professors that you're looking to become involved in research. Explain that you hope to work closely with someone on their research and ask questions about their work. Demonstrate honest intellectual curiosity and motivation. If you are perceived well, word will get around that you're an excellent student looking for research experience.

Remember that classroom behavior is an important indicator of a student's maturity and motivation that influences professors' views of students. If you do well in your courses and present yourself as competent, motivated, wanting to get involved, and committed, you may even be approached by a faculty member who wants to mentor you. Students with excellent literature searching, critical analysis, and writing abilities are helpful assistants. Students with expertise and interest in research and statistical analyses are often especially appealing to faculty because they require less instruction and therefore can become deeply immersed in research at a faster pace.

As you look for a mentor, remember that the most popular professors may have more students coming to them than they can mentor. Working closely with a student in a mentoring relationship entails a great deal of time, attention, and intellectual focus; faculty can only mentor so many students at once. Some faculty may not be able to take on additional students. Remember that popularity, whether a particular professor is liked by the majority of students, should not be your main criterion for selecting a mentor. Look to faculty who are actively involved in research and whose interests parallel yours as closely as possible. Visit during office hours to ask a question or two about graduate school or your career interests; get a feel for the professor's approachability. If he or she seems interested in discussing these questions, express your desire to gain some experience in research.

In the vast majority of cases, there is no pay involved for assisting professors with their research. Instead, you'll get a free learning experience that will improve your skills and abilities as well as make you more appealing to graduate schools and employers. Sometimes you may earn course credit for your work. Finally, volunteer to work closely with a professor only if you have the time to commit. Remember that falling behind or dropping out will reflect negatively on you—much more so than if you hadn't become involved at all.

What to Look for in a Mentor

The role of a mentor is to provide guidance so that students are aware of resources and opportunities and understand their options. Successful mentoring relationships are not an accident. Mentoring relationships are most successful when students make careful and conscientious efforts to find mentors who possess certain characteristics and who complement their needs. A successful mentoring relationship requires chemistry, or the ability to work together.

In order to find a helpful mentor, be aware of your needs and career goals. Where are you now, in terms of skills? Who do you want to become? How must you grow and what skills and experiences must you obtain to do so? A well-chosen mentor can help you to find the answers to those questions, while a poorly chosen mentor might leave you hanging, frustrating you with more questions than answers. Effective mentors are professionally skilled but also have positive attributes and are skilled interpersonally (Appleby, 1999). Some desirable characteristics to look for in mentors are listed in Table 4.2. No one person will have all of these characteristics; you must decide which are most important to you and find someone who approximates them (Exercise 4.4).

TABLE 4.2 ● Characteristics of Effective Mentors

Check off the characteristics that match the attributes of a faculty member from whom you are considering seeking mentorship.

Effective mentors are interpersonally skilled. They:

❑ Are responsive, warm, and encouraging

❑ Are nonjudgmental

❑ Help students develop positive self-concepts

❑ Help to open doors to career and graduate school opportunities by telling others of the positive aspects of protégées

❑ Provide emotional support

❑ Challenge and motivate students to attempt new tasks that stretch their abilities.

Effective mentors have positive personal attributes. They are:

❑ Mature and wise

❑ Providers of accurate and useful advice, and they enjoy providing advice

❑ Friendly, optimistic, and positive in their life outlook

❑ Admired and respected by students and peers

❑ Trustworthy and dependable

❑ Ethical and have high moral standards

Effective mentors have attained professional competency. They are:

❑ Qualified, competent, and experienced

❑ Knowledgeable with up-to-date information

❑ Able to communicate well

❑ Actively involved in professional or academic organizations

❑ Involved in research

❑ Interested in lifelong learning

Source: Appleby (1999).

EXERCISE 4.4
LEARNING ABOUT POTENTIAL MENTORS

Learn about the faculty in your department. Visit the department website and review faculty biographies. Visit their websites. Review their lists of publications.

1. Choose two or three faculty to study in more depth. Who are they and why did you choose them?

2. Next, choose one professor. Review his or her research. Look up the abstracts of articles that sound interesting. Write a two-sentence summary of the professor's area of expertise and research. Do you find it interesting? Why or why not?

3. If you're interested in the professor's work, read more and devise three questions to ask about his or her work. List the questions here.

4. Visit the professor's office hours to speak with the professor about his or her research. What did you learn?

5. Consider your overall impressions: How comfortable do you feel speaking with this faculty member? If you're uncomfortable, try to identify why.

6. Complete this process for each faculty member, and you'll begin to get ideas about which faculty you're more inclined to work with. Discuss the results of this exploration.

As you consider potential mentors, ask yourself the following questions:

1. Is the professor in a position to share his or her time and advice?

2. Does he or she conduct and publish research?

3. Is the professor interested in mentoring you?

4. Are you comfortable with the professor's demeanor and personality? Does it fit your academic style and needs?

5. From your perspective, does the professor exhibit the ability to communicate openly and clearly?

Choose a mentor who you admire and with whom you can communicate and whose interpersonal skills and interactional patterns work well with your own.

Get Research Experience

Many students get involved in research as research assistants. A research assistantship is an opportunity for undergraduate students to assist a faculty member in his or her program of research. Assisting a faculty member in research is an exciting opportunity to do the research rather than just read about it.

Why Become a Research Assistant?

Research generates new knowledge. When we engage in research, we make new discoveries and learn new things. Sure you read about psychology research, but carrying it out is an altogether different animal that will help you learn more than you have in any class. It's an opportunity to be on the cutting edge of psychology. Aside from the thrill of generating new knowledge, assisting a professor with research provides many other valuable opportunities (Grover, 2006; Landrum, 2008), such as the following:

- Gaining specialized skills and knowledge by working one-on-one with a faculty member

- Learning methodological techniques that will be helpful in completing your senior thesis or, perhaps, graduate work

- Practicing written and oral communication skills by learning how to express research findings and preparing papers for submission to, and presenting at, professional conferences and journals

- Developing a mentoring relationship with a faculty member

- Obtaining experiences that will enhance your applications to employers and graduate programs

- Acquiring outstanding letters of recommendation, as faculty who work closely with you can write more detailed letters that fully demonstrate your capacities and strengths.

Engaging in research is a worthwhile experience for all students because it provides opportunities to learn how to think, organize information, and solve problems, as well as demonstrate commitment to a project—all skills coveted by employers and graduate admissions committees. In fact, graduate school admissions committees rate research experience as a "very important" factor in the admissions process and more important than GPA (Keith-Spiegel & Wiederman, 2000; Walfish & Moreira, 2005).

What Does a Research Assistant Do?

What will be expected of you as a research assistant? We cannot predict the specific tasks that you will be assigned, as a research assistant's tasks will vary by faculty member, project, and area of psychology. Some might be involved in data collection by administering surveys or maintaining and operating lab equipment. Others might code and enter data, make photocopies, or write literature reviews. Here are some general tasks that research assistants perform (Landrum & Davis, 2014):

- Collect data by administering surveys, interviews, or running research protocols.

- Score, code, and enter data into a spreadsheet or statistical analysis program.

- Conduct library research, including performing literature searches using databases (e.g., PsycINFO, Social Sciences Citation Index, PsycARTICLES), making copies of articles, and ordering unavailable articles and books through interlibrary loan.

- Assist the faculty member to develop new research ideas.

- Use computer skills such as word processing, spreadsheet, scheduling, and statistical analysis programs.

- Assist in preparing submissions for local or regional conferences and, if accepted, work on poster or oral presentations for professional conferences.

- Assist faculty in preparing a manuscript to submit the results of your collaborative research to a scientific journal.

Frequently students who work with faculty members as research assistants develop their own ideas for research projects that stem from the faculty's work. For example, one of my students worked with me on several related projects and developed her own hypothesis to extend my work by adding additional variables. She carried out her project under my supervision as her senior thesis, presented it at a regional psychology conference, and together, we published it in a scholarly journal with the student as first author. Research assistantships provide substantial educational and professional development opportunities.

How Do You Become a Research Assistant?

First and foremost, you should perform well in class and be motivated and visible in your department. Let faculty know that you're interested in getting involved in research, but do not send out a mass e-mail or a form e-mail notifying them of your availability. Instead, approach professors during their office hours and ask for leads on who might be looking for research assistants. Before you approach a professor you would like to work with, learn about his or her work. Read some of the professor's articles, especially the most recent ones. When you find a professor who is looking for an assistant, carefully and honestly describe what you can offer (computer skills, Internet skills, statistical skills, and the number of hours per week you're available). Let the faculty member know that you're willing to work hard (be honest). Ask thoughtful questions, such as those in Table 4.3. Ask questions about the professor's expectations and how you will be evaluated. Professors are often unintentionally vague in describing their expectations for students during the research assistantship as well as for the products of the collaboration (such as a paper).

It may be tempting to consider turning the professor down because the hours don't fit your schedule or the research isn't interesting enough, but the opportunity to work as a research assistant is a coveted prize that will enhance your academic and professional development in many ways. Don't be hasty in turning down such an important opportunity. You may not work on a project that you find mind-blowingly exciting, but you will obtain excellent experience. Also, research projects often become more interesting once you're immersed in them. Your academic interests most likely will change as you gain more experience and education.

Why Do Professors Seek Student Research Assistants?

You're now aware that there are many benefits of getting involved in research. Did you know that there are benefits for faculty too? They get a hard-working student to do some labor-intensive parts of research. Faculty, especially those at undergraduate institutions without graduate programs, often depend on undergraduates to further their research programs. Many faculty members have ideas for studies that they don't have time to conduct. Motivated students can help them to carry out these studies. If you develop a relationship with a faculty member, you might be able to help him or her conduct a project that may otherwise remain shelved for lack of time.

Involving undergraduates in research also offers the opportunity for faculty to develop a relationship with a student and witness his or her professional growth, which most professors find quite rewarding. Student-professor research relationships offer benefits to all involved; however, the commitment to become a research assistant is a big one. You will be given responsibility to

TABLE 4.3 ● Questions to Ask About a Research Assistantship
• Are the work hours set or is there some flexibility? Will they change each week?
• What will I do? What are specific kinds of examples?
• Will I be evaluated? How?
• Will I be asked to submit a paper or other project at the end of this experience?
• How long will the project last?
• How long is the commitment (full semester, part semester)?

ensure that aspects of the project get done. The faculty member will count on you to be responsible and complete your assignments correctly. This includes asking questions and seeking assistance if you don't understand the task. Your performance as a research assistant can give a professor lots of good things to write in a letter of recommendation, including specific examples of your skills, competencies, and personal characteristics. If you complete tasks competently, you might be asked to take on more responsibility, and you will learn more as well as earn a reputation as an excellent student and potential future colleague (and thereby earn excellent letters of recommendation). However, there is a positive payoff from conducting research with faculty only if you consistently perform competent work. If you don't take the commitment seriously, are unreliable, or make repeated mistakes, your relationship with the professor will suffer (as will your standing in the eyes of other faculty, because professors often share information about their experiences with students). If you decide to work with a faculty member on his or her research, treat it as a primary responsibility.

Conduct a Research Study

Taking an active role in your education entails looking for opportunities to learn and develop useful skills. We have seen that engaging in faculty research promotes a host of abilities and skills that employers and graduate programs seek. Another way to obtain research experience is to carve out your own opportunity by conducting an independent study. As you're aware, research generates new knowledge. When we engage in research, we make new discoveries and learn new things. Sure you read about psychology research and may have assisted faculty with their research, but carrying out your own study to examine your own hypothesis is an altogether different animal that will help you learn more than you have in any class.

Although student-developed studies are often referred to as *independent studies*, they are far from the isolated experiences that the name conveys. All are closely supervised by faculty. Some psychology departments require students to carry out their own research projects in order to demonstrate their competence; these studies often take place in capstone courses.

If you are interested in developing and conducting your own study, take the steps we have described to find a faculty member whose interests match yours and who is willing to oversee your study. Together you will determine your research question and how to address it. Frequently students' ideas for independent studies come from their work on faculty projects. It is often said that research often generates more questions than answers. These are often the best studies to conduct because they already have a faculty member's attention and interest. However, you may also consider approaching faculty with whom you have not conducted research. The specific steps entailed in designing and conducting your research study will be determined by the topic and by your interactions with your faculty supervisor. Pay attention to the advice in this chapter about how to choose and make contact with faculty.

Get Applied Experience

Taking an active role in your education entails seeking opportunities for personal and professional development. As you consider your own academic and professional development, attempt to gain experiences that will round out your competencies. Research experience is an important contribution to your academic development, but applied experiences such as working as a teaching assistant or completing field experiences such as internships or practica also build important competencies.

Teaching Experience

Teaching assistants have opportunities to learn a variety of skills, although these opportunities are less common than research assistant positions. Many professors, myself included, observe that teaching a topic helps them to develop a new, more complex, understanding of that topic. Explaining material to another person helps you identify gaps in your own knowledge and prompts learning.

What do undergraduate teaching assistants do? They work with a faculty for one semester, offering assistance with a specific course such as Introduction to Psychology. They may help an instructor plan discussion questions or in-class group assignments, run discussion or laboratory sessions, and serve as class assistants. More specifically, a teaching assistant might do any of the following, depending on the instructor and institution:

- Attend lectures
- Conduct review sessions for exams
- Facilitate discussions
- Prepare lectures as needed
- Request or acquire necessary equipment
- Hold regular office hours
- Tutor students
- Manage and respond to course-related e-mail
- Update course webpages
- Participate in online discussions
- Organize assignments
- Proctor exams
- Maintain course attendance records
- Attend instructor/TA meetings
- Act as a liaison/mediator between students and professors

Not every department and college offers teaching assistantships. Some departments have formal programs with application procedures that entail completing forms, submitting a statement of intent, and soliciting recommendation letters. Others have no formal program, but students informally assist faculty as volunteers. Still others offer teaching assistant opportunities as an independent study course, in which a student earns course credit for working as a teaching assistant and completing an academic project such as a paper examining his or her experiences. Ask your professors if teaching assistant opportunities exist. Ask even if no one you know has worked as a teaching assistant. Sometimes opportunities exist, but they are largely unadvertised. Ask and you may be pleasantly surprised. At any rate, asking never hurts and will only make you appear motivated and eager to learn and gain experience.

PRACTICAL TIP

CONSIDER PEER-TO-PEER TUTORING

If your department does not offer teaching assistantships, consider getting some teaching experience by tutoring other students. Check whether your department has tutoring facilities or a tutoring program. If not, check with the study skills center and student services center to locate your university's tutoring program. Tutoring is an opportunity to learn, to help others, and to determine if further study in psychology is for you. Couple tutoring with research and applied opportunities to round out your experience.

Field Experience

Field experiences in the form of internships or practica involve students in relevant academic experiences and provide a useful service to agencies and communities. Examples of field placements include being an intern at a social service agency (where you might observe or assist in intake of clients, psychological testing, report writing, and behavior modification) and working in a human services department of a company or business (where you might observe and learn to administer structured interviews, write performance appraisals, and coordinate special projects or programs). As an intern, you have a chance to get an idea of what it is like to work in a particular setting. For example, you might sit in on a group therapy or parent training session or help personnel plan sessions and analyze the outcomes of sessions. You may learn new skills and hone others, and you may come to recognize that you have skills to contribute to practical settings.

Why Seek Field Experience?

There are many benefits to participating in field experience. If you hope to become a mental health professional and provide services to others, it is important to seek practice opportunities as an undergraduate in order to clarify your interests. It is not uncommon for students to believe that clinical or counseling psychology is for them until they gain some experience and realize that they don't like working with people. Therefore, one of the most important reasons for seeking field experience is to become more certain of your career choice. Working in the field helps you to identify not only what work-related outcomes you value (e.g., pay, autonomy, responsibility) but also what interests and abilities you need to be satisfied in that work. It is a job tryout. You'll learn about a particular job environment, duties, and support. You'll learn about typical clientele you might work with and what you can expect in terms of resources. If you choose to apply to graduate school, field experiences will suit you well. Admissions committees and directors of applied subfields of psychology, such as clinical, counseling, or school psychology, look favorably on field experience because it is a good indicator of a student's interest, motivation, and competence in applied settings.

Other benefits of field experience include the opportunity to apply what is learned in class in a real-world setting, acquire knowledge and new skills, and learn about the practice of psychology. Depending on the placement, you may learn more about psychological problems, ways of helping, agency functioning, professional relationships, interviewing techniques, psychological testing, report writing, consultation, behavior modification, and group therapy. Field experience gives you a chance to develop useful skills that may be hard to practice and develop in class, and it helps you to integrate what you've learned. Personal benefits include developing responsibility, maturity, and confidence.

Aside from educational and personal benefits, field experience offers professional benefits. These include gaining a realistic understanding of work environments, developing professional contacts, and enhancing your résumé. Interns get formal and informal job sources and contacts, are evaluated positively by recruiters, earn higher salaries in the workplace, and report greater satisfaction in jobs (National Association of Colleges and Employers, 2018). Students who work as interns are more likely to be satisfied with their jobs after graduation, and they may even have a job lined up before graduating. They also remain in their jobs longer than the students who do not obtain field experience. Students who obtain field experience are able to consider the match between their academic preparation and work requirements (e.g., students are often poorly equipped for the stresses of work, including the realities of politics, difficult clients, and the conflict between theory and application) while they're still in school. Doing so gives you time to learn more and to resolve the conflicts early. Therefore it may not be surprising that after graduation, students who obtain field experience often have a smoother, easier transition to work, without the "reality shock" that other graduates often experience.

How Do You Get Field Experience?

The organization of field experiences varies by institution and department. Many departments have a faculty member who serves as a campus coordinator for field experience and internship programs. This individual makes sure that internship sites are appropriate, develops working relationship with them, and evaluates student performance. Other departments may not have one coordinator; in some cases, different faculty are responsible for each internship site, depending on their relationship with the site. Some colleges have an office that specializes in placing students in internships. Sometimes these offices and opportunities are referred to as co-operative education.

Your department may require that you obtain an internship through the co-operative education office. Sometimes a department may require a student to find his or her own practicum site. If you are in this position, begin at least 2 to 3 months early, as it takes time to locate a site, make contact and meet with the director, obtain a faculty supervisor, and get permission to proceed. Look up the social service agencies in your area, such as women's centers, shelters, and not-for-profit agencies that help individuals and families. E-mail the director and explain that you are a student and are looking to volunteer and perhaps get course credit for your work. Attach a résumé (see Chapter 9). Alternatively you might call and ask if they'd like more information. Anticipate meeting and interviewing with the agency staff. Be prepared to have a faculty speak with the agency, vouching for you and taking responsibility for providing academic supervision. Field experience is challenging. It will test your knowledge and will help you learn much about yourself.

Get Involved in the Discipline

Research, teaching, and field work offer important educational opportunities, but there are many other ways to learn and advance your competencies. Show your interest in psychology and open up new avenues of learning by seeking opportunities to get involved in the field as a whole. Disseminating the results of research—formally telling others about what you have found—requires another set of competencies and offers many benefits. Another way of becoming active in the field is to become active in a local or national psychology organization, as described in the following sections.

Attend Psychology Conferences

Conferences are good places to see what psychology research is all about. Professional organizations such as the American Psychological Association (APA; http://apa.org) and the Association for Psychological Science (APS; http://psychologicalscience.org) hold annual meetings in various cities around the United States. Psychologists from all types of settings attend to share and learn about the latest research, as well as socialize. National conferences attract thousands of people. National conferences usually take place at hotels in cities near airports so that attendees can easily arrive and leave, as well as have a place to stay, as most conferences last several days. Regional psychology associations also hold annual conferences, some of which might be within driving distance. These conferences are smaller, with a few hundred people, depending on the conference. A list of regional psychology associations is provided in Exercise 4.5.

EXERCISE 4.5
REGIONAL PSYCHOLOGICAL ASSOCIATIONS

Eastern Psychological Association (EPA): http://www.easternpsychological.org

Southeastern Psychological Association (SEPA): http://www.sepaonline.com

Southwestern Psychological Association (SWPA): http://www.swpsych.org

Rocky Mountain Psychological Association (RMPA): http://www.rockymountainpsych.com

Western Psychological Association (WPA): http://westernpsych.org/

Midwestern Psychological Association (MPA): http://www.midwesternpsych.org/

New England Psychological Association (NEPA): http://www.nepsychological.org/

Prompt

1. Which association represents your area of the country?

2. Visit the association's webpage. What kinds of resources are offered?

3. When is the annual conference? Where is it?

What can you expect to do at a conference? You'll listen to presentations by researchers who will discuss their latest work, usually work that is not yet published. You'll also view poster sessions. Posters are another format for presenting research, in which the study's purpose, methods, results, and discussion are presented on poster board. The author of the study stands by to answer questions and to talk informally about the work. Poster presentations are a great opportunity to make contacts with students and faculty who share your interests. Most conferences also have practical presentations on topics such as getting into graduate school, publishing, and teaching. Other reasons to attend conferences are to peruse and purchase the latest books in the field and to network. You'll have opportunities to meet student researchers, possible advisors, and possible employers. If you are interested in graduate school, you may have opportunities to talk to current students in programs you're considering and to possibly meet faculty with whom you'd like to work. Many students find attending their first conference an eye-opening experience because it's a glimpse into the world of research psychology and academia. Distinguished researchers you've studied become real people, lecturing about their latest work, right in front of you.

If you are interested in attending a conference, speak with students and faculty involved in the department club or Psi Chi. Many departments organize informal trips to conferences. If your department is not sponsoring an informal trip, seek another interested student or two and consider attending together.

Disseminate Research

If you conduct research with a faculty member and the results of the research project turn out favorably, the next step in the project is to disseminate the results and tell the scholarly community about your findings. Most students obtain their first experiences with research dissemination through presentations at local or regional professional conferences. Presenting research results at a conference is a wonderful learning opportunity that is an impressive addition to a résumé or graduate school application.

Typically, conference presentations take two forms—papers and posters. A paper is a 10- to 15-minute presentation made to an audience in which you describe your research concisely, with the aid of handouts, overheads, or slides. Posters are more common formats for student presentations. A poster presents your research concisely on a 3- by 5-foot or 4- by 6-foot freestanding bulletin board. All posters are displayed in a large room for a period of time (usually 1.5 to 2 hours), and the audience wanders through, browsing posters of interest. A poster presentation offers opportunities for lots of one-on-one interaction, as audience members stop at posters of interest to them and ask questions about the project.

If the research that you are conducting with a faculty member turns out especially favorably, you might prepare the results for submission to a scholarly journal. If you decide to submit to a journal, recognize that it will take a great deal of time and effort. The time it takes to prepare a paper for submission is always longer than anticipated. Once the paper is submitted, there will be a long wait (typically several months) to hear from the publisher. Even if a paper is accepted, it is usually under the condition that further revisions be made. It is important to understand that not every paper submitted to a journal is published. The standards for publication are much higher than those for getting an "A" in a course. Journal editors expect articles to make a contribution to the literature, and "nonsignificant results are typically not a big contribution in their eyes" (Powell, 2000, p. 28). Despite these cautions, the rewards of publishing are great. Publishing in a scholarly journal is a major achievement that employers and graduate schools look upon favorably.

While professional journals in psychology abound, there are a handful of journals that specialize in publishing the work of undergraduates. The most prestigious of the undergraduate journals is the *Psi Chi Journal of Psychological Research,* which is sponsored by Psi Chi and published quarterly. Submissions to the *Psi Chi Journal of Psychological Research* are reviewed by three psychology professionals. Other undergraduate journals in psychology are listed in Table 4.4.

TABLE 4.4 ● Undergraduate Psychology Journals	
Journal Title	**Website**
Journal of Psychology and Behavioral Sciences	http://view2.fdu.edu/academics/becton-college/psychology-and-counseling/jpbs/
Journal of Young Investigators	http://www.jyi.org
Modern Psychological Studies	https://www.mpsjournal.com/
Psi Chi Journal of Psychological Research	http://www.psichi.org/?page=journal_main
University of California Los Angeles Undergraduate Research Journal of Psychology	https://urjp.psych.ucla.edu/
Yale Review of Undergraduate Research in Psychology	http://www.yale.edu/yrurp/

However, research experiences do not always result in submissions to scholarly journals. Fortunately, there are respectable non-refereed outlets for students to demonstrate initiative and writing skills. Newsletters published by psychology departments, student organizations, and other groups on campus offer opportunities to write about topics related to psychology. Professional organizations such as APA, APS, and regional psychological associations (such as EPA, NEPA, and WPA) have student publications or member publications that are open to student writers. Finally, Psi Chi and Psi Beta offer opportunities for students to contribute to their newsletter magazines. Although these publications are not peer reviewed, and the articles are not empirical, they demonstrate initiative, writing ability, and interest in psychology—all of which are valued by employers and graduate admissions committees.

Participate in Professional Organizations

One of the simplest, most effective, yet underappreciated ways of forming an identity as a lifelong student of psychology is to get involved in professional organizations, on and off campus (Exercise 4.6). Likely the most visible resource for psychology students on your campus is Psi Chi, the National Honor Society in Psychology. Psi Chi is a psychology organization designed for students. Founded in 1929, its purpose is to encourage, stimulate, and maintain excellence in scholarship and to advance psychology as a science. Students enrolled at institutions that have a chapter must meet minimum qualifications and apply for membership to Psi Chi. Students at community colleges are eligible to apply to Psi Beta, the sister organization of Psi Chi.

Get involved in your institution's chapter of Psi Chi and you'll have the opportunity to get to know other psychology students, develop leadership skills, and get involved in departmental activities. Psi Chi also offers opportunities for students at the regional and national level. Psi Chi sponsors sessions at most regional and national conferences that promote the research and scholarly achievements of undergraduate psychology students. In other words, Psi Chi sponsors opportunities for students to present their research. Psi Chi offers programming relevant to psychology students at these conferences, such as presentations on careers in psychology and how to apply to graduate school. Another important benefit of membership in Psi Chi is the quarterly magazine, *Eye on Psi Chi*. Each issue includes articles on psychology as well as practical advice on how to pursue a career in psychology. As discussed, the *Psi Chi Journal of Psychological Research*, published by Psi Chi is a national peer-reviewed scholarly journal that is dedicated to research conducted by undergraduate students. Because there are so many benefits to becoming a member of Psi Chi, if your institution does not have a chapter, discuss with a faculty member the possibility of starting a chapter.

Another opportunity to get involved in psychology and promote a campus culture oriented toward psychology is to join (or start) a psychology club. Most psychology clubs are open to anyone with an interest in psychology, regardless of major. Many students who do not meet the academic criteria to join Psi Chi get involved in a school's psychology club. Frequently the psychology club and Psi Chi work together to organize psychology-related activities for students.

When considering ways of getting involved in psychology-related activities, don't forget to pay attention to what's happening in your department. Departments often invite guest speakers to campus or faculty members give presentations on their research interests. Attend these activities to support the department's efforts and to demonstrate your interest and commitment to learning more about psychology.

Finally, the American Psychological Association and the Association for Psychological Science offer resources that are helpful to students. Both associations offer advice on entering the field of psychology and obtaining student affiliate memberships that permit you to join for a reduced fee and offer discounts on psychology journals and books. As discussed earlier, APA and APS sponsor annual conferences in which thousands of psychologist researchers and practitioners gather to learn about the latest research, attend workshops, and network. Attend either of these conferences, or any of the conferences sponsored by regional psychological associations, for an amazing learning opportunity.

There are a variety of ways to take an active role in your education, but all involve stepping back and recognizing the covert, unstated, college curriculum (Appleby, 2001); you can learn much more in college than just theories and facts. Taking an active role in your education means that you must seek out opportunities to learn and enhance your skills. It means that you must develop relationships with faculty and do more than just attend class. Although taking an active role in your education takes effort (it's much easier to sit back and just attend class), the benefits are immense.

EXERCISE 4.6
ACADEMIC AND PROFESSIONAL ORGANIZATIONS

Several professional organizations offer opportunities for students to learn about the field of psychology and make contacts with other students and professionals.

1. Visit the Psi Chi website (http://psichi.org). What is the purpose of the organization? Under the publications link, what is *Eye on Psi Chi*? Browse the collection of articles organized by category. Read three articles from three different categories (such as career preparation, fields of psychology, or promotion of research). Write a one- to two-sentence summary of each article.

2. Visit the Psi Beta website (http://psibeta.org). What is the purpose of the organization? How does it differ from Psi Chi?

3. Visit the American Psychological Association website (http://apa .org). Locate the Students page. Identify two helpful resources. What are they? How are they helpful? Can students join APA? What are the benefits? How much does it cost?

4. Visit the Association for Psychological Science website (http:// psychologicalscience.org). Locate the Students page. Can students join APS? What are the benefits? How much does it cost? Identify two ways of getting involved in APS.

REFLECTION PROMPTS

My Advisor

Who is your advisor? Write down the contact information for your advisor. Now reflect on your meetings with him or her. Did you set up an appointment or just visit during office hours? What kind of advice has he or she given you? Do you feel comfortable interacting with your advisor? Identify questions to ask during your next meeting.

Relationships With Faculty

Explore your feelings about interacting with faculty. How often do you interact with professors? List the professors you interact with. Explore the context of your discussions. For example, is it after class or in the professor's office? Are your discussions focused on the course material or do you talk about other things, like life and career goals? What, if anything, is holding you back from interacting with professors? Explore your feelings. How can you overcome these obstacles?

My College Career

An important part of taking an active role in your education is planning your coursework. Look through your college handbook, and write down the requirements for your major. What courses are required? Are any other experiences required? Now list all the courses that you have taken. Make a list of all the courses that you need to take. In what ways have you been active in shaping your education to match your goals? What steps can you take to be more active?

5

Self-Management Skills

Chapter Outline	

Attitudes, Beliefs, and Achievement
    Motivation, Attributions, and
        Mindset
    Self-Talk and Motivation
	*Exercise 5.1: Become Aware of Your
	    Positive and Negative Self-Talk*

Time Management
    How Do You Use Your Time?
    Make Choices About How to
        Spend Your Time
    Time Management Is Project
        Management
    Create Your Schedule
	*Exercise 5.2: Time Management
	    Self-Assessment*
	Exercise 5.3: Keep a Time Log

Strategies for Efficiency
    Digital Distraction and
        Multitasking
    Create a Study Environment
    Organize Your Materials
	Exercise 5.4: Study Environment Quiz

Academic success is influenced by ability and opportunities, but also by attitudes and behaviors. How you view yourself and the world and how you approach problems influences your success in college and life. Improving your study habits requires taking a hard look at yourself. Knowing yourself—your motivations, habits, preferences, and needs—is critical to devising study strategies that work for you. In this chapter we discuss self-management and how to regulate your behavior to achieve goals. The most successful students are self-aware. They understand their motivation, manage their time well, and are organized.

Attitudes, Beliefs, and Achievement

Students differ in their academic performance. In addition, most students perform better in some subjects or types of assignments than others. How you make sense of these differences influences how you approach problems and how you account for your successes and failures. How well you do in college and life is not just a matter of your ability. Your beliefs, attitudes, and motivation also matter.

Motivation, Attributions, and Mindset

What motivates you to achieve your goals? Why do you want to earn good grades? Why read, study, and do the work involved to succeed in school? Is your academic behavior motivated by intrinsic or extrinsic goals? The source of your motivation influences your success. For example, is your primary reason for reading to get good grades on quizzes? Do you stick it out to complete difficult math problems because you like the challenge? Students who are *intrinsically motivated* focus on the internal rewards of completing tasks, such as mastering the material and increasing knowledge. Other students are *extrinsically motivated* and focus on the outside rewards that come with success, such as earning good grades, rewards, and positive attention (Ryan & Deci, 2000). People tend to be more highly motivated and persist longer when they find a task personally interesting or gratifying, when they are intrinsically motivated to succeed. In contrast, the outside rewards that fuel extrinsic motivation often aren't enough to sustain activity in the face of overwhelming challenges. The best students study not just to earn good grades but to master the material. Generally speaking, students who are intrinsically motivated tend to perform better in college than those who are extrinsically motivated (Taylor et al., 2014).

A second factor associated with success in college and life is one's beliefs about the causes of success and failure. How people attribute their successes, failures, and circumstances of their lives is influenced by the degree to which they believe that internal or external forces control their lives. This pattern of beliefs is known as *locus of control* (Rotter, 1990). People who adopt an *internal locus of control* believe that they have the power to influence most aspects of their lives. They gravitate toward internal attributions, emphasizing their own role in academic achievement, such as through skills or choice of study techniques. In contrast, people with an *external locus of control* tend to believe that outside forces are more important contributors to their circumstances. Performance is attributed to outside factors such as test difficulty, instructor quality, or luck. Students with an external locus of control may lose their motivation to improve because they view their success or failure as out of their control. They feel powerless (so why try?).

In addition to attributing success or failure to internal or external causes, students vary in their *mindset*, the degree to which they believe that their abilities and characteristics are modifiable (Dweck, 2017). Can you improve your own abilities or are they set in stone? Some students show a *growth mindset*, viewing their skills and characteristics as malleable or changeable. In contrast, others show a *fixed mindset*, believing that their characteristics are enduring and unchangeable. Students who believe that they are able to learn and improve their skills and abilities (growth mindset) tend to persist longer in challenging tasks and ultimately earn higher grades than other students (Richardson, Abraham, & Bond, 2012).

What does all of this mean? These qualities—motivation, locus of control, and mindset—contribute to students' academic tenacity, the tendency to persist in order to achieve goals (Dweck, Walton, & Cohen, 2011). Successful students tend to be intrinsically motivated. They are motivated to master the material for its own sake rather than to simply earn a grade. They tend to adopt an internal locus of control, attributing grades to factors within themselves such as effort rather than luck. They have a growth mindset, believing that they have the ability to improve their performance. Successful students believe that they control their academic destiny, their effort makes a difference in their performance, and they have the ability to succeed.

Self-Talk and Motivation

Beliefs about yourself and your abilities matter in determining your success. Change the way you view your competence and the tasks you face, and you will be more likely to meet success. It requires patience, but you can train yourself to think in empowering ways. Pay attention to how you talk to yourself. We all engage in self-talk and have an inner critic, a voice that monitors and comments on all that we do. Self-talk influences your self-esteem, confidence, motivation, and success.

Positive self-talk contains words of encouragement and support. Positive self-talk is the voice inside you telling you that you can do it. It helps you to persevere, boosts self-esteem, and is motivating. *Negative self-talk*, on the other hand, is deflating. It is discouraging, belittling, and negative. It pulls you down, creating and sustaining self-doubt. Negative self-talk is the nagging voice telling you that you don't have the ability, you aren't smart enough, or you will not succeed. Negative self-talk makes us more likely to quit.

Try to pay attention to your inner voice, your self-talk. As you work on challenging math problems or read a lengthy passage, what does your inner voice say? Train yourself to recognize when you're using negative self-talk, then turn it around into positive self-talk. When you find yourself saying, "I'm just not good at this. There's no point trying," reframe your negative self-talk into motivating positive self-talk. Instead tell yourself, "I can do this. I've done so in the past and I've learned from my mistakes. I'm willing to work hard." The self-talk you use doesn't need to be sophisticated. A simple "I can do this" is motivating. Becoming aware of and changing self-talk is challenging but is well worth it because self-talk influences our motivation, sense of control, and efficacy (Exercise 5.1).

EXERCISE 5.1
BECOME AWARE OF YOUR POSITIVE AND NEGATIVE SELF-TALK

1. Identify examples of negative self-talk that you have used. In what situations did they occur?

2. How might you reframe negative self-talk into positive self-talk?

3. Identify specific positive self-talk phrases that you will use during your next challenging situation.

Time Management

At one time or another, most of us feel overwhelmed, like there is not enough time in the day to get it all done. Although we can't add more hours to the day, we often have more free time than we realize. How do you find those free hours and allocate them as you choose? Use time management strategies to regulate your use of time. *Time management* refers to planning how to divide your time between activities and tasks. Become more efficient at using your time and you'll get more done and make time for friends, family, and—most importantly—yourself.

How Do You Use Your Time?

The first step toward gaining control over time is to understand how you use it. Most people could use some help in managing their time. Take the time management quiz in Exercise 5.2 to examine your use of time.

EXERCISE 5.2
TIME MANAGEMENT SELF-ASSESSMENT

Indicate your response (true or false) to each item below.

1. _____ I do a lot of my work at the last minute.

2. _____ I use a calendar to keep track of my work and activities.

3. _____ I struggle to begin unpleasant tasks.

4. _____ At this very moment, I can identify three things that I have planned to do today.

5. _____ I often find myself daydreaming when I should be working.

6. _____ I have a workspace that I can go to that requires minimal planning or setup.

7. _____ I feel like my friends are much more organized than me.

8. _____ I have a to-do list for this week.

9. _____ I check e-mails and texts as I hear the delivery notifications.

10. _____ I know what time of day I work best.

11. _____ I often feel overwhelmed with work.

12. _____ My calendar lists all of the important deadlines that I face this semester and year.

13. _____ I often attend class unprepared and wish I had done more reading.

14. _____ I prioritize my work and activities.

15. _____ I often find myself on Facebook, Instagram, or online when I should be working.

16. _____ I have time set aside to relax and have fun with my friends.

17. _____ I often forget to complete assignments.

18. _____ I write down what I need to do.

19. _____ I often lose important papers or articles.

20. _____ I rarely hand work in late.

Scoring

Exercise 5.2 assessed the time management and organization skills that we will discuss in this chapter. Give yourself 1 point for each even item marked "true" and 1 point for each odd item marked "false." Sum your points for a total score. Higher scores indicate greater use of time management strategies.

Prompt

1. Is your score as high as you'd like? Look over your answers. What aspects of time management seem most challenging for you? Why?

2. Choose three items in which you'd like to improve. Explain your choices.

3. After reviewing this chapter, discuss specific ways of improving the items you identified.

Before you can begin studying, you must gain control over your time—be its master, not slave. Many students and professors are poor judges of their time use. One of the most accurate ways to learn about how you spend time is to keep a time log. There are 168 hours in a week. How are you spending yours? If you're like most people, you will find the results of Exercise 5.3 ("Keep a Time Log") surprising. That 10-minute coffee break might really be closer to 40 minutes! You might not like to admit the amount of time you spend on social media or playing video games, but it is important to construct an accurate picture of your time use so that you can identify areas to change (and those to keep).

EXERCISE 5.3
KEEP A TIME LOG

For several days or a week, record how you spend each half-hour of the day. As your day progresses, record what you're doing as you're doing it. There are many apps that can help you log your time. Run a search for time-tracking or time-logging apps for some options. Or use a spreadsheet. Set an alarm to ring every 30 minutes and record what you're doing. You may find it difficult to remember to record your activity but do the best that you can. After a few days or a week, analyze your patterns of time use.

1. What do you spend the most waking time on?

2. What do you spend the least waking time on?

3. How much time did you spend on school work? With friends? At work? Online?

4. Does your time use reflect your priorities? Is there an area where you'd prefer to spend more time? Less? Explain.

5. Do you think you are using your time most efficiently? What can you change?

Make Choices About How to Spend Your Time

Many of us let too much time slip through our fingers because we aren't taught how to manage it. Keeping a time log can increase our awareness of how we spend our time and the need for a solid plan for managing this limited resource. Juggling school, a job, extracurricular activities, and a social life is difficult and nearly impossible to manage successfully without a plan. I often hear students say that if they just tried harder, they'd be able to do it all. They resign themselves to all-nighters and walk around campus like zombies. This approach of trying to do everything without acquiring the skills to manage your time will lead to burnout. Life may seem busy now, but it doesn't suddenly get easier after graduation. In fact, demands on time often increase with career and family responsibilities.

Planning your time isn't about squeezing more activities into your schedule; it's about taking a serious look at your commitments and priorities. Take a moment and analyze the demands on your time. Now that you've listed all of your activities, you might realize that you are quite busy—and perhaps overextended. Are you committing yourself to too many activities? You might love music, but can you juggle jazz band, a guitar trio, and an off-campus rock band? Can you write for the school paper and maintain several blogs at once? Recognize that sometimes you can't do it all. Decide what is important and what isn't. Difficult as it might be, you must remove activities that aren't meaningful to you in order to devote time to those that are. Don't eliminate all fun activities, but prioritize them and make decisions about what's important to you and what will help you meet your goals. Make conscious choices of how to spend your time so that you have more control over your days and your life, rather than running late on everything and constantly feeling harried and behind.

Time Management Is Project Management

Time management is about more than schedules and time logs. It is about planning and strategizing how to divide your time between activities and tasks in order to achieve your goals. It's not just time that we're wrangling when we engage in time management techniques: It's really our tasks that are managed. Time itself is not the problem. Instead, the problem is our ability to get everything done (our tasks) that we need to get done.

The first step in getting a handle on your time is determining what has to be done. Create a to-do list. To-do lists can be created from the perspective on the day, week, month, semester, year, or even as a 5-year plan. Most students will find it most helpful to consider the semester as a whole. Look over all of your course syllabi. Record assignments, exams, and due dates. Add other tasks and dates to remember for work, outside activities, and your personal life. This is your master to-do list. Most of the tasks on this list, however, are likely huge and cannot be completed in one sitting. For example, the term paper due on the last day of class requires more than one work session the night before.

Create a plan for each large task, such as paper assignments. These big tasks are often referred to as *projects*. List the actions that are required to complete the project. In the case of a paper, those actions might include brainstorming topics, reading to choose a topic, selecting a topic, gathering sources, reading and taking notes, preparing an outline, writing a draft, and so on (see Chapter 7 for more on writing papers). Think about how much time you need for each task and work *backwards* from the due date. For example, if the paper is due December 15th, complete your first full draft of the paper by December 5th, write your outline by November 30th, finish reading and note taking by

November 15th, and so on. Create multiple informal personal due dates for each part of each project. Backwards planning ensures that you make progress on your project over a stretch of time, which gives you time to think it through, find errors and ways to improve, and ultimately turn in a better assignment. This process sounds like a lot of work, and it is; but planning will make your semester run much more smoothly because you will know what you need to do for each assignment and when you will do it. You'll also hone an important career skill. Devising a plan to accomplish a project is known as *project management*, a key skill that employers seek.

Apply this same approach to each week. Determine what tasks you'll complete to make progress on your major projects and record specific assignments and tasks for the upcoming week. Consider the following questions: What reading is due when? Do you have any homework assignments? Is there anything you need to prepare for group assignments? Then determine which of these tasks needs to be completed on each day. It takes some planning to ensure that your semester-long to-do list gets done and that you keep on top of the rest of your life and enjoy it. The rewards of planning include feeling in control, reducing stress, and making time for the people, events, and activities that are important to you. Table 5.1 presents additional benefits of time and project management.

PRACTICAL TIP
TO-DO LIST MANAGERS

Paper to-do lists are easy to maintain. Some students prefer digital to-do lists. If you're looking to go the digital route for maintaining your to-do list, you're not limited to text files or the standard app that comes with your phone. There are hundreds of to-do list apps to help you get organized and manage your time. Some of the most popular apps include:

Any.do: http://any.do/

Asana: http://asana.com

Remember the Milk: http://rememberthemilk.com

Todoist: http://todoist.com

Toodledo: http://toodledo.com/

There is a dizzying array of ways to organize and keep up with your to-do list. However, be warned: It's easy to let searching, trying, and playing with new to-do list apps become a form of procrastination. Don't let yourself fall into the trap of spending more time searching for a way to organize your list than actually acting on the list.

TABLE 5.1 ● Benefits of Time Management and To-Do Lists	
You'll know where to begin.	One of the primary benefits of creating a schedule is that you won't waste time deciding what to do. Removing the thought and planning can free your energy to actually complete what's on your list and spend your time productively.
You'll be less likely to avoid distasteful tasks.	It's human nature: we spend time on activities that we like and that we are good at. Many students put other tasks first and find that they've run out of time to study subjects that they dislike. A schedule prevents this type of forgetfulness.
Planning frees your mind.	Recording your to-dos (tasks that you need to complete) relieves them from your mind. Once you've written an item down, there's no need to worry about forgetting it, so you're free to focus on other things.
You'll set priorities.	What is important to you? How important is each of the classes that you are taking to your academic standing and future plans? How many assignments does each of your courses entail? What is the relative weight or value of each assignment? It's easy to spend lots of time doing busy work that is not worth much of your final grade while not allocating enough time to study for a test or prepare a major paper.
Planning ensures time for fun.	Good time management skills permit you to make time for friends and enjoy leisure without feeling guilty that you're not studying. If you schedule time to do your work, you know that it will get done. Then you can enjoy "play time" without worrying or thinking about studying.

Create Your Schedule

After creating to-do lists to manage all of your projects and assignments, the next step is deciding when you'll complete the tasks on your list. Selecting specific times to work on specific tasks will ensure that they get done. Some students and faculty balk at the idea of a schedule, instead preferring to keep their days open and allow for spontaneity. The philosophy behind time management is that by controlling or planning *part* of your time, you are able to be more flexible with the rest of your time. Create a schedule and determine when you're in class, working, or engaging in other activities, and mark specific times for completing your tasks.

We can all benefit from keeping a schedule and working on time management. However, the form that the time management system takes will vary.

Look over the possibilities and decide what works for you. Is there one approach that you prefer more than the others?

- An old-fashioned analog paper set of daily, weekly, and monthly calendars

- A plan notebook that you fashion into a personal calendar

- A simple text file that you sync among your devices

- Your phone's basic calendar and to-do list app

- An app that can sync with your phone, laptop, and tablet computers

Whatever format you choose, make sure that it works for you, is easy to use, and is always present so that you will be motivated to use it. You may find that it takes time to figure out what works, and you may try more than one system.

Once you settle on a system, use it consistently. Create a plan or a schedule for each day. That is, choose what tasks to accomplish and when to accomplish them.

- Schedule time for your reading and class assignments.

- Think ahead and schedule time for work on major projects early in the semester. As we discussed, work back from the due date and create mini-deadlines. Work on these each week.

- Plan short blocks of time, preferably half-hour or (at most) hour-long blocks. Give yourself breaks.

- Schedule the most difficult tasks during daylight hours, when people tend to be most alert and awake.

- Don't schedule every moment. Allow for some flexibility, last-minute changes, and play. For example, you might decide to end the scheduled part of your day at 4 p.m., leaving open time for whatever you choose.

- Allow time for sleep. You need 7 to 9 hours of sleep each night (this is supported by psychological research: Hirshkowitz et al., 2015). Without sleep, you are less likely to remember material, which means that you're less likely to learn (Landmann et al., 2015).

- Know your arousal pattern and work with it. We all have a natural rhythm of times in which we are alert and awake and times in which we are less alert. Arrange your study times around your natural rhythm. Study when you're alert and sleep when you're sleepy.

- Schedule down time, exercise time, and social time. The only way to ensure that all of your needs are met consistently is to plan ahead. Care for yourself by setting aside time just for you.

As a student, the most important activity to schedule is likely your class work. By scheduling regular periods to work, you will have opportunities to think about what you are learning rather than just simply prepare for looming deadlines. Without the pressure of cramming for an exam, you have time to consider what you're studying and how it fits with your experience and perspective. Learning can become more interesting, enjoyable, and meaningful, which contribute to retention.

To summarize, the cardinal rule of time management is that you must capture everything. Record your tasks, assignments, and obligations in one place, including class times, study times, project due dates, assignments, appointments, and social events. Consistently write everything down so that you don't forget and so that you're free to think without worrying that you've forgotten something. Always carry your schedule and to-do list so that you can bring order to your life and have peace of mind. Make no mistake about it; this will take some time and practice, but creating a schedule and maintaining a to-do list produces important returns. You'll feel like you have extra time. You'll feel more in control.

PRACTICAL TIP
CAPTURE LOST TIME

Each day we lose time as we go about the tasks of our day, such as walking from one place to another, waiting in line, and traveling. This time isn't really lost. We can use it, if we choose. For example, while walking from class, try to think of the main points of the lecture and how they apply to what you know. While exercising on the elliptical machine, brainstorm topics or titles for papers or think about how to organize papers. Another way to use in-between time is to carry pocket work (an article, flash cards) that you can do while waiting in lines, standing at the bus stop, sitting, and so on. Cell phones make it easy to always have a task at hand. Ten minutes here, 15 minutes there; it adds up. In addition, cognitive psychology and memory research has shown that we can recall more information if we study in short periods rather than long ones, so you just might learn more. However, also remember that you don't need to be productive all the time. Sometimes staring into space while you wait in line is a good thing!

Strategies for Efficiency

Excellent project management skills can help you plan and schedule your work, but your success is influenced by your organization and self-management skills. The ability to control your attention is one of the most important self-management skills that you can cultivate.

Digital Distraction and Multitasking

You sit down to study, open your books, and then hear a *ding* as a notification pops up on your phone. What do you do? If you're like most people, you peek. You might read the message and reply, read it and decide to reply later, or just mark the notification as read. Regardless of which action you choose, you've distracted yourself and fallen out of the study zone. It may seem like taking 15 seconds to check a notification is no big deal, but it takes you away from your task and regaining your focus takes time. Your study time will be most efficient—that is, you'll learn the most in the least amount of time—if you eliminate distractions.

"But I can multitask. It's no big deal," many people argue. Instead, as you study psychology you will learn that our attention is limited. Contrary to the term *multitasking*, our minds unitask; that is, we focus on one stream of stimuli or information at a time (Monsell, 2003). Multitasking is instead *task-switching*, directing our attention from one stimulus to another and back again. There's a cognitive cost to task-switching or multitasking, and we ultimately perform more poorly on both tasks. Students who multitask while studying tend to perform more poorly on exams (Carrier, Rosen, Cheever, & Lim, 2015; Patterson, 2017). This is true when it comes to reading and studying but is also true in class. That moment you check your phone and read a text or quickly scan Instagram for updates draws your attention away from class. Most multitaskers believe that they can successfully attend to multiple sets of stimuli, such as class, Snap Chat, and a group discussion, but research suggests that they are mistaken and multitaskers tend to perform more poorly on exams and generally score lower in academic achievement (Uncapher et al., 2017; Zureick, Burk-Rafel, Purkiss, & Hortsch, 2018).

So what should you do? You don't need to ignore your phone and social media entirely. Instead, limit your consumption. Set times when your phone is off limits, such as during class and study time. Silence notifications and you'll remove some of the temptation to switch tasks. It's difficult. With practice you'll build stamina and get better at resisting that urge to check your phone. Set a timer to allocate study time (try 30 minutes). Work. Then you might use screen time as a reward. Set a timer to ensure that you don't spend more than 5 to 10 minutes. Repeat. Slowly increase your off-the-grid time to an hour or two. If you're finding it especially difficult, there are a number of apps that can block websites or cell phone use for a period of time. Control your digital devices rather than let them control you.

Create a Study Environment

Improving your skills in time management means that you will set aside consistent periods for reading, writing, and studying. Setting aside time is the first step to ensuring that you keep up with your studies. Another part, however, is creating a place conducive to your work. It is one thing to set aside time, but you need to ensure that you will be productive during that time. As a psychology student you will learn about how our environment influences us. Take advantage of that knowledge and create a study environment that will support and encourage your work. Where do you work? Is it conducive to learning? Exercise 5.4 will help you to evaluate your study area and determine if it is conducive to work.

EXERCISE 5.4
STUDY ENVIRONMENT QUIZ

Check off items that you find are true for your study environment.

❑ There is a clutter-free table or desk with space to spread out books and papers.

❑ The area has good lighting.

❑ No television, music, or another loud distraction is nearby.

❑ A sturdy and comfortable chair is available.

❑ The temperature is comfortable.

❑ My calendar, schedule, and to-do lists are handy.

❑ My laptop, tablet, and phone notifications are turned off.

❑ Books and supplies are handy.

❑ My phone is silenced.

❑ People interrupt me rarely here.

❑ There are few things in my field of vision that have nothing to do with school work.

❑ I work well and feel that my studying is effective here.

Scoring

Count your checkmarks. The closer your score is to 12, the better your study environment.

Reflection

1. How does your study space rate? Reflect on your score.

2. In what ways might the quality of your workspace influence your learning and academic achievement?

3. In what ways can you improve your study space to make it a place more conducive for working? Identify three strategies for improving your workspace.

Designate an area just for studying. Choose a quiet place with adequate light. Make your study area pleasant and motivating. Avoid distractions; don't set up a study area in a high-traffic place (like the kitchen). If you are prone to distraction and procrastination, be sure to set up your study area away from the television or anything else that might draw your attention (e.g., a big window). Create a barrier between you and the world. If possible, shut the door or at least create an invisible barrier by facing the wall. Your study area should be convenient—a place that's easy to use, so you'll use it often. Some students need light background noise to study, but be careful that it's not distracting. Generally speaking, television and music with lyrics tend to be distracting because we naturally try to process what we're hearing even though we're trying to focus on our work. Before you decide that you need background noise like the television or radio, try spending some time without any noise to see how it feels. Many people find white noise helpful because it's simple background noise without content, such as static or a subtle hissing like the motor of a fan. There are a number of websites, apps, and downloads that offer free access to white noise (e.g., I like Simply Noise at http://simplynoise.com but there are many other options, including playlists on YouTube).

Many students don't have an ideal work space, a place that is just for studying. What then? Create consistent circumstances that prepare you to work. Find a handful of places where you can distance yourself and work. Don't rely only on studying in your dorm, in case your roommate has friends over. Find a place in the library but also a quiet student lounge so that you have options. Avoid open spaces where students congregate to chat. The conversations taking place around you will interfere with your concentration. Seek a barrier, whether physical or mental. Turn yourself away from others so that their activity won't disturb you. Play white noise through your ear buds. Wherever you choose, enact the same ritual each time you prepare to work: Lay your stuff out, find your barrier, use your ear buds, and focus.

PRACTICAL TIP
SET A ROUTINE STUDY TIME

Your energy and attention tends to fluctuate over the course of the day. Determine your best study time, when you're awake, alert, and more ready to work. Try to study at the same time each day. When you set a discrete period of time aside for studying each day, your mind gets used to the pattern. It becomes easier to work during that time. If you stick to a routine study time and place, you'll find it easier to get into the "zone" and you'll spend less time warming up and more time studying effectively.

Organize Your Materials

Studying is easier if you're organized. Have you ever sat down to study only to realize that you needed materials from another room or files that are on your tablet rather than your laptop? Not having your materials together is a time trap, because you'll need to spend extra time gathering them and risk getting sidetracked. Save time by keeping all your study materials in one place.

Think about your filing system. Do you know you where you put last week's notes? The handout from class? Do you know where to look to find your work? There are various ways of keeping your class material organized. If you prefer to use paper, follow this simple binder method. Use a three-ring binder for your schoolwork. Keep lecture notes and handouts from each class together, marked by a tab. Use one large binder for all of your classes, separating each class with tabbed dividers. You can also add a section for other necessities such as calendars, weekly schedules, lists, and phone numbers. All that you have to carry around is a single binder, and not five notebooks, folders, and many scraps of paper. You're also less prone to losing handouts if they're in your binder. If your binder is full or gets too bulky, empty the contents into file folders marked for each class. Some students do this weekly. If you move your notes and handouts into folders, date each page and, if applicable, add page numbers. If you drop a folder, you'll be able to reorganize it easily. At the end of the semester you'll have at least one file folder for each class.

Today there are many digital options that provide more flexibility and are more durable than the binder-paper approach. Data management websites and apps like Evernote, OneNote, or Google Keep allow you to create notes, scan handouts, and save photos of whiteboards and other presentations. Some students take handwritten notes in class and scan them into their desired app. Some apps can convert handwriting to searchable text. Notes can be tagged for easy searching. Each of these apps is available online, as computer programs, and as phone apps syncing across all of your devices, ensuring that your work is safe and easily accessible.

If you save your notes as word-processing files, create a set of folders on your tablet or laptop to organize your materials from class. You might have a folder labeled by semester (Fall 2021) with subfolders for each class (e.g., Child Psych, Biology, Experimental Psych, and so on). A hierarchical set of folders ensures that you can find your files easily. Also develop a standard way of labeling files to help you find what you need quickly. For example, your notes from Tuesday's Experimental Psychology class would be filed in the Experimental Psych folder and might be titled "Exp_notes_01_20_2021" to indicate that they were recorded on January 20. A simple labeling system will be very helpful when you need to search for notes recorded on a specific date.

As we have discussed, self-management skills contribute to your success in college and beyond, and you can improve your competence. In Chapter 6 we examine study skills, another contributor to academic success, as effective study skills can help you learn more in less time. However, your ability to apply study skills is influenced by your competence in self-management. In order to take advantage of study tips, you must effectively manage your time, attitudes, and environment.

REFLECTION PROMPTS

I'm at My Best When . . .

When are you at your best? When do you find it easiest to concentrate on difficult tasks? Are you a morning person, someone who accomplishes the most in the early morning? Do you work better at night? Why do you think you have these working patterns? What are the implications for scheduling classes and studying? How can you use this knowledge to help yourself?

Making Time for Health

Usually when we talk about time management, the emphasis is on ensuring that we get our work done. Good time management also ensures that we make time for our social life and for fun. Many students (and professors), however, prioritize work and friends over self-care. Ever notice how nearly everyone has a cold around exam time? Use your time management strategies to ensure that you make time to take care of yourself. Identify at least three times this week in which you will do something special for yourself to focus on your own health. It might be taking a yoga class, making a special meal, or doing an activity that you love. What are those times and what will you do?

Ideal Day

Suppose that you managed your time well. What would an ideal day look like? Write about it, realistically. Deal with life as it is now, not as a fantasy. What would you do, and how would you handle yourself in all situations? What two things could you do to bring yourself closer to that ideal?

Two Extra Hours

Suppose you suddenly had an extra 2 hours each day. How would you spend the time? Why? How does this proposed activity compare with the rest of your schedule? Is it more important than any of your current activities? If you believe it is, identify steps that you can take to make time for this activity.

Evaluating Time Management Strategies

After you've had a chance to try the time management strategies described in this chapter, write about your experience. Which strategies worked well? How might you modify them to fit your style and needs?

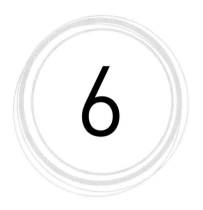

6

Study Tips

Tools for Academic Success

(Continued)

(Continued)

Chapter Outline	

Preparing for Exams
    Get the Lay of the Land
    Space Study and Prep Time
    Anticipate Questions
    Create Study Sheets
	Exercise 6.4: Create a Study Sheet

Test-Taking Tips
    Read the Directions
    Multiple-Choice Tests
    Essay Tests
    Reduce the Stress That
        Accompanies Tests
            Care for Your Physical
            Well-being
            Don't Psych Yourself Out
            Reduce Anxiety During
            Your Exam
    Learn From Returned Tests	

Have you ever spent hours studying for a test, only to get a mediocre grade? Meanwhile, your friend says he only studied for an hour and got an A. What's the deal? Consider this scenario:

Tom gets home from his part-time job and fixes himself a snack. It's almost 6 p.m., and he knows that he has to start studying for tomorrow's test. It's been a rough semester and he's gone to all of his classes, but he doesn't have a lot written in his notebooks. Tom finds that his mind wanders in class and it's difficult to understand the point of the professor's lectures. Sometimes class is so boring that Tom scrolls through Instagram. The professor just repeats himself anyway. Tom usually doesn't read before each class because it's hard to keep up with five classes while working over 20 hours a week. Tom decides to complete the reading tonight, hoping that he'll remember some of it for tomorrow's test. He brings his snack to the kitchen and clears a space among the breakfast dishes piled on the table. He tries to read while eating his snack. He begins reading but finds it difficult to concentrate. Tom exclaims, "Those dishes! That's why I can't focus." He takes a break to wash them. Twenty minutes later, after washing the dishes and clearing off the counters and stove, Tom sits down to read. Thirty minutes into Tom's reading, his roommate comes home and tells a long story about his day. Soon they decide to order a pizza. Tom vows to study after dinner. "This will be an all-nighter," he thinks to himself.

Sound familiar? After reading Chapter 5, you probably recognize that Tom has poor time management skills and is simply studying in the wrong place at the wrong time. Tom has good intentions and is motivated to study, but he's developed poor study habits (such as cramming) and is having trouble keeping up with his classes. Tom's predicament is common, but don't fall prey to this damaging cycle.

An important theme of this chapter is somewhat counterintuitive: Spending lots of time studying will not guarantee you good grades. Instead, it's the *quality* of your studying that counts. It doesn't do you much good to spend countless hours poring over your books if you don't retain anything. Work hard, but also work smart. This chapter describes techniques to help you improve your study habits. Couple these study habits with the self-management skills discussed in Chapter 5 and you'll be less likely to find yourself in Tom's shoes. Improving your study habits will take time and effort, but the work that you put in now will pay off. With effort and consistent practice, you'll find that you can study more efficiently and be more productive.

Are You Prepared to Succeed?

Before you can improve your study skills, you must take a hard look at yourself. In this chapter we discuss general strategies but you will need to tailor these ideas to fit your own needs and capacities. There is no one right way to study. However, the most successful students are self-aware. They monitor their learning to figure out what works for them.

How do your study skills rate? If you're like most students, they can use improvement. Complete the study skills assessment in Exercise 6.1 to learn more about your study needs.

EXERCISE 6.1
STUDY SKILLS ASSESSMENT

Use the following scale to respond to the study skills assessment below. Be honest!

1 = None of the time

2 = Some of the time

3 = Most of the time

4 = All of the time

(Continued)

(Continued)

How often do you do the following?

_____ 1. Manage your time to meet school and job responsibilities, as well as relax.

_____ 2. Set and monitor academic and personal goals.

_____ 3. Read your textbooks before class.

_____ 4. Pause to think about how well you understand something.

_____ 5. Maintain attention during classes.

_____ 6. Use active listening in class.

_____ 7. Take notes that are useful for later studying.

_____ 8. Study well ahead of exams.

_____ 9. Use a variety of strategies for recalling information.

_____ 10. Test yourself to determine whether you understand the material.

_____ 11. Have a well-defined study space.

_____ 12. Distinguish essential and nonessential information in lectures.

_____ 13. Identify the main points in your reading.

_____ 14. Take notes on readings.

_____ 15. Vary your learning and study strategies according to the material at hand.

Scoring

Add the points for each item. Higher scores indicate more effective use of study skills. Specifically, items 1, 2, and 11 refer to time management and organization skills (Chapter 5). Reading skills are assessed by items 3, 4, 13, and 14. Skills in listening and taking notes in class are assessed by items 5, 6, 7, and 12. Items 8, 9, 10, and 15 examine study skills.

Prompt

1. Consider your overall score. How well do you think it reflects your skills?

2. Compare your scores across the four areas. What pattern do you see?

3. What areas need improvement?

4. What three activities (items) do you engage in most often? Provide an example of each.

5. Choose three activities (items) that you engage in least often. How might employing these skills improve your academic achievement?

6. After reading this chapter, identify opportunities to use the activities you listed in item 5. Discuss specific strategies to employ.

Carefully consider your answers to Exercise 6.1 and you may glean clues about where to focus your efforts to improve your studying. No one can do this part for you. You'll need to develop your own formula for academic success, based on your understanding of yourself. Once you learn what works for you, you'll increase your academic efficiency and get more work done in less time.

Reading Tips: Improve Your Comprehension and Efficiency

Have you ever read a chapter yet were unable to remember much about it? Many students have difficulty retaining what they read. We discussed how our beliefs, attributions, and attitudes influence our academic achievement. They also influence how we approach tasks such as reading. As you sit down with a textbook in front of you, stop and think about how you feel. Are you dreading the task? Are you multitasking? Sometimes students say that they hate reading, but I don't believe it's true. We read almost all day every day. Whether in the form of text messages, social media posts, Tweets, or webpages, gathering virtually any information online comes from reading. Given how most of us are glued to our smartphones, it's a safe bet to say that most people do not hate reading. Instead it is the context that sometimes turns us off to reading. Sometimes students dislike reading textbooks. While reading a textbook will never come as easily as reading an exciting fiction book or posts about your favorite musician, reading a textbook can become more enjoyable and, more importantly, you can become more efficient so that it takes less time. As you begin to read, take note of your attitudes. Are you engaging in self-defeating negative self-talk? Remember to use positive self-talk to empower you as you accomplish challenging tasks like reading dense material.

Reading Textbooks With the SQ3R Method

Reading a textbook is very different from reading novels or magazines for pleasure, yet students often attempt to read textbooks and other scholarly books as if they were novels. Textbooks require a different set of strategies. Particularly suited to reading dense college textbooks, the SQ3R method (Robinson, 1970) is designed to help students read faster and retain more. The name stands for the steps in reading: survey, question, read, recite, review. Let's examine each step of this technique.

Survey or Preread the Assignment

This step is important; regardless of whether you carry out all of the SQ3R steps, you should always survey the material before reading it. Often referred to as *prereading*, an initial perusal of the reading assignment will help you grasp its organization and main points and will activate prior knowledge. Prereading prepares you for learning.

How do you survey or preread? Glance through the topic headings to get an overview of the chapter. Skim the sections, and read the summary paragraphs to get an idea of where the chapter is going. Look at the illustrations and read the captions. Take note of highlighted vocabulary terms. Read the study questions that often appear at the end of chapter sections. Your survey will highlight the main ideas of the chapter and provide an initial orientation that will help you to organize the material as you read it. Surveying a chapter gives you background knowledge to link with other material that you are learning and what you already know and gives you an idea of what is to come. Your survey should take only a few minutes. If you spend more than 15 minutes, you're likely not surveying but reading.

In addition to previewing the text, stop and think about your instructor's purpose in making the assignment. What does your professor want you to get out of this reading? How does this assignment contribute to the course content? Identify your purpose for reading: What can you gain from this reading assignment? The most obvious response might be "an understanding of the course material," but other responses might include "consider a possible topic for my paper" or simply "learn something new and interesting." Reading with purpose makes it easier to stay engaged and focused as you read.

Question

Look at the first heading in the chapter. Turn it into a question. Your task in reading the section following that heading is to gather information and answer that question. Posing questions will help you remember information that you already know and will arouse curiosity about the reading assignment, which will increase your comprehension. This step requires conscious effort but is worth it because active reading is the best way to retain written material. For example, if the heading is "Prevalence of Substance Use and Abuse in Adolescence," you might ask "How many adolescents use illegal drugs?" If the heading is "Multiple Personality Disorder," you might ask "What are the characteristics of multiple personality disorder?" Asking questions focuses your concentration. Take an active role in your reading. Don't read passively: Interrogate the author.

Read

Read to answer the questions you pose. Actively search for answers. If you finish the section and haven't answered the question, reread the section. Read reflectively. Consider what the author is trying to say and think about how you can use that information. If you haven't answered your question, consider the following: What question did the author answer? How does that differ from your initial expectation?

Recite (and/or Record)

Now that you've read enough to answer your question, look away and try to recite the answer to your question. Use your own words and examples. If you can do this, it means that you understand the material. If you can't, glance over the section again. Record the answer in your notes. Once you've said each answer, record it. You might also reconsider your initial question, fine-tune it, write it in the margin of the text, and underline the key words that provide an answer.

Review

Once you have read the entire chapter, test your memory by asking yourself the questions that you've identified. Review your notes and get a bird's-eye view of the chapter. Consider how it fits with what you know from the course, experience, and other classes. What is the significance of the material? What are the implications or applications of this material? What questions are you left with?

Sometimes the SQ3R method is too detailed for a particular assignment. A shorter reading method, known as P2R (Wong, 2015), is useful for material that you don't need to cover comprehensively. P2R has three steps. First, preview the entire chapter. Next, read actively. Finally, review the material. The key to making P2R work lies in using an active strategy to read, such as by reciting the important points, taking notes, answering chapter review questions, or writing in the margins. Doing something active while you read ensures that you are thinking about the material and are much more likely to retain it. Reviewing the material helps to reinforce the information (Exercise 6.2).

●
EXERCISE 6.2
SQ3R PRACTICE

Practice SQ3R on your next reading assignment.

1. What activities did you plan to do in each step?

2. Review the list of questions and corresponding notes you've created.

3. How well do they capture the main points of the reading?

4. How does this technique compare with your usual strategies?

5. What are the pros and cons to the SQ3R method?

More Tips on Reading

By now you understand that reading for comprehension often requires more than one pass. It usually takes two, three, or even more readings to grasp difficult concepts. Rereading takes time and may seem inefficient; however, thoroughly understanding what you have read and integrating it with your existing knowledge will save you time in the long run, such as when it is time to study for a test. It is easy to remember material that you understand, so you will spend less time studying.

Here are some additional pointers:

- Use a dictionary to look up unfamiliar words. If your cellphone is nearby, there's no excuse for not looking up a word. After looking up an unknown word, consider its meaning in the sentence.

- Pace yourself. Note that difficult readings will require more than one pass. Permit yourself the time to read such assignments over more than one session.

- Read the chapter before attending the lecture so that you're familiar with the material beforehand. Note unanswered questions or particularly difficult material and seek answers during the lecture.

- If you underline text, do so minimally and stay focused on the important details. Avoid the temptation to highlight every line. Heavy highlighting can be a procrastination technique because you're often marking what you should learn instead of focusing on learning it.

- Instead of underlining or highlighting, take the briefest of notes while reading by adding brackets in margins or underlining minimally. Note pages where you might want to take formal notes. After reading, take more extensive notes. Write the main points, in your own words.

As you finish each section or even each paragraph when reading dense material, take a moment to write down what you've learned. Be sure to use your own words and not those of the author (to lift the author's words is plagiarism, as we will see in Chapter 7). Your notes will be a valuable resource when it comes time to study. However, don't write down concepts that you don't understand. Reread the section until you understand the concept or explain as much of it as you can and indicate your questions so that you can ask your instructor for assistance. When reading and note taking are complete, reread all of your notes, think about what you've read, and add more notes based on your reflections. Ideally, your notes should be complete enough so that you can rely on them without returning to the text.

Getting the Most Out of Class: Note-Taking Tips

Class is not the time to sit back and relax. If you expect to learn and retain information from lectures and discussions, you can't simply listen; you must actively do something with the material. You must take notes. Without notes, even professors find it difficult to stick to the main points they'd like to make. Your class notes are an important study resource, a sort of privately constructed textbook that may contain information that is not available anywhere else. When you take notes, you listen more actively and are more involved in the subject, promoting learning, enhancing memory, and reducing boredom. Note taking is a lifelong skill. Most careers require at least some note taking (for example, how else can you remember what happened in that staff meeting?). How can you improve your note-taking skills?

Come Prepared

Listening to a lecture, participating in class, and learning are easier if you are prepared. Professors assign reading prior to class to ensure that students have the background knowledge needed to help them understand the day's lecture. Read before class so that the lecture material isn't completely new. Another reason for reading beforehand is to determine how closely the instructor follows the textbook. You might take notes differently in a class where the professor follows the textbook organization as compared to one in which the professor lectures on different topics entirely. The familiarity that comes with reading before class also means that you'll be able to recognize and organize the main ideas and terms more easily. Other reasons to read include feeling prepared (which can reduce anxiety) and anticipating the professor's lecture and class plan, which means you can ask better questions, process the material on a higher and more critical level, and be more engaged (and less bored).

Be Selective

Don't write everything the instructor says. Beginning note takers often make the mistake of trying to write every word and become frustrated when they find that it's impossible. Try to determine the main points and take notes in your own words. Identifying the main points requires active listening. Listen actively; that is, think about what you are hearing, evaluate it, determine your understanding, and make connections with what you already know.

The instructor usually provides clues to what is important. One clue is repetition: Instructors repeat important points. Repeated use of examples indicates important points. Notes written on the board or presented in PowerPoint slides offer other clues. Remember that when you copy notes from the board or follow along with the PowerPoint slides, you will need to write more than the phrase or words indicated. Also write an explanation. The instructor's tone of voice might signify important information. Pay attention to pauses that offer time for students take notes. Finally, instructors often highlight essential information by using specific phrases. Table 6.1 lists signal phrases that instructors might use to draw attention to critical information.

Beware of PowerPoint

One bad habit that many students fall prey to is relying too heavily on a professor's PowerPoint slides. It is tempting to simply copy the information on the overhead slides, but professors require you to know much more than what is on the slides. Likewise, many professors make PowerPoint slides available for students to download. Some students print the slides as a substitute for taking

TABLE 6.1 ● Signal Words and Phrases

Listen For	Type of Phrase
To illustrate, for example, for instance	Provides examples to make a point more clear
Before, after, formerly, subsequently, prior, meanwhile, first, second, last	Specifies the time relationships among ideas or enumerates them
Furthermore, in addition, moreover, also	Indicates additional information to add to a list
Therefore, as a result, if . . . then, accordingly, thus, so	Suggests cause and effect
On the other hand, in contrast, conversely, pros and cons	Offers contrast words to discuss both sides of a controversy
More importantly, above all, remember	Emphasizes important information
In other words, in the vernacular, it simply means, that is, briefly, in essence	Repeats the information presented in a simpler form

notes in class. Printing the slides is an excellent idea but it's critical to remember that slides are not class notes. Downloading and printing a list of points and terms for the day's class is deceptively simple and can feel as if you have already recorded the content of the day's class. Professors explain much more than is on their slides. Use the slides as an outline of the professor's lecture and add information to support each bullet point. Consider what the bullet point is saying. Listen to the professor's explanation. Practice active listening and listen for information. Try to pull out what information supports or refutes this point. How does it relate to theory?

Streamline Your Notes

If you are taking handwritten notes, use a shorthand style that includes only the essential elements and leaves out unnecessary words. For this purpose, don't write in full sentences or worry about grammar rules. Grammatical sentences require more time than you have while taking notes. Create your own abbreviations for common words used in class (just be sure to record what each abbreviation stands for). For example, as a student of developmental psychology, most of my notes referred to "dev" instead of development and "Ψ" for psychology.

Use wide margins and an outline or bullet-point method to record a streamlined account of the main points of the lecture. As you take notes, indent your paragraphs and points deeply to help you note the organization of the lecture (like an informal outline) and to provide room for later notes and comments. If you find note taking particularly difficult in a class, leave extra blank space at the end of each section or paragraph so that you can add more later after asking a question or reading the text. Focus on legible rather than pretty handwriting. Some students write more sloppily because they plan to type their notes after class, but if they run out of time they might end up with notes they can't read.

Take Notes During Class Discussion

Discussion is not the time to put your pen down and relax. Instructors use discussion to steer students toward grasping major points. It's not simply chatting. Listen actively during class discussions. The instructor will comment on important points and draw conclusions from the discussion. Record these.

Organize Your Notes

Review your notes soon after class, making corrections or adding information as needed. Identify follow-up questions to ask your professor. Some students type their notes after class. Typing class notes can be a waste of time if you focus *only* on the typing or transcribing what you've written. Typing your notes in order to organize and integrate them with prior lectures and readings is useful *if* you remember to focus on integrating information and creating links among sources of information, rather than simply getting it into a typed form.

One of the challenges of handwritten notes is that they can be lost. Organize your notes in a loose-leaf binder so that you can't lose pages easily. A binder also lets you rearrange the pages as needed, add handouts from class, and remove pages neatly. Write notes on only one side of each loose-leaf page so that you can see all the information at once and later add additional pages of notes easily. Or consider the digital route by saving your notes in an app such as an Evernote or OneNote notebook. Scan or take pictures of your notes and you'll have an easily accessible, portable, and searchable database of your notes.

Reconsider Your Use of a Laptop or Tablet

Some students choose to take notes on a laptop or tablet. Check with your professor beforehand, as some have policies prohibiting electronic devices in class. Students with excellent typing skills often prefer taking notes on their laptop because it's quick, editable, and searchable and can be easily linked to data management apps. On the other hand, professors and often other students find student use of laptops distracting because of the clicking of keys, digital displays that draw the eye, and the ability to view students' off-task activity (how easy is it to tear your eyes away from an unknown Instagram profile on a student's screen?). Research shows that students are distracted by peers' laptops, hampering their learning (Sana, Weston, & Cepeda, 2013). The concerns about laptop use in class are not simply social—they are also academic. Students who use a laptop take more notes, but those notes tend to be verbatim transcriptions of what the professor says. Students who take handwritten notes tend to show stronger conceptual understanding of the material and are more successful in applying and integrating material (Mueller & Oppenheimer, 2014). As we've discussed, learning is an active process: You need to manipulate material to learn it. Transcription is a passive process. Taking handwritten notes requires judging what material to record and finding ways to record it simply in ways that you understand, and both lead to learning.

Note taking is important not simply for recording information but for learning. Explaining ideas in your own words will ensure that you understand the material and can recall and apply it later to achieve your goals as a college student. The act of writing helps you retain material (Exercise 6.3).

●

EXERCISE 6.3
ANALYZE YOUR CLASS NOTES

How well do your notes capture what you learn in class? Analyze your class notes. Choose one class session and answer the following questions.

1. What did you do in class? Did the professor lecture? Was there discussion? Was there group work? Note all of the activities that occurred that day. (If you can't recall, it suggests that you probably need to do a better job of taking notes.)

2. What did you record? What form did you use (e.g., paragraphs, lists of words, or phrases)?

3. Do the detail and depth of your notes reflect the day's work?

4. How helpful are your resulting notes?

5. Identify challenges to taking useful notes. How can you overcome these challenges?

What If You Miss Class?

Regardless of how good a student and how detail-oriented, hardworking, or diligent you are, you can be certain that you will miss a class at some point in your academic career. What do you do after missing class? Do you just show up at the next class and start fresh? What about material that you've missed? How do you get the notes and find out what happened?

First, be aware of class attendance, late work, and make-up policies. This information is listed in your course syllabus. Some professors do not accept late work or offer make-up exams, regardless of the reason. Others offer opportunities to make up lost work but have very strict policies about when they will accept it. Read the syllabus to ensure that you don't miss any opportunities.

If it is possible, e-mail your professor before missing class. Remember the tips for e-mail etiquette offered in Chapter 4. Understand that most faculty do not consider family vacations, early flights home for break, or work obligations as appropriate reasons for missing class. If you're ill or have an emergency, try to send an e-mail to inform the professor that you cannot attend class and, if you wish, provide an excuse. Be professional; offer a concise explanation without going into personal details. If you cannot e-mail your professor before class, do so afterward. If possible, hand in assignments or e-mail them to your professor beforehand and offer to hand in a hard copy when you're back on campus (e-mailing them shows that they were completed on time).

Upon returning to class, never ask if you "missed anything important." Most professors feel that class time itself is important. This is a surefire way to make a professor's eyes roll (maybe inwardly, at least!). Also, do not ask your instructor to "go over what you missed." The professor lectured and discussed the material in class and likely will not run through an hour-long class for you now. To confirm what you missed, instead ask whether your instructor covered the material listed on the syllabus. Then demonstrate to your instructor that you care and are willing to try by reading the course material and handouts, and ask questions about specific material that you don't understand. This is a more productive use of your (and the professor's) time. It also demonstrates initiative.

Finally, turn to your classmates for information about what happened in class and ask whether they will share their notes. Be sure to read more than one student's notes because students have different perspectives and might miss some points. Read notes from several students and you're more likely to get a complete picture of what happened in class.

Preparing for Exams

We've discussed habits of studying, reading, and note taking that should keep you immersed in the subject matter of your courses. A test is on the horizon; how do you prepare?

Get the Lay of the Land

Well ahead of the test, conduct an overview of all work that needs to be done. Apply your project management skills to make a list of tasks and allocate time to complete them. If you're behind on your reading, approach the unread material with a plan. What do you need to get from the readings? Decide how much time you have to catch up. Preview the reading, deciding which parts are most important to focus on and which can be omitted. Use the reading techniques described earlier in this chapter.

Space Study and Prep Time

Studying begins on day 1 of the course. If you follow the strategies for reading, class preparation, and note taking described in this chapter, you will retain material as you learn it. To save more time and retain more, use cumulative review throughout the semester. Set aside a few minutes each week to review your notes, even if an exam is not on the horizon. This small step will help you learn more and you'll find that you have to devote less time to studying for exams. The more often that you encounter material, the more likely you are to remember it. By distributing your learning sessions over the semester, you'll find that you learn more and don't need to cram.

When it comes time to study, ignore the advice of students who plan to devote an entire day cramming for an exam. Contrary to popular belief, long study periods (e.g., 4 or more hours) aren't effective. The best way to retain knowledge and prepare for exams is to squeeze in short review periods throughout the day. For example, distributing four 30-minute sessions throughout the day is less fatiguing and more effective than a single 2-hour session. In addition, try to recite the information at odd moments (say it out loud while you are taking a shower or walking to your car). By verbalizing the material, you'll get an idea of how well you know it and where your weaknesses lie. Slow and steady really does win the race.

Anticipate Questions

Ask yourself, "If I were making up this test, given what we've focused on in class and the readings, I would probably ask my students . . . ," and then answer the questions. How do you anticipate questions? Think about how the various course topics relate to one another. Are there any repeated themes? Examine your notes and readings to determine how the course content supports the major themes of the course (you can often find these in the syllabus, the first few lectures, and the first chapter of the text).

PRACTICAL TIP
REREADING IS NOT AN EFFECTIVE STUDY STRATEGY

Frequently students report rereading the textbook to study for exams. Rereading the text is not a good study strategy. Preparing for an exam requires that you actively manipulate information, think about it, and quiz yourself. Rereading is often a passive activity, especially when students review only the highlighted areas. Self-quizzing is a more effective strategy.

Create Study Sheets

Create a series of study sheets that summarize important information for each major topic. A study sheet is a one-page synopsis of the relevant factual information, vocabulary, and theories relating to the topic. It requires you to identify, condense, and organize material from your text and the lectures. Preparing a study sheet requires actively processing all that you have learned and determining what you need to learn. The result is a comprehensive but condensed explanation of a topic, much of which you might retain simply from engaging in the active processing required to prepare it. Create a study sheet for each major topic (Exercise 6.4). Also, study sheets are excellent preparation for open-book exams.

EXERCISE 6.4
CREATE A STUDY SHEET

Choose a topic in one of your courses and create a study sheet to integrate all the information you have about it. Identify the main points and concepts. Compare your class notes with the textbook. Construct a study sheet that synthesizes all that you know about the topic. Identify any remaining questions. Based on your work, consider the following:

1. How might you use this technique in the future?

2. What are the advantages and disadvantages of creating and using study sheets?

3. Is this technique better suited to some kinds of information and topics than others?

Test-Taking Tips

An essential element to performing well on tests is preparation, applying good study skills; however, preparation is not always enough to perform at your best. Test-taking skills also count. Students who excel understand *how* to take tests. They tailor their strategies to the type of test (e.g., multiple choice or essay) and know how to prepare themselves emotionally. Let's examine test taking.

Read the Directions

The first step after receiving any test is to read the directions carefully. This is true even if it is a multiple-choice test. For example, some instructors might require that you choose the *best* answer, while others might require you to mark *all* correct answers. If you are asked to choose the best answer and you mark more than one response, you'll lose credit. On the other hand, if you are asked to mark all correct answers, you may lose credit if you don't choose more than one answer. Read the directions carefully. If they are not clear, ask your instructor to explain them.

Once you have carefully read the directions, preview the entire test. Check to be sure that your test has no missing or duplicate pages. Read through the test and decide how to allocate your time. If your head is swimming with information that you're afraid that you'll forget, jot it down quickly. The following sections present strategies for taking multiple-choice tests and essay tests, as well as for test preparation in general.

Multiple-Choice Tests

When answering a multiple-choice test, begin each item by reading the question. Then read all of the options. Don't rush; take your time to read the question and each option completely. If the question is difficult, cross out any options that don't fit. In other words, eliminate distracters. If you can eliminate all of the distracters, you'll have the correct answer. How do you identify distracters? Combine the question and each option into a complete statement. If the resulting statement is false, you've found a distracter. Stick with the subject matter of the course. If an option includes terms that seem out of place or that you don't recognize, it's probably a distracter. Here are some other tips:

- If one of the options is "all of the above," all that you need to do is determine whether two of the other options are correct. If so, then "all of the above" is your answer.

- Multiple-choice tests often include options that look alike; two options might be identical except for one or two words. It's logical to assume that one of the pair is correct.

- Note that correct answers are often longer and more inclusive than distracters.

- Tests often give away relevant information for one question in another question.

- After you have selected your answer, read the entire statement to be sure that it makes sense.

- Don't waste time on difficult questions. Eliminate as many distracters as possible. If you still don't know the answer, guess, mark the question, and return to it later.

- Don't leave any items blank.

- Don't read into questions. Sometimes questions are simple. Don't make the question more complex than it is intended to be.

- Students' first choice is usually correct. Unless you encounter specific material to change your mind or you are confident that your new answer is right, don't change your answers.

- Look for clues in other questions.

Essay Tests

Your first step in taking an essay test is to read all of the questions thoroughly. Jot down any ideas and examples that come to you, so they don't clutter your mind. Consider the difficulty of each question and answer the questions in a strategic order. Complete the easy questions first to reduce anxiety and facilitate clear thinking. After completing the easy questions, move on to those with the highest point value. The last questions you answer should be the most difficult, take the greatest amount of writing, or have the least point value.

As you consider each essay question, determine what is being asked. What do you know that is related to the question? Take a moment and organize your essay. Jot some notes or an outline of points that you want to make. Once you have a list of points or a basic structure, start writing. Don't meander but get right to the point. Use your first paragraph to provide an overview of your essay. Be sure to state your main point within the first paragraph. Use the rest of your essay to discuss your points in more detail. Back up each point with specific information, examples, or quotations from the class readings and notes. Leave space at the end of each paragraph to allow you to add further information, if needed, as you proofread. Write on every other line and on just one side of the page, not only to allow space for adding information but also to make the answers easier for your instructor to read.

Budget your time for each essay question. When you reach the end of your allotted time for a given question, list your remaining points, leave extra space, and move on to the next item. Partially answering all questions (especially by listing all of the points that you want to make) is better than fully answering only a few questions and skipping others. You won't earn credit for the questions that you skip. After you've completed the rest of the test, return to items that are incomplete.

Once you're done with the test, proofread your answers. Modify them for clarity, adding details (if needed) to make your answer complete. Check for spelling, grammar, and punctuation errors. Remember that students tend to lose points on essay tests because they fail to answer the question asked, don't provide examples or evidence to support their statements, don't write enough, are disorganized, or don't follow directions. Finally, avoid the "kitchen sink" method of answering essays, which entails writing all that you know about a subject and hoping that the answer is somewhere in your essay (Landrum & Davis, 2014).

Reduce the Stress That Accompanies Tests

Everyone finds taking exams at least a little bit stressful. Many students are surprised to find they experience that exams in some classes are very stressful, while exams in other classes are a breeze. Why? We are more likely to feel anxiety taking exams in classes that we feel are very important to our success or when taking "make it or break it" tests. We also feel more anxiety taking exams in subjects in which we feel less efficacious. Recall that self-efficacy refers to our feelings of competence in completing a task, such as an exam. Understanding why you might feel more anxiety in one class than another is an important step in approaching exams with more confidence and feeling less stressed.

Care for Your Physical Well-being

Success on exams is not just about your mind, or showing what you know; it also requires some physical preparation. Let your body and mind rest so that you are ready to work hard. Get a good night's sleep. Set your alarm a little bit early and take the time to have breakfast. Arrive 10 to 15 minutes early for your test, allowing time to acclimate yourself, relax, and prepare. Bring all the materials you will need for the test, including pencils and pens, a calculator, and a watch. Having all the materials necessary and arriving early will help you focus on the task at hand. Choose a seat that is well lit and located where you can't see many other students (and can't be easily distracted).

Don't Psych Yourself Out

Try not to talk with other students just prior to the test, especially if they seem anxious. Anxiety can be highly contagious. Feeling stress is normal, but you can control how you respond to that stress. Students who are anxious tend to engage in negative self-talk (e.g., "Everyone in this class is smarter than I am," "I always screw up on tests," or "If I don't do well on this exam, I'll flunk the course."). Negative self-talk just brings you down and increases your stress level. When you find yourself engaging in negative self-talk, catch it and stop. If you feel anxious, take some slow, deep breaths to relax and use positive self-talk to raise your confidence. Try to encourage yourself as you would a friend. Repeat positive statements to yourself in place of the negative. Remind yourself that you are well prepared for the test and believe that you are going to do well.

Reduce Anxiety During Your Exam

If you find it hard to focus your eyes to read, use a physical object to help you focus. Place your pencil along the line you're reading or use a sheet of paper to focus your eyes. If you feel that your mind has gone blank, don't panic. Close your eyes, breathe, and return to the question. Try reading it "out loud" in your head, or silently mouth the words to yourself. If you're stuck, mark the question and return to it later. If you find it hard to focus your concentration, draw your attention to the page. Circle or underline significant words to mark the page and draw your attention to the task at hand.

If you're feeling overwhelmed, try using a progressive relaxation technique to help reduce your muscle tension. Breathe in deeply and flex your toes. Release and breathe out. Do the same for your calves, then your thighs, buttocks, stomach, chest, arms, shoulders, and neck. Repeatedly tense and release your major muscle groups; it takes only a moment and produces big results. You'll feel more relaxed and able to concentrate.

Learn From Returned Tests

Think that your learning is over once the test is? It's not! There's a lot you can learn from returned tests, so don't fall into the trap of checking your grade without reviewing the test. When you get a test back, you should examine it carefully and consider your errors. Why was the correct answer correct? Identify why you missed a question. Did you read it correctly? What do you need to learn to fill in these gaps in your knowledge?

Get clues for the next test. Look for the origin of each question (tests, lectures, labs, supplementary readings, discussions). Check the level of detail and skill of the test. Were most of the questions about vocabulary, or did they ask for precise details and facts? Were the questions about main ideas, principles, applications, or all of these?

Decide which strategies worked and which didn't. Were you prepared for the test? Did you run out of time? How might you have better allocated your time? Identify those strategies that didn't work well and replace them. Use your tests to review when studying for final exams. Did you have any problems with anxiety or blocking during the test? Did you really know the answer to a question but failed to read it carefully enough to recognize it?

Academic success requires work; it's an active process. Practice the tips in this chapter and refine them based on your needs. Not everyone studies in the same way. Be flexible in your study habits, and do what works for you. Above all, remember that a little work on getting organized, creating a schedule, and staying on top of your reading can save you from cramming later. Perhaps even better is knowing that you'll retain what you've learned well beyond the test, the course, and college.

REFLECTION PROMPT

My Last Exam

Review your last exam. How did you feel when you finished it? Did you do as well as you thought? If not, what went wrong? What kinds of problems did you have difficulty with? What kinds of errors did you make? How did you prepare for this exam? Given what you learned in this chapter, do you think you prepared adequately? Why or why not? What will you do differently next time?

7

Writing a Literature Review

(Continued)

(Continued)

Chapter Outline	
Read and Record Your Research Material 　　　How to Read a Journal Article 　　　How to Read Scholarly Books 　　　Keep Your Purpose in Mind 　　　Take Notes	
Avoid Plagiarism 　　　Appropriate Use of Quotations 　　　Appropriate Paraphrasing	*Exercise 7.5: Understanding and Avoiding Plagiarism* *Exercise 7.6: Academic Honesty Policy*
Write Your Paper 　　　Prepare an Outline 　　　Write 　　　Revise	

It's the first day of class and the professor has just handed out the course syllabus, which includes a 10- to 15-page paper that is due on *"a topic of your choice."* "Ten pages! How am I supposed to know what I want to write 10 pages about before taking the class? How can I write a paper on anything without knowing something about it first?" Sound familiar? Don't know where to begin? The typical ambiguous term paper assignment can make even the best student feel queasy. Don't stress. Take control of your academic destiny by beginning your paper immediately. It's tempting to put off challenging or work-intensive assignments, but waiting until the last minute to write your paper will only increase your stress and make writing even more difficult. This chapter will walk you through the steps in writing a literature review, from selecting a topic to proofreading the final draft.

What Is a Literature Review?

The term paper assigned by most professors usually is more appropriately called a *literature review* because it is intended to present and critically evaluate the research literature on a given topic. The purpose is to present an organized discussion of current or historical research on a topic. Writing an effective review of the literature entails choosing a method to organize the studies that you will discuss in your paper (such as by thesis, methodology, or theoretical approach) and then identifying, synthesizing, and evaluating the published work relevant to your topic. Your paper should present the research in a way that tells a story about your topic, such as how theoretical perspectives on your topic or methods used to study your topic have changed over the decades. The studies you review should support your points and lead readers to draw conclusions regarding your argument.

Another way of thinking about the literature review is that it answers a question. What's the question you'd like to answer? Pose your question and then synthesize an answer, using research to support it. Ultimately your paper will give readers a detailed summary of the existing knowledge base on your topic as well as your informed evaluation of the literature.

At this point most students wonder, "Is my instructor a masochist? Why assign such a difficult project?" The answer is that writing is an integral part of learning psychology. It's an opportunity to learn about a topic of interest and acquire a host of skills, such as those in Table 7.1. These skills are useful well beyond academia, as they're coveted by employers. The work you put into writing papers now can help you in the future too.

TABLE 7.1 ● Skills Entailed in Writing a Psychology Paper
• Learning how to locate information about topics and subjects within psychology
• Collecting information
• Reading and understanding research articles in psychology
• Developing your own perspective on a topic
• Deciding what points and arguments are relevant
• Evaluating an author's claims
• Integrating ideas from multiple sources to support your ideas
• Developing writing skills and vocabulary
• Developing critical thinking skills
• Thinking and writing like a psychologist

Perhaps the most important skills you'll rely on to complete your paper are information-seeking and critical thinking skills. Information-seeking skills enable you to find useful research articles and other materials and to scan the literature efficiently. Critical thinking skills entail applying principles of analysis to identify appropriate research studies, evaluating the literature, and organizing your review in sections that identify themes, major issues, or trends. Your job in writing a literature review is not to list as many research articles as possible, but rather to carefully select those that support a comprehensive discussion about what has been published on your topic. A literature review should accomplish the following objectives:

1. Define the scope of the topic.

2. Discuss the major findings relating to your topic.

3. Summarize what is and is not known about the topic.

4. Evaluate the existing research, identifying controversy when it appears in the literature.

5. Discuss further questions for research (e.g., identify gaps in the knowledge base. What questions remain? What direction should further research take?).

As you might imagine, constructing a quality literature review takes work and insight. The degree of difficulty entailed in writing your paper is directly influenced by the topic you choose.

How to Select a Topic

Choosing a topic is one of the most important tasks in writing a paper, because "the paper can be no better than the topic" (Sternberg & Sternberg, 2017, p. 67). How can you choose a topic that is well researched and will sustain your (and your reader's) interest? Plan ahead, and pay attention to the tips discussed in the following sections.

To write a good paper, you must begin to think about it early—when you receive the assignment. Don't underestimate the amount of time that it will take for you to decide on a topic for your paper. Choosing a topic obviously requires thinking, but students are sometimes surprised to discover that it also requires reading. How are you to decide what to write about without knowing a little about the course and the topic? You cannot. Scan the literature and learn a little bit about each topic to inform your decision.

Sources of Ideas for Paper Topics

Believe it or not, it may not feel like it but you're surrounded by ideas for papers. Paper topics might come from watching television programs and the news, observing people or yourself, or reading magazines, newspapers, books, and websites. Pay attention to the social world around you, observe people's behavior, and ask "Why?" You'll never be at a loss for ideas. You may also find ideas by using the following resources, which are often overlooked.

Your Textbook

Your class textbook should be your first stop. Leaf through it and carefully scan the table of contents, which lists all of the topics covered in the text (and your course). Once you find a topic that sounds interesting, turn to that section of the text and skim through it. Textbook chapters usually provide very short overviews of topics that condense broad areas of theory and research into a few pages. If you're still interested after reading more, you've found a potential paper topic. You may have to read several sections of the text to get to this point, so it's important to start early in the semester and try not to get discouraged. Once you've found a topic of interest, use the material in your text as a starting point to expand the topic into a paper. Reread the appropriate sections of your text, and take note of any references that look promising. Write down vocabulary and ideas that you can use as key terms in your literature search. Although a textbook is a good source of ideas, you should not use it as a reference for your paper. Most professors require students to review original research from journal articles rather than rely on the broad summaries provided in textbooks.

Professors

If your instructor has provided a list of suggested topics, give them serious consideration. Recognize that professors can be an important source of information and ideas. However, they are more likely to offer you help if you've done some work first. Approach your professor for feedback, but understand that you should come with several ideas and ask for advice. Don't expect your professor to provide you with a topic for your paper.

Print and Online Dictionaries and Encyclopedias

Reading a short definition and overview of a topic can quickly tell you whether to pursue it. Reference tools such as encyclopedias and dictionaries were once found only in the reference section of libraries. While you can still locate these volumes in the library, many libraries also provide online access to these tools and some are available to the public online and for free. Table 7.2 lists some commonly available psychology reference books and websites. These resources can often help you in selecting and narrowing a topic, but remember that they are only a starting point. The short summaries characteristic of encyclopedia entries can help you to develop an initial understanding of the breadth and depth of the topic at hand. In most cases you will not cite the encyclopedia or reference book or website in your paper. Instead your professor will expect you to use journal articles as sources. A reference book, however, can point you toward useful sources.

Media

Television, magazines, and newspapers can offer ideas for papers. For example, each Tuesday, the *New York Times* newspaper includes a science section that usually has at least one article about health and psychology. These articles are a fantastic source of information and ideas. As you read or watch television, stop and consider the topic of the program or article. Ask the following questions: Why does the problem occur? How can it be prevented? What do we know about it? Ideas are everywhere; finding them requires an enquiring mind.

Internet

The Internet is usually the first place students turn in searching for a topic. A quick Google or Yahoo search can be invaluable for identifying interesting topics, but treat information found on the Internet with caution. Unlike scholarly journals

TABLE 7.2 ● Psychology Dictionaries and Resources

Books

American Psychological Association. (2015). *The APA dictionary of psychology.* Washington, DC: APA.

Colman, A. M. (2015). *A dictionary of psychology.* New York, NY: Oxford University Press.

Hayes, N., & Stratton, P. (2012). *A student's dictionary of psychology.* New York, NY: Hodder Education.

Matsumo, D. (2009). *The Cambridge dictionary of psychology.* Cambridge, MA: Cambridge University Press.

VandenBos, G. R. (2016). *APA college dictionary of psychology.* Washington, DC: APA.

Weiner, I. B., & Craighead, W. E. (2010). *The Corsini encyclopedia of psychology and behavioral science.* New York, NY: Wiley.

Online Resources

All Psych Online Psychology Dictionary: http://allpsych.com/dictionary/

AmoebaWeb: http://www.vanguard.edu/psychology/amoebaweb/

American Psychological Association: http://www.apa.org

Association for Psychological Science: http://www.psychologicalscience.org

Encyclopedia of Psychology: https://psychcentral.com/encyclopedia/

Psychology Dictionary: http://psychologydictionary.org/

or books, anyone can post anything online, so it's up to you to think critically when evaluating the credibility of the source and determining how to use the content (Exercises 7.1 and 7.2).

How do you evaluate a site's credibility? The URL can provide some information about a site's trustworthiness. Sites hosted by the government (.gov), universities (.edu), and organizations (.org) are often trustworthy sources of information. Professional organizations such as the American Psychological Association (APA) and the Association for Psychological Science (APS) are also a good source of information about psychology. For example, APA and APS publish monthly magazines, *Monitor on Psychology* (http://www.apa.org/moni tor/) and the *Observer* (https://www.psychologicalscience.org/observer), that are excellent sources of paper ideas.

Wikipedia is another source of ideas, as it is an online encyclopedia with short articles on a seemingly endless number of topics. Take great care, however, in considering information from Wikipedia articles because the entries vary widely in reliability and value. Wikipedia articles are not reviewed for accuracy or quality. They are often modified by multiple contributors, but anyone with access to the Internet can contribute. The APS sponsors a Wikipedia

Initiative, encouraging psychologists and students to contribute to Wikipedia to share accurate information about psychological science (https://www.psy chologicalscience.org/members/aps-wikipedia-initiative). However, there is no way to tell which articles have been written by scholars. That said, perusing Wikipedia with a healthy dose of skepticism can lead to useful ideas for class papers. Similar to textbooks, however, websites can offer useful information to generate ideas, but you will need to locate scholarly articles to actually write your paper.

EXERCISE 7.1
DEVISE CRITERIA FOR EVALUATING INTERNET SOURCES

Don't take what you read online at face value. Critically evaluate the source to determine the credibility of the information and whether you should rely on it. The following exercise encourages you to examine advice from university and library websites on evaluating Internet sources.

1. Locate and list three webpages hosted by .edu addresses that provide advice on evaluating Internet sources.

2. Discuss the advice offered by each site. Identify similarities and differences in the range of advice offered as well as specific tips.

3. Identify the three to five most important tips for evaluating Internet sources that you have learned from comparing these three resources.

EXERCISE 7.2
PRACTICE EVALUATING INTERNET SOURCES

1. Using the criteria identified in Exercise 7.1, list qualities that describe a trustworthy Internet source.

2. List qualities that signal an untrustworthy source to avoid.

3. Search Google for a topic of your choice. Peruse the results and choose an example of a trustworthy article. Explain why it is a credible source.

4. Provide an example of a poor, untrustworthy website or article. Explain why it is a poor source for a paper.

Reference Librarian

Your best source of information about the library resources and holdings is the reference librarian. Discuss your paper with him or her, and explain what you're looking for (that's why it's important to have selected a preliminary topic beforehand). Ask the librarian to suggest sources of information. He or she can help you to devise specific search strategies to help you find what you need more quickly and efficiently; however, you must approach the librarian with a topic(s) in mind. Do not expect the reference librarian to give you a paper topic, but he or she can assist you in locating important resources, such as psychology journals.

Psychology Journals

Most professors require that students cite articles from psychology journals in their papers. Journals can be viewed as scientific magazines consisting of collections of articles written by scientists describing their research. Journals are published monthly or several times each year. Many psychology journals specialize in a particular subfield, such as health psychology or cognitive psychology. As we will discuss later in this chapter, articles from psychology journals are radically different from magazine articles. For now let's consider their value as sources of paper ideas.

For a paper in an Introductory Psychology course, browse through general psychology journals that have articles spanning all of the fields within psychology. Either locate the print version of the journal in the library or view the journal online, which you can find using PsycINFO (which we'll discuss shortly) or the journal webpage. You'll notice a link for each issue. Click through and read the titles. Browsing without a specific topic in mind may feel like you're fishing without a fishing rod, but reading with an open mind will help you to get a feel for the wide range of psychological topics that you have to choose from. For example, *Current Directions in Psychological Science* publishes short review-type articles (in a student-friendly writing style) that may spark some ideas. Also take a look at *American Psychologist* and the *Psi Chi Journal of Psychological Research* (in which all articles are written by college students). If you're writing a paper for a class in a particular subfield, such as developmental psychology, look through more specialized psychology journals to find recent articles and get ideas. For example, if you're searching for a topic for your Adolescent Psychology paper, leaf through recent issues of journals specializing in adolescent development (e.g., *Journal of Adolescence*). Once you find an article that's interesting, read it carefully and examine the reference section to find related articles.

Define and Narrow Your Topic: Focus on Refereed Journal Articles

By now you should have one, preferably two, topics in mind. Your next step is to gather information to narrow your topic. Review the literature, specifically research articles from psychology journals, for each topic to determine if it is appropriate for your paper assignment. Is the topic well researched? Is the topic narrow enough? Is the topic too narrow? You won't be able to determine the answers to these questions without searching and reading through some of the literature. How do you locate additional readings to narrow your topic and get started? While many of the resources that we have discussed are excellent sources of paper ideas, most instructors prefer (and often require) that students rely only on journal articles for writing papers. Consider the strengths and weaknesses of various sources of information and it is easy to see why professors prefer journal articles as references for student papers. Why are journal articles so special? Why do professors prefer them as references?

What Are Refereed Journal Articles?

How are articles from psychology journals different from magazine articles? Magazines pay writers, whereas journals do not pay their authors. Magazine articles might be checked for accuracy, but they are not scrutinized to the same extent as journal articles. Journal articles more extensively document the sources of ideas and evidence; magazines are rarely as extensively documented. Most importantly, journal articles in psychology are chosen for publication only after a process of *peer review*, whereby several professionals review article submissions before an acceptance decision is made. When an author submits a manuscript to a journal, the editor sends copies of the paper out for review by the author's peers. This means that other psychologists are asked to read the article and determine whether it is suitable for publication. The peers who do the review are called *referees*. Sometimes peer-reviewed journals are referred to as *refereed journals*.

How do referees evaluate manuscripts? Although each reviewer may use slightly different criteria, manuscripts are reviewed based on scholarship. A scholarly manuscript offers an important contribution to the field of psychology and includes a comprehensive review of the literature, concise writing, appropriate methodology and statistical analyses, and an understanding of the audience. Once the editor has received the reviews, a decision is made whether to reject the paper, accept it, or suggest that the author make some changes and resubmit. As you might imagine, this is a long and arduous process, but it ensures that the articles appearing in scholarly journals have scholarly merit.

Even those who are unfamiliar with journal articles quickly see that research articles have a specific format and layout. Understanding the layout will make articles more comprehensible. An empirical article consists of several sections: the abstract, introduction, method, results, discussion, and references. Each section has a specific purpose. The *abstract* (usually located underneath the article title and before the text of the article) briefly summarizes the study. The *introduction* is the first section of an article. It provides an overview of the research question, reviews the literature, and identifies the purpose of the study (the specific purpose and hypotheses are usually found at the very end of the introduction section). The *method* section explains how the research was conducted; it describes the participants, measures, instruments, equipment, and procedure. The *results* section presents statistical analyses that address the research questions. Here, the study findings are presented, with information displayed in graphs and tables. In the *discussion* section, the author examines the significance of the study's findings in light of prior research, discusses limitations of the study, and offers suggestions for further research. For more information about empirical articles, see Chapter 8. How do you find refereed articles for your paper?

Use Reference Databases (PsycINFO, PsycARTICLES)

The APA publishes an important resource for locating journal articles: PsycINFO. PsycINFO is an online database of abstracts from journal articles, book chapters, books, and dissertations published in psychology and the behavioral sciences. Each article entry includes bibliographic information (which helps you locate the article) and an abstract (which provides summary information to help you decide if the article is useful for your paper). PsycINFO is updated frequently and indexes articles from 1887 to the present, permitting a thorough search of the literature. Most institutions maintain a subscription to PsycINFO and some also have a subscription to PsycARTICLES, a service that provides full-text articles from journals published by the APA from 1894 to the present. Most institutions permit students to log into these databases off campus and on their own computers, making it possible to search the literature wherever and whenever they choose.

Entering a search term into PsycINFO usually will yield a long list of articles. You'll see the article title, authors, date, and journal. Click on a title and you will see the full bibliographic information for the article plus the abstract. An abstract is a short 150-word summary of the article. Read the abstract to decide whether it is worth reading the article itself. Note that the abstract is *not* the article—it's a very short summary. If you plan on using the article as a reference for your paper, you must locate and read the entire article, not just the abstract. Depending on your library's resources, a pdf of the article may be linked to the entry, you may be able to obtain a copy in your library, or you may have to request it by interlibrary loan. PsycINFO and other reference databases make it easy to conduct a thorough literature search, which saves you lots of time in your research *if* you know how to use them effectively. Skill, flexibility, and creativity are required to get the most from computerized reference databases. Sometimes the search for a topic yields few results because the wrong search words are used.

How do you determine the appropriate search terms? The *Thesaurus of Psychological Index Terms*, published by the APA (last updated in 2015), lists all of the standardized, agreed-upon words or phrases used to represent concepts in PsycINFO. Review this thesaurus rather than try to figure out all of the ways authors might refer to the same concept. Use the thesaurus before beginning your search to brainstorm the most appropriate descriptors, and you'll save time and hassle. After locating an article that is useful to your paper, look for the key terms under which the article is labeled. Use these key terms to find additional articles. The *Thesaurus of Psychological Index Terms* is linked to PsycINFO and is also available at http://help.psycnet.org/en/term-finder/.

Additional features that make PsycINFO especially useful are the tools for refining searches; you can combine the results of several searches and limit the results of a search. Table 7.3 illustrates the steps in using an electronic database, including how to combine the results of several searches and how to limit the results of a search. Finally, note that if your institution does not subscribe to PsycINFO, you can access it online for free through the APA website (http://www.apa.org). You'll have to obtain the articles through your school (or purchase them for a fee online), but this online resource permits you to do a great deal of research at home.

TABLE 7.3 ● Conducting a Literature Search With PsycINFO

Before beginning your search, remember that you won't find everything in one pass. Instead, you'll need to refine your searching strategies and, depending on your topic, you may conduct several searches. For example, consider a paper about risky behavior in adolescents.

1. **Run an initial search:** *risky behavior*

   To gather articles about risky behavior, I type in *risky behavior* as keywords and find that over 2,457 articles have *risky behavior* in their title, abstract, or subject.

2. **Use OR to expand a search:** *risky behavior* **OR** *problem behavior*

   I remember that *problem behavior* is a similar term. I search for *problem behavior* and find 57,058 articles. I decide to see how many articles use either term, so I enter *risky behavior OR problem behavior* and find 63,706 references—this is clearly too many to use in my paper!

3. **Narrow the search with quotation marks:** *"risky behavior"* **OR** *"problem behavior"*

   I decide to look for articles that use the specific terms "risky behavior" or "problem behavior", so I add quotation marks to search for *"risky behavior" OR "problem behavior"*. I get 7,711 results.

4. **Narrow the search with AND:** *"risky behavior"* **AND** *"problem behavior"*

   I combine the terms to identify articles that address both risky behavior and problem behavior terms. I enter *"risky behavior" AND "problem behavior"* and find 22 articles. After reviewing them, I decide that they don't quite fit my topic. I want to find more articles.

5. **Broaden the search by dropping a term:** *"risky behavior"*

   I decide to look only at "risky behavior" and get 1,552 references—this is still too many.

(Continued)

TABLE 7.3 ● (Continued)

6. **Narrow the search with AND:** *"risky behavior" AND adolescents*

    My paper is about risky behavior in adolescence, so I add the term *adolescents* to the search. I enter *"risky behavior" and adolescents* and find 700 articles.

7. **Further narrow the search with additional terms:** *("risky behavior" AND adolescents) AND (parents OR peers)*

    I'm particularly interested in parents and peers. I narrow the search to articles that examine parents or peers, since I'm interested in either. This is a more complicated search, so I use parentheses to keep my sets of search terms separate. The term *("risky behavior" AND adolescents)* searches for articles that meet both criteria, as before. I also search *(parents OR peers)* because I'm interested in articles that examine either parents or peers. I combine the two sets of terms to search for articles about risky behavior in adolescence that examine both parents and peers: *("risky behavior" and adolescents) AND (parents OR peers)*. I find 604 articles.

8. **Further narrow the search:** *("risky behavior" AND adolescents) AND (parents AND peers)*

    I decide that I really want to review articles that look at <u>both</u> parents and peers, so I change my search to *("risky behavior" and adolescents) and (parents and peers)* and have 124 results.

9. **Narrow by year**

    I can further narrow my results by year of publication. I narrow my search to those articles published since 2014, using the year limiter in the left-hand column. After limiting my search to articles published after 2014, I find 42 articles (a manageable number).

Don't Rely on Google

Many students turn to Google in search of sources, but Internet search engines are not likely to yield the sources that you will need to write a decent paper. Most Google searches result in websites and popular press articles. Remember that a literature review is a scholarly paper that integrates information from reputable academic sources, such as journals and scholarly texts, which can be difficult to find using Google or another search engine. In addition, most professors require that students only use scholarly sources and no Internet sources. Instead of searching Google, turn to your college library. College libraries subscribe to a number of electronic databases that index journal articles and books, permitting users to search by topic, author, title, and more. In addition to using your college's online databases, make a trip to the library. Walking the stacks (that is, browsing books on their shelves) can lead you to sources and help shape your paper.

Narrow Your Topic and Determine If There Is Enough Research

Once you have an initial idea for a topic, you're not yet ready to begin writing your paper. Before committing yourself to a topic, be sure that there is adequate literature on it. Can you find articles that address your topic, or do you find too many? The most common mistake that students make in choosing a paper topic is to choose one that is too broad. A literature review, by its very nature, provides comprehensive coverage of a topic. In order to provide comprehensive coverage, you'll need to choose a narrow topic (otherwise you're writing a book, not a class paper). Try Exercise 7.3 to practice narrowing a broad topic into a paper topic.

EXERCISE 7.3
NARROWING A TOPIC

Practice refining your search terms to obtain a manageable list of results when using PsycINFO.

1. Enter the following term into PsycINFO: *depression*. How many articles did you find?

2. Narrow the topic by considering the population of interest (children, adolescents, adults, adoptees, etc.). Enter *depression* and your population (e.g., children). How many articles did you find?

3. Further narrow the topic by considering what aspect of the topic you'd like to cover. For example, is it treatment, prevention, or causes? Add your chosen term to the search. How many articles did you find?

4. Further narrow the topic by choosing specific dates of publication (e.g., since 2017). How did the results change?

5. What other terms might you add to further narrow the results?

Narrowing your topic means that you'll focus your paper on a specific line of research or aspect of your topic. Unless you are already knowledgeable about the research area, you can't preselect a topic that is narrow enough. This is another reason why you shouldn't procrastinate because choosing an appropriately narrow topic requires reading and getting a handle on the literature. Once you have tentatively chosen a topic, scan the literature (using the techniques described earlier in this chapter) to determine how well researched it is and narrow your topic, if necessary. This is a good time to visit your professor or teaching assistant to get some feedback on your choice. Think you have a good understanding of how to use PsycINFO to locate articles as well as broaden and narrow searches? Try Exercise 7.4 to test your competence.

EXERCISE 7.4
USING PSYCINFO

Choose an area of research in which you are interested. Be specific in order to narrow the results of your PsycINFO search to yield a manageable number of articles.

1. What is your research question?

2. Write the search terms that you will use.

3. Enter your search terms into PsycINFO. How many results did you get? Were your terms too narrow or too broad? Print out the first page of your results.

4. Try narrowing your topic. Write down the search terms used. How many results did you get? Print out the first page of your results.

5. Take a closer look at the results from the first page of your narrowed search. How do these results differ from those in your first search? Discuss any patterns that you notice in article titles.

6. Try broadening your topic. Write down the search terms used. How many results did you get? Print out the first page of your results.

7. Take a closer look at the results from the first page of your broadened search. How do these results differ from those in your narrowed search? Discuss any patterns that you notice in article titles.

8. Return to the results page of your narrowed topic search. Choose one article that is particularly interesting. Retrieve the first page of that article using your library's full-text or print resources. The reference librarian can assist you if you're experiencing difficulty. Print the first page of the article.

Choose an Appropriate Match to Your Abilities

Try not to choose a topic that is too easy or "safe" for you. The purpose of writing your paper is to learn something about a subject. Choose a topic that you're relatively unfamiliar with, to maximize the learning opportunity. Choosing a safe topic (e.g., one you've already written papers on) deprives you of the opportunity and challenge of gaining competence in a new area. The opposite is also true; try not to choose a topic that is too difficult. Scan the abstracts of articles in your topic to be sure that you can understand the purposes and the underlying concepts and ideas. Avoid topics that you can't adequately present and evaluate from the information presented in articles. In other words, be "certain that the topic you choose does not require an understanding of concepts that your background does not permit you to grasp" (Sternberg & Sternberg, 2017, p. 69).

Begin considering your paper early so that you have time to select a topic that will maintain your interest. Allow yourself the opportunity to consider several topics, and choose the one that appeals most to you. In other words, don't procrastinate. Too often, students wait until the last minute to select a topic. Then they choose hastily and end up with a topic they are only marginally interested in. Be nice to yourself by taking the time to find an interesting topic. Few scholarly tasks are less fun than working on an uninteresting paper.

PRACTICAL TIP
SUPPLEMENT YOUR SEARCH WITH GOOGLE SCHOLAR

While a general search engine like Google likely will not yield helpful results, the Google Scholar specialized search engine (http://scholar.google.com) can be helpful. Google Scholar is a dedicated search engine that filters only scholarly research articles, reports, and books. Google Scholar is not limited to psychology. It searches all fields. Your search may reveal many articles unrelated to psychology. Like PsycINFO, you can sort items by year. Perhaps what's best about Google Scholar is that pdf links are listed, if they're available online. Type in the title of an article that you are unable to access through your library and you might find that it is posted online (click to see "all versions" to determine if pdf copies are available). Type an author's name and you'll see links to his or her work. While Google Scholar cannot replace specialized psychology databases such as PsycINFO, it is a useful supplement and can help you find needed articles.

Read and Record Your Research Material

As we have discussed, the primary sources that you will use in writing your paper will be published articles from psychology journals. Most professors prefer journal articles as sources over books because scholarly journals are published more frequently and have a more rigorous review and acceptance process than do books. Journal articles are the most important sources for current findings in psychology. As a psychology major, you will need to become familiar with journal articles.

How to Read a Journal Article

Thoroughly reading an article requires several passes. Your first pass should be an initial scan to determine whether the study is essential for your paper.

Reading and taking notes is time-consuming; therefore, you want to be sure that the article will suit your needs before you spend a great deal of time on it. During your initial scan of the article, determine the research question, specific hypotheses, findings, and interpretation. After you've scanned for this material, stop and consider whether the article fits with the purpose of your paper. Is it relevant? How does the article apply to your paper? How will you use it?

If you've decided that the article is relevant to your paper, your next task is to read for depth. What is the problem or issue addressed? Discern the theories tested and the methods used. Who were the participants, and how were they tested? How were the findings interpreted? Consider the items in Table 7.4.

As you read, remember that journal articles can lead you to other articles and sources for your research. When you find a current article that is especially useful, examine the references and you'll find other sources that are relevant to your paper. If you examine the reference list for each article that you cite in your paper, you'll find that a great deal of your research is complete. However, it is

---

TABLE 7.4 ● Guidelines for Reviewing Research Articles

1. Is the author's hypothesis ambiguous or clearly articulated?

2. What is the author's research orientation and theoretical framework? What are the author's underlying assumptions? From what theoretical framework does the author address the problem? (You can find clues in the author's choice of citations and how often particular references are cited.)

3. Could the problem have been approached more effectively from another perspective?

4. Has the author evaluated the literature relevant to the issue? Were any areas of literature excluded from the author's review?

5. Does the author take a balanced perspective and include articles that take contrary positions?

6. Is the sample large and representative of the population the author wishes to address? How were participants selected?

7. What measures were used? Are the instruments' psychometric properties presented? How valid are the instruments? Do you think the instruments measure the intended constructs?

8. Were the data analyzed properly? What are the findings? Are the findings meaningful? Sometimes researchers find differences between variables that are statistically significant, but small; these differences may not be meaningful when applied.

9. How are the findings interpreted? Do you agree with the interpretation?

10. What are the strengths and weaknesses of the study (every study has strengths and weaknesses)?

11. Do the findings have applied or policy implications?

important not to rely on this as your only strategy for locating articles because you may end up with a distorted view of the literature. Some authors may not cite other seminal works because of differences of opinion and bias. If you obtain all of your sources from the references of other articles, you might miss some important pieces of research, and you will certainly miss out on new research.

How to Read Scholarly Books

When you consider books as sources for your paper, remember that the more recently a book was published, the more likely it is to contain current theory and methodology. Edited books, which contain chapters written by many different authors, are often good sources of information. Because each chapter is written by a different author, it usually presents a different view of your topic.

Before you spend a great deal of time searching for books, be familiar with your instructor's recommended and required resources. Some professors advise their students not to use books as sources because they're too long for student papers. Or simply that the material in books is older than what you'll find in journals. In addition, many books are not scholarly. Many popular self-help books, for example, are of questionable scientific value. Therefore, some professors discourage students from using books as sources because it can be difficult to evaluate their merit.

If you decide to use books as source material for your paper, examine each one carefully. How do you determine the academic trustworthiness of a book?

- Examine the author's background. What are the author's academic credentials and experience?

- Examine the reference section, because the number and type of references can indicate how well the book has been researched. How many of the references are the author's?

- Does the book have an index? Scott, Koch, Scott, and Garrison (1999) suggest that "in addition to making your search for relevant material easier, an index suggests a certain amount of professionalism on the part of the authors" (p. 109).

- Skim the introduction, preface, forward, or first chapter to find clues about the book's purpose, intended audience, and scholarly quality.

- How sound are its facts, methodologies, and findings?

Before beginning a scholarly book, preview it. It's easy to get lost in the prose within and later find that you cannot explain the author's perspective and supporting points. Savvy readers learn about the author's purpose and thesis *before* they read the book. It is counterintuitive but true: To get the most out of a book in the least amount of time possible, know what you're getting into and what you're looking for before you begin.

What is the book about? Read the back cover and book jacket. More importantly, read the preface. Most students skip the preface; however, the preface contains essential information for understanding the book's thesis. The preface usually provides information about the author's objective, the organizational plan of the book, how the book is different from others on the market, and the author's background and qualifications. Once you know the author's objective or goal, it's easier to see relationships among the facts presented. The organizational plan is like a road map explaining where the author will take you. Reading the author's view of what the book contributes to the field and learning about his or her background and qualifications gives you more insight into his or her perspective, perhaps making it easier to comprehend the ideas that appear in the book.

In addition to (or sometimes in place of) a preface, most books begin with an introduction section or chapter. Read the introduction because it is a window into the book. It provides an overview to a text, making it easier to digest information in the subsequent chapters. The introduction usually is packed with facts and ideas so as to lay the foundation for the book.

As your mass of research sources grows, you may feel a sense of unease and wonder how you will sift through the pages and pages of information. Reading the articles and synthesizing the ideas into a cohesive paper may seem like a daunting task, but break it down into smaller pieces and it will seem more manageable. If you've taken your time in choosing a topic and narrowed it down appropriately, you've already begun reading some of the literature, or at least scanned some of it, and you have a better sense of how to organize your paper than you think.

Keep Your Purpose in Mind

Once you begin reading, it's easy to forget the purpose of your paper. Instead, you may find yourself describing every detail of each article. Stay focused. Before you begin reading and taking notes, clarify the purpose of your paper. Remain focused as you read and consider articles, and your paper will seem more manageable. Consider your thesis, problem, or research question. What is your angle? Are you considering issues of theory, methodology, or policy? What is the scope of the review? How have you limited the literature? For example, a student might limit the scope of a paper about conduct disorder to examining evaluations of behavioral interventions. Defining the scope of the review involves restating your narrow topic and setting rules for including or excluding articles. Write down your ideas about the purpose, angle, and scope of your paper. Write the purpose on a note card or sticky note and keep it near you. Refer to it often to remember and focus.

At first, concentrate on reading the abstracts for the articles that you've chosen. If you've defined your purpose well, you may find that after reading only the abstracts, you can eliminate some articles from consideration because they're not relevant to your paper. As you read, take occasional breaks to reread your stated purpose. Consider whether what you've read is within the scope that you delineated for your paper. Where does the article fit? Perhaps your reading has suggested that you change your focus or narrow your paper. Realize that your ideas about your paper will change and become more refined with your reading. Be open to change, and take notes on how you might refocus your paper.

The most important tip about reading is to begin early. Notice a trend? Lots of time and effort will be spent before you begin to write but ultimately you will write your paper more quickly. You'll need plenty of time to think about your paper, collect articles, and read them before any writing occurs. Reading for your paper is a process of information gathering and synthesis. As you read, you might encounter references that seem important. Return to the library to gather these new sources.

When do you stop reading? One clue that you have done a thorough review is when you notice that article authors cite studies that you have already reviewed. But this doesn't mean that you're ready to write the paper. Understand your sources, take notes, and think carefully about their implications before beginning to write. Consider how the articles fit together and how you might organize your review.

Take Notes

As you read, summarize the main findings and methods of each study that you think are important enough to include in your paper. Summarize each article in a page or less. If you consistently take the time to write a brief summary of each article that you plan to include, your literature review will be largely done by the time you sit down to formally write. Take the time to record the reference, using correct APA style. Take it from my own experience, hunting for an unrecorded reference is very frustrating! It can sometimes take an hour to locate a source once you've begun writing, whereas it takes only a few minutes to record the information properly while you're taking notes.

The method that you use to take notes is a personal choice. Traditionally, experts advocated using an analog (hard copy) note-card system comprised by 5- by 8-inch cards, organized by topic. This system requires that you use a separate card for each article. Write the APA-style reference on the back of the card and notes on the front (if you're not sure what an APA-style reference is, see Chapter 8 for a discussion of APA style). Note cards allow you to physically organize information and sort it into topical categories that will help you to organize the outline of your paper. Note cards travel well and offer a handy way of arranging and rearranging information

Apps such as Google Keep, Evernote, and OneNote offer platforms that can simulate note cards, with many advantages. Consider each page or note in these programs as an individual note card, to take notes on an individual study. If you take digital notes, clearly mark each reference and back up all of your work each day. E-mail it to yourself, save it on a cloud drive, or print a hard copy to ensure that none of your work is lost. Digital notetaking offers several advantages over the old note-card system: search, portability, and pretyped notes. You may find that most of the notes that will become the prose of your first draft are already typed. Import (or cut and paste) your notes into a word processing program to write your paper. You can cut and paste the material to organize it, then edit, and add transitions, analysis, and interpretation. Always back up your work and make a "safe copy" to edit during each writing session.

Be precise in indicating paraphrases and direct quotes. Take great care to ensure that any direct quotations you copy from a source are indicated as such. This is especially important if you choose to keep digital notes. I find it helpful to highlight direct quotes in a bright color as a precaution. Sometimes students forget that a sentence or two was copied from a source—and is not their own summary—and inadvertently commit plagiarism. Regardless of whether it was intended, plagiarism is a serious breach of academic honesty.

Avoid Plagiarism

The cardinal rule that applies for all subjects and all writing assignments that you'll ever complete is to avoid plagiarism. *Plagiarism* refers to using another person's work (i.e., ideas, research, writing, websites, charts, data, or other original work) without giving credit and without clearly acknowledging its source. The rules of plagiarism apply to all sources, both published (books, magazines, newspapers, websites, and textbooks) and unpublished (class lectures, notes, handouts, speeches, and student papers). Writers must give credit any time they use information from a source. Citations giving the source of information must accompany the following: (1) discussions of another person's ideas, arguments, or theory; (2) facts that are not common knowledge; (3) quotations of a person's spoken or written words; and (4) paraphrases of another person's spoken or written words.

How can you avoid plagiarism? Use your own words to express the ideas of others, and then give credit to the originators of those ideas. Try to convey the author's main idea without using his or her words or sentence structure. Always cite information and ideas that are learned through your research, no matter where you find them (even if it is on the Internet or in an encyclopedia). Common knowledge is not cited, but be careful of what you consider to be common knowledge. Examples of common knowledge are well-known dates and familiar sayings. Generally, information that could be found in a number of general sources (e.g., popular magazines) may not have to be cited. Whenever you are in doubt, cite the source. It is better to be safe and overcite your sources than to accidentally plagiarize.

Appropriate Use of Quotations

When you repeat an author's exact words, you must indicate that the material is a direct quote and give its source. APA style requires that you enclose the material in quotation marks and cite the author's last name, year, and the page number for the quote (American Psychological Association, 2010). Here is an example of a short quotation, given in text:

Bornstein and Arterberry (1999) argued that "perception begins our experience and interpretation of the world, and is crucial to the growth of thought" (p. 231). This is . . .

If the quotation contains 40 or more words, it should be displayed as a free-standing block, with the quotation marks omitted:

Bornstein and Arterberry (1999) argued that

> Perception begins our experience and interpretation of the world, and is crucial to the growth of thought, to the regulation of emotions, to interaction in social relationships, and to progress in most aspects of our development. The input, translation, and encoding of sensory information in perception is requisite to reflection and action. (p. 231)

In summary, it is permissible to include a direct quote in your paper as long as it is appropriately documented. Enclose the material in quotation marks, and cite the authors, year of publication, and page numbers. Quoting a source without providing documentation is plagiarism. That said, check with your instructor, as some professors prefer that students not use direct quotations in their papers.

Now that you've reviewed the appropriate use of quotes, be aware that it's best not to use too many of them in your paper. A paper represents the synthesis and analysis of what you've read. When you use direct quotes too often, the resulting paper is just a string of other people's words, rather than your own analysis, interpretation, and expression of their ideas. Be careful not to quote because of laziness; it is much easier to use direct quotes than it is to paraphrase. Quote directly from a source only when you cannot capture the original ideas in your own words. Use quotes only when the author's language is distinctive and enhances your argument. In other words, record quotations only when the wording is particularly vivid, precise, or authoritative.

PRACTICAL TIP
CITE ONLY WHAT YOU'VE READ

Your reference list should include only articles that you have read. If an article is cited in your paper and its citation appears in your reference list, it means that you have read the article and used it to write your paper. Your professor will expect you to have the article and be able to explain its findings and how you used it in your paper. Listing articles in your reference list that you have not read is a form of academic dishonesty.

Appropriate Paraphrasing

Like any paper, yours will discuss a great deal of research conducted by other people, and you must give appropriate credit to the authors you have read. How do you relay the sources of ideas and give credit? Enter paraphrasing. Paraphrasing refers to restating an author's ideas or information in your own words. Even though you are using your own words, you must cite the source of your information. The American Psychological Association (2010) has published a style book describing the nuts and bolts of writing papers. According to APA style, appropriate citation of paraphrases includes the author's last name and year of publication; you are encouraged but not required to provide a page number. Note that you are required to provide the page number only when quoting directly from a source. For example, a paraphrase of the text quoted earlier might read as follows:

> Perception is essential to cognitive, emotional, and social development because it determines how we interpret and react to the sensory world around us (Bornstein & Arterberry, 1999, p. 170).

As you can see, the paraphrase concisely restates the main idea of the passage, using different words and sentence structure. The page number is optional.

How do you paraphrase? First, be sure that you understand the information you wish to paraphrase. Your goal is to restate the idea and convey the same meaning, so it is essential that you understand the original passage before trying to paraphrase it. Realize that you may have to edit your paraphrase several times. Write your paraphrase; then reread the original passage to check for accuracy and to be sure that you haven't borrowed language or structure. Revise your paraphrase as needed. Use your own grammatical structure, restate the material in your own words, and cite the source. Pretend to explain the idea to a friend, then write what you say. Practice is important because appropriate paraphrasing is difficult. Paraphrasing allows you to summarize an author's main points concisely and in your own writing style, contributing to the "flow" of your paper. Test out your ability to quote and paraphrase as well as learn about how your institution views plagiarism and its consequences by completing Exercise 7.5.

EXERCISE 7.5

UNDERSTANDING AND AVOIDING PLAGIARISM

1. Identify an interesting passage from your textbook. Write a short paragraph about the topic, including the quotation, using appropriate APA style to indicate that it is a quotation and not your own words.

2. Now write a short paragraph that paraphrases instead of quotes the passage. Note that paraphrasing entails more than using a thesaurus to replace a few words. Appropriate paraphrasing requires conveying the ideas in an entirely new set of words and sentence structure from the original.

3. Reflect on the process of paraphrasing. Was it challenging? Why? How might you gain experience and become more comfortable with this new skill?

4. Identify reasons why students might plagiarize.

5. Look up your institution's definitions and policies about plagiarism. What are the consequences of plagiarism at your institution?

Frequently students commit plagiarism without realizing it, by incorrectly quoting and paraphrasing material. Remember that ignorance of the rules (or laziness) is no excuse for plagiarism. Many instructors don't provide a "get out of jail free card." In other words, if you inadvertently plagiarize, you might find yourself with an F or a zero on an assignment and no way to make it up. Unfortunately, plagiarism, whether intentional or unintentional, can mark a student as dishonest, lazy, and a cheat. This is not an exaggeration. Plagiarism is a serious offense that marks offenders as unethical (Exercise 7.6).

EXERCISE 7.6
ACADEMIC HONESTY POLICY

Locate your college's academic honesty policy. Conduct a quick search of your institution's website to locate the policy.

1. Provide a link to the page.

2. Summarize the policy.

3. What behaviors and activities are listed?

4. What is the process for addressing cases of academic dishonesty?

5. What is the range of consequences for academic dishonesty?

6. What does the policy imply about the importance of academic honesty? What do you think?

PRACTICAL TIP
AVOID DISHONEST SHORTCUTS

Writing papers is difficult. It is tempting to take shortcuts. Some of these shortcuts may seem harmless, but all of the following are forms of academic dishonesty:

- Recycling an old paper used in a prior class
- Buying a paper online
- Downloading a paper online
- Cutting and pasting from Internet pages
- Using a service that writes papers for students
- Asking someone else to write a paper
- Using a sibling, parent, or friend's paper

Recognize that these are dishonest and unethical ways of completing paper assignments. You'll cheat yourself of the learning and skills that are developed by researching and writing papers. Professors also have ways of discovering the use of these techniques, so success with these devious methods is unlikely.

Write Your Paper

Now that you've read your articles, taken notes, and spent time thinking about the articles, it is time to organize and write your paper. Where do you begin?

Prepare an Outline

Before you begin writing, prepare an outline. It's much easier to prepare an outline once you've read and taken notes, so save this step until you have a set of notes from your reading, have had time to think about the reading, and have made lists of the material that you think is important to include in your paper. Consider the theme, issue, or research question that you plan to explore in your paper. What have you learned so far? Outlining helps you to get a better understanding of your paper because it forces you to list your ideas and to arrange them logically. Perhaps most important, an outline is a concrete plan for your writing. It will not only help you to stay on track (i.e., keep you from introducing irrelevant topics) but also keep you from leaving important material out of your paper. You'll find that you can write your paper more quickly because you'll know exactly what to put in each section. An outline doesn't have to be fancy. Just jot down the points you want to make and then order them so that they make sense. It's easier to do this using a word processing program to cut and paste your ideas as you wish. You might start simply by reordering your notes.

Some students dislike using outlines and think they are a waste of time. Typically, if you are experiencing difficulty structuring your outline, it means that your ideas are too vague and fuzzy. Read and think about your project, and organizational themes will emerge. Outlining is a valuable skill; but if you really can't write an outline, then just begin writing. Some authors prefer to write a rough draft of their paper, allowing thoughts and creativity to flow freely. Once you're written a rough draft, read through it and outline what you've written. This is called *reverse outlining* and it will help you to see the structure of your argument. You can then reorder the outline as needed to make sense and present your argument skillfully.

All good literature reviews have a clear outline. The first sentence of each paragraph should provide an overview of the paragraph. Therefore by examining the first sentence of each paragraph, one can compile an outline of the structure of the paper. Check the first sentence of each paragraph of your paper. Examine the structure. Does each paragraph have a purpose? Then examine the ordering of paragraphs. What idea is expressed in each paragraph? Are the ideas ordered in a logical fashion? Reorder as needed.

Write

Students often worry about how to start writing, and then don't begin. A simple list of points to address (an outline) helps prevent writer's block. Once you have an outline or list, your paper is organized and you can work on filling in the outline. Don't worry about starting at the beginning. Don't get stuck on a first sentence or paragraph. Just start anywhere. Use a word processing program on your computer, which allows you to cut and paste your writing into endless patterns. Take advantage of this technological capability and begin writing whatever part of your paper flows most naturally. You can arrange and rearrange your writing later. Be sure to save your original notes and original outline in separate files so that your notes are safe and you can undo any changes that you make.

PRACTICAL TIP
REFERRING TO SPECIFIC ARTICLES

In scholarly writing, articles are referred by their author's last names only. Do not introduce an article by writing out its title. Refer to articles using the author's last name and year. Full names and first names are generally not used nor are institutional affiliations. For example, instead of "In an article entitled 'Psychology Is for the Birds,' John T. Smith of New York College found. . . ," you would write "Smith (2014) found. . ." Listing the article title and author names and affiliations might be viewed by some instructors as padding, or an attempt to artificially lengthen a paper.

Ultimately your paper will be organized into several sections. The first section of your paper, the introduction, explains the research question and explains why it is worth examining. The last paragraph of the introduction section should outline the organization of the paper. In the body of the paper you will present evidence from research studies to support your points. Describe and evaluate each study, and make comparisons among the studies. Compare studies based on assumptions, theories tested, hypotheses, research designs, methods, findings, and interpretations. How do the studies support the theme of your paper? In the final section of the paper, draw conclusions, discuss implications, and suggest avenues for further research. Based on the studies reviewed and the comparisons and evaluations made, what conclusions do you draw? What research is left to be done? Recommend future studies. By now you should have a list of all the important ideas you hope to convey in your paper.

As you begin to write, remember that this is only your first draft. Not every word will stay, and not every word has to be perfect. Don't worry about errors. Just get the ideas out; you'll catch the errors later as you edit. Write anything that appears relevant, and think about where to put it and how to reorganize it later. Regularly save your work on your computer and on a cloud drive or flash drive so that your work is protected in the event of a computer catastrophe. It's not uncommon for a hard drive to crash or a file to seemingly disappear. Flash drives fail and are lost. Save your work in multiple places (on your device and in the cloud, for example). If you can, print a hard copy at the end of each writing session and preferably more often (e.g., after completing two or three pages).

Begin working early, to give yourself time to write and rewrite. Time is essential to writing a comprehensive review of the literature; take time to read, let ideas simmer, write, gain perspective on what you've written, and revise. As you write, you may find that some elements of your research are incomplete. Go back to the library and gather additional resources to fill in any gaps in your research or argument.

Revise

A big part of writing is rewriting, so be prepared for lots of editing and rewriting. Many students neglect this part of the writing process and instead print out a paper and submit it right away. The best papers ferment over time. Once you have a draft, spend at least 24 hours away from it. Let it sit for a day or two and you'll be able to approach it with fresh eyes. With time, you'll find it easier to separate yourself from your work and become more objective.

Before you begin the editing and revising process, make a "safe" copy of your paper in case you decide to undo some of your revisions. Create a new file each day you edit your paper, include the date in the file name (e.g., "dev_paper_01_12_2019").

Read through your draft and note what needs to be done. Is the organization consistent with your outline? Are you happy with the outline, or should it be modified based on your paper? As you read, you might want to list gaps in the paper's organization that need to be filled, missing details to provide, and other tasks to complete such as checking spelling and grammar or tracking down an errant reference. Recognize that you will revise the paper several times; don't feel the need to complete the final draft right away.

Read your paper aloud. Reorganize sections, edit them, or even delete them if you deem them unnecessary. Examine the order of sentences and paragraphs. Sometimes moving a sentence up in a paragraph (or even deleting it) makes a world of difference. As you revise your paper, consider whether you've left anything out. Can anything be deleted? Are there extraneous details or sections? Are the paragraphs and sections coherent and logical? Have you used transitions between paragraphs and sections so that the paper flows? Have you used consistent style throughout? Have you used the proper guidelines, as stipulated by your instructor or APA style? (See Chapter 8 for more on APA style.)

Think you're done? Print out your final draft and proofread it aloud. Check for the placement of commas and your use of grammar. You might be surprised by the errors that you find. Take your final draft to the writing center at your college or university. You'll get an extra pair of eyes to read your work and some helpful feedback on how to improve your paper. Now make your corrections and print out your final draft.

Remember that good writing is the result of practice. The process gets easier with experience, but we all begin a paper with at least a little trepidation. Start early and take time to read and mull over your articles. Revise your paper several times, waiting a day or two between each draft to gain distance. Use the checklist in Table 7.5 as a guide to writing your literature review. Finally, don't procrastinate or let fear stop you from writing.

TABLE 7.5 ●   Literature Review Checklist

❏ Is the topic appropriate (e.g., is it a topic within the field of psychology)?

❏ Does the title of your paper describe the topic of your review?

❏ Does your review include an introduction section that defines the purpose of the review and its significance?

❏ Does the introduction section explain the organization of the literature review?

❏ Are journal articles included as sources?

❏ Do you include current (and appropriate) articles as sources?

❏ Does your review discuss the major findings relating to your topic?

❏ Do you evaluate existing research?

❏ Have you explained why particular studies and sets of findings are strong?

❏ Have you explained why particular studies and sets of findings are weak?

❏ Have you included enough detail about each study to help the reader determine the significance of each article?

❏ Have you described relationships between studies?

❏ Have gaps in the literature been noted and explained?

❏ Have any controversies in the field been described?

(Continued)

TABLE 7.5 ● (Continued)

❏ Have you chosen a method of organizing the literature reviewed in your paper?

❏ Have you outlined your paper after writing it to examine its organization?

❏ Does your literature review answer an identifiable question?

❏ Does each study you reviewed correspond with a specific part of your topic outline?

❏ Have you deleted studies that do not relate to your purpose or argument?

❏ Does each part of your review flow logically from the preceding part?

❏ Do you use transitions between paragraphs to indicate the flow of major points in your outline?

❏ Does your review include a conclusion section?

❏ Does your review discuss further questions for research?

❏ Does your conclusion address the purpose identified in the introduction?

❏ Did you revise your manuscript several times?

❏ Did you spell check the manuscript?

❏ Are quotations used only when needed?

❏ Are quotations appropriately cited? Can any quotations be paraphrased?

❏ Are all paraphrases appropriately cited?

❏ Have you avoided the use of slang, abbreviations, and contractions?

❏ Have you used the past tense to refer to research studies?

REFLECTION PROMPTS

How I Feel About Writing

How do you feel about writing? Imagine receiving a paper assignment in class. What are your initial thoughts and emotions? Would you like to change any of these reactions? Which ones? How would you prefer to react? What small steps can you take to make it easier to react in a more satisfactory way?

My Writing Interests

Which writing experiences do you find fun? Do you prefer free writing, or do you like writing papers, essays, or creative pieces? How are these different for you, and what do you prefer about each? What topics do you most prefer writing about? Why?

My Writing Habits

What are your habits and typical ways of completing a writing assignment? Do you find that you procrastinate? How? Is there any way that you can prevent this? How can using some of the techniques described in this chapter make the writing task quicker and easier?

Writing an
Empirical Paper

The ability to write literature review papers is a critical skill for success as a psychology major. Unlike many other majors, psychology students must learn how to write a second kind of paper. They must learn how to report the results of empirical work—that is, research studies. Psychology is a science; as a psychology major, you'll learn how to read and understand scientific literature and contribute to the literature by writing empirical papers and lab reports. All colleges and universities require psychology majors to complete courses in research methodology in which students must conduct research studies and write empirical papers to describe their research. An empirical paper discusses the question under study, the methodology used to gather information about the question, and the findings and their implications. Understanding how to write an empirical paper is essential to your academic success. In this chapter we discuss the mechanics of the empirical paper. After a brief discussion of the *Publication Manual of the American Psychological Association* (2010), we will examine each section of an empirical paper. The chapter closes with a sample template for your empirical paper.

APA Style: The *Publication Manual of the American Psychological Association*

As you've read journal articles, you've probably noticed the distinct style of scientific writing. Why is the style so structured? Consider the purpose of written reports (i.e., communication) to tell readers about your research and explain what you did and what you found. Excellent scientific communication provides readers with enough information to enable them to critically evaluate the procedures, judge the quality of the research, and replicate (or reproduce) the results. Scientific writing is filled with facts that are appropriately paraphrased and documented. Because publication space in scholarly journals is limited, authors attempt to provide complete information in as few words as possible. Each word is carefully chosen for its precision. Scientific writing promotes clear communication, but it is very different from other types of writing and often requires more practice to master.

In psychology, authors are expected to follow the standard format specified by the sixth edition of the *Publication Manual of the American Psychological Association* (2010). Although learning the format known as APA style is challenging, ultimately a standard style of scientific communication makes it easier for researchers to report findings and for readers to comprehend them. This chapter provides a brief overview of APA style and the structure of research reports. Remember that this presentation is brief and cannot replace the *Publication Manual*, which is over 250 pages long. If you have questions about specific issues, consult the *Publications Manual* or your professor.

Structure of the Empirical Paper

An empirical paper or research article is a highly structured, concise, professional way of communicating the results of a research study. It consists of several sections, each with a specific purpose. The *title page* communicates the title, the authors, and the authors' institutional affiliations. The *abstract* provides a brief summary of the study. The *introduction* is the first section of an article. It gives an overview of the research question, discusses the relevant literature, and identifies the purpose of the study. The *method* section explains how the research was conducted; it includes a description of the participants, measures, instruments and equipment, and procedure. The *results* section presents statistical analyses that address the research questions, with information displayed in graphs and tables. The *discussion* section explores the significance of the study's findings in light of prior research, limitations of the study, and suggestions for further research. Last but not least is the *reference* section, which provides accurate references for all material that was cited in the paper. Now let's examine each section of the empirical paper.

Title Page

Don't underestimate the importance of a title. The title gives readers a mini-introduction to your paper and helps them to decide if they want to read the abstract and paper. The title should offer a concise summary of the paper—the topic, variables, and theoretical issue under study—all in no more than 12 words. According the *Publication Manual*, "a title should be fully explanatory when standing alone" (American Psychological Association, 2010, p. 23). A good title is hard to write; plan to spend some time on it. It's often easier to write the title once the paper is complete.

- The paper title is written in uppercase and lowercase letters (i.e., title case), positioned in the upper half of the first page and centered between the right and left margin.

- Center the author's name, written in uppercase and lowercase letters, on the line below the title.

- The author's institutional affiliation appears in uppercase and lowercase letters, centered on the line below the author's name.

- The running head is a short version of your title that appears at the top of the pages of a paper or published article. The running head is typed flush left (all uppercase) following "Running head:" on the first page, then appears on its own (without the "Running head:" label) on all subsequent pages. The running head should not exceed 50 characters, including punctuation and spacing. With most word processors, the running head and page number can be inserted into a header, which then automatically appears on all pages.

- The page number appears in the top right-hand corner.

- Similar to the entire paper, the title page is double-spaced, in 12-point font, with 1-inch margins.

- The title is not in bold type, italics, or underlined.

- For a sample title page, see the sample template in the Appendix at the end of this chapter.

- Note that you may decide to change your title as you complete your research study. Revise your title, if needed, to reflect the findings and the content of your paper.

Abstract

Like the title, the abstract gives readers a glimpse into your paper. The abstract provides a brief comprehensive overview of your study, offering enough information for readers to determine if they want to read the article itself (that is, to determine if the article is likely to provide information to address their questions). Write the abstract after you've completed your paper and have a firm perspective of the findings and their importance. Describe the problem under investigation, presenting the major hypotheses, participants, materials, and procedure. Summarize the results and conclusions, indicating the implications or applications. A good abstract interests readers and convinces them that the study is worth reading. An abstract should be self-explanatory and should range from 150 to 250 words. Sticking to the word count is very difficult, but well-written shorter abstracts are best. Most writers begin by composing a longer summary and slowly pare down unneeded words. The abstract appears on the second page of your paper. The word "Abstract" should appear centered at the top of the page. The abstract begins on the second line and is left justified with no indentation.

Introduction

The title of the paper appears on the first line of page 3, centered and capitalized (often referred to as "title case.") The introduction begins on line 2, flush with the left margin and indented approximately five to seven spaces (or ½ inch). Do not add the title "Introduction." Simply begin your text. The introduction is your opportunity to introduce readers to your research question and describe what is known about the topic, why the topic is important, and how your study contributes to what is already known. Consider the introduction as three separate sections. The first section, a paragraph or two in length, introduces the problem: What is the topic under study, and how will it be approached? Why is it important? The second section of the introduction provides a review of relevant literature to explain what is known about the specific question under study (review Chapter 7 for suggestions on how to conduct a literature review). Be specific and present only research that is directly relevant to the research question. What has prior research shown? What are limitations in prior research? How is your study an extension of prior research? The third section of the introduction states the purpose and rationale of the research study and provides a brief overview of your study. Now, let's consider each part of the introduction in more depth.

The first paragraphs are introductory and act to lure readers into your paper. These paragraphs often are the most difficult to write, so consider saving them for later, after you've written the rest of the paper. Use the funnel approach to structure the introduction. Begin with a general statement (the wide opening of the funnel) and get more specific (narrow the funnel) with each sentence, until the final sentence introduces the purpose of your study. An additional introductory paragraph may explain why the research question addressed by your study is important. Your goal is to make readers see the point of your study and to convince them that your project tackles an important question or issue.

The next section of the introduction reviews the literature relevant to your study. It typically is several pages long and cites theory and research that expands and supports the rationale for your study. The literature searching and summarizing strategies discussed in Chapter 7 illustrate how to search the literature, take notes, and organize a literature review. Your goal is to inform readers of the published literature on your problem, demonstrate the importance of the question, and justify the rationale for your methods. As you review the literature, it is important to remain focused on your research topic. Discuss only research that is pertinent to your project. The review is selective and should "avoid nonessential details; instead emphasize pertinent findings, relevant methodological issues, and major conclusions" (American Psychological Association, 2010, p. 28). Refer readers to published reviews that examine more general issues, so that they can obtain additional information, if desired.

An effective review of the literature orients readers to what is known and answers several questions:

- What is the purpose of the study?

- What do we know about this area of research?

- How does the study relate to prior research? How does it draw upon and extend prior work? What is the nature of your contribution?

- Why is the study important or interesting?

- What rationale links the research questions and research design? How did you choose the research design, and how does the design address the question?

It is vital that you demonstrate the logical continuity between prior research, your research question, and your research design. Unquestionably, this is the most difficult part of writing the introduction. As you write, keep your purpose in mind: Your goal is to interest readers, explain why your study is relevant, and motivate them to continue reading. Finally, be very careful to appropriately cite the sources of information in your literature review. If you are unsure of the overall use of citations or how to appropriately quote or paraphrase sources, see the section on plagiarism in Chapter 7 and the *Publication Manual*.

The final component of the introduction section explains the purpose and rationale for your study. Explain your hypotheses (your specific predictions about the research results), and provide a brief overview of your study. How does your research design relate to the theoretical issue that you wish to address (this is particularly important if you are employing an unusual design)?

PRACTICAL TIP
REFERENCE MANAGERS

Writing a paper requires a great deal of organization. One way to keep track of the articles you read and make parenthetical citation easier is to use a reference manager. A reference manager is a program that allows you to record citation information for an article as well as your own notes. The best part of using a reference manager is that it syncs with your word processing program to organize your citations. For example, when you discuss an article by Smith, you can direct the reference manager to insert the parenthetical citation. It automatically updates itself too. Even better is that the program tracks your references and can automatically generate your reference list. There are a variety of reference managers to consider. Two free popular reference managers are Mendeley (http://www.mendeley.com) and Zotero (http://www.zotero.org). Start using a reference manager early in your academic career and you'll build an easily accessible library that can help you throughout college and beyond.

Method

The introduction answers the questions "What?" and "Why?" The method section explains "How." The purpose of the method section is to clearly explain how you conducted your study. The method section should provide enough pertinent details so that readers can replicate your research. Typically the methods section contains several sections: participants, apparatus (or materials or measures), and procedure. Begin the method section, titled "Method," on a new line, bolded and centered between the right and left margin.

Participants

On a separate line, flush with the left margin, list "Participants" in bold. The next line is indented and begins the participants section, which answers the questions, "Who participated in the study?" "How many participated?" and "How were they selected?" In this section, describe the demographic characteristics of the participants. Explain any demographic details that might affect your study, including age, sex, ethnicity, geographic location, and number of participants assigned to each treatment group. Explain how participants were selected and how they were assigned to groups. What were the circumstances in which they participated, and were any inducements offered (e.g., extra credit)?

Apparatus, Materials, or Measures

Depending on your study, this section might be entitled apparatus, materials, or measures. Similar to the participants section, this section begins on a new line with the bold label "Apparatus," "Materials," or "Measures." Indent the next line and describe the equipment or instruments used to conduct the study. If you used specialized equipment to conduct the research, describe it and explain how it was used. If the equipment is a manufactured item, include information on the manufacturer and the model number. If you developed an apparatus or any materials for your study, describe it in enough detail so that readers could reproduce it (including exact dimensions and physical properties of any apparatus that you construct). If standardized tests or measures were used, describe them, include their psychometric properties (e.g., reliability and validity), and explain how they were coded or scored. As you write this section, remember that your goal is to describe how you measured your variables and what methods you used to collect data.

Procedure

On a new line, type "Procedure" and set it in bold and flush left. This section describes the steps you took in conducting your research. Tell readers what was done, how, and in what order. Clearly describe what happened to participants from the time they walked into the lab until the time they left the lab, from the beginning to the end of their experience. If you administered surveys to participants, describe the survey conditions and instructions provided. If your research was experimental, describe how participants were exposed to the independent variable; include a description of any instructions that participants received. Describe your methodology and any control features of the design, such as counterbalancing or the use of control groups. Again, your goal is to provide sufficient detail so that a reader can replicate your study.

Results

The heading for the results section appears centered and in bold between the right and left margin. On the following left-justified and indented line, begin your results section. Ask yourself, "What did I find?" Report the most interesting results first, or those that are most relevant to the hypotheses tested. Save results that are less interesting and relevant for later in the results section. In other words, think about the importance of your findings and present them accordingly. Don't just give your readers a laundry list of findings. Instead, carefully consider how to present the results, including the order and style of presentation.

The results section provides answers to your research questions in the form of reports of descriptive and inferential statistics. Descriptive statistics summarize the data. Inferential statistics examine your hypotheses and test the likelihood that the results are not due to chance. As you report tests of statistical significance, the *Publication Manual* recommends that you include the name of the test, value obtained, degrees of freedom, significance level, and effect size. Note that these guidelines are intended for publication in scholarly journals; your professor may modify these guidelines for your class. Tables are an effective way of concisely conveying a great deal of information. The *Publication Manual* recommends including tables to list means, medians, standard deviations, and confidence intervals. Any tables that you use must be self-explanatory (i.e., with titles and fully labeled) and should not repeat information that is presented in the text. Review the *Publication Manual* for detailed explanations of how to construct tables to represent your data.

Discussion

The discussion section begins with the word "Discussion" bolded and centered. The text on the following line is flush left and indented. Here you will describe the significance of your findings, place them in context, and discuss their implications. In other words, the discussion takes a big-picture, bird's-eye view perspective. As you structure the discussion section, ask yourself the following questions: What did I set out to learn? What was the purpose of the study? What did I find?

Begin the discussion section by reminding readers of the purpose of your study. Then consider your data. Was there support for your hypotheses? Explain. Was anything surprising? If the data do not support your hypotheses, can you provide another interpretation? If so, clearly state that your interpretation is speculative and that further research is needed to confirm it. Now, discuss your findings within the context of prior research. How do your findings compare with those of other researchers? Does your work extend prior findings? If your findings do not replicate prior work or do not make sense given the literature you have reviewed, you might explore methodological differences or other factors that may account for the disparate findings. What are the theoretical and practical implications of your findings? As you write this section, remember that your goal is to connect your findings with prior research. Do not present new statistical analyses not included in the results section. Instead, the discussion section is a place for you to explain the value of your findings, and not the data itself.

The discussion section should also explore limitations or shortcomings of your study (every study has weaknesses). What factors might limit the extent to which you can generalize your results? Try to think of objections someone might make to the conclusions that you draw (whether the objections are correct or not), and either answer them or qualify your conclusions to take them into account. If you think that possible objections are weak, explain why. Help readers to understand exactly what can and cannot be concluded from your study. Finally, consider avenues for future research. Do not end your discussion section (and therefore article) with the sentence, "More research is needed." Be specific. What are the remaining unanswered research questions? Given what you have learned, what research is the next step? Provide specific questions and topics for further research (Exercises 8.1 and 8.2).

EXERCISE 8.1
TEST YOUR UNDERSTANDING OF JOURNAL ARTICLES

Using PsycINFO, locate an empirical journal article in an area of interest. Retrieve the article using your library's full-text and print resources. The reference librarian can offer assistance if you experience difficulty. Read the article and complete the following:

1. Write the article's citation in APA style.

2. Examine the abstract of the article. Based on the abstract, what do you expect to learn in this article?

3. What was the purpose of the study? Where did you find that information?

4. How was the study conducted? Describe the methodology. Where did you locate that information?

5. What were the findings of the study? Where did you look to learn about the findings?

6. What were the author's conclusions? How did the results of this study compare with prior research? Where did you look to learn about the findings?

7. Reflect back on the abstract. How well did it reflect the content of the article? Did you learn what you thought you would?

EXERCISE 8.2
WRITE AN ABSTRACT

Choose an empirical article. *Do not read the abstract*. Read the article very carefully.

1. Once you feel that you grasp the article well, write an abstract describing the research study.

2. Compare your abstract to the published abstract. How well do they match?

3. What details should you have included? Are there any that were unnecessary?

References

The reference section begins on a new page with the word "References" centered and bolded. The reference section lists all articles or books that you cited in your paper, including enough information so that an interested reader can locate them. If a source is listed in the reference section, it must be cited within the paper. List only the sources that you used. The most common sources of reference material in student papers are journal articles, books, and perhaps material from reputable sources on the Internet. References are listed in alphabetical order by the author's last name. The first line of each reference is set flush left, whereas the subsequent lines of each reference are indented. The second and following reference lines are indented. The *Publication Manual* lists slightly different formats for journal articles, books, and Internet sources, as well as slight differences depending on the number of authors. Table 8.1 illustrates how to cite journal articles, books, and Internet sources. Let's examine each type of citation.

List journal articles in the following way:

- List journal articles by the author's last name and first initial.
- The year of publication follows the author's name and is given in parentheses, followed by a period.
- The article title comes next. Don't capitalize each word of the title; only the first word of the article title is capitalized (i.e., use sentence case). If the article title contains a colon, the first word after the colon is capitalized as well. Follow the article title with a period.
- The title of the journal and volume number come next and are italicized. Capitalize each word of the journal title. Place a comma after the journal title and after the volume number. Note that only the number is used to indicate volume; don't use "V," "Volume," or "Vol." If an issue number is needed, list the issue number in parentheses immediately after the volume number without a space and follow this with a comma.
- Last are the page numbers, followed by a period. Again, note that only the numbers themselves are used to indicate pages (don't use "page," "p," or "pg").
- The digital object identifier (DOI) is placed after the page numbers and is not followed by a period. References that are obtained online (such as through subscription services such as PsycINFO) are labeled with a DOI, which is a unique string of numbers and letters that labels an article for database searches. The DOI usually appears on the first page of an article, near the copyright notice. Older articles may not list DOIs. If you include a DOI, it appears after the period following the page numbers as "doi:" and gives the DOI number without a space after the colon. Check with your instructor regarding whether to include the DOI, as including the DOI is a recent addition to the *Publication Manual*.
- The first journal article example in Table 8.1 illustrates an article by one author, the second example illustrates two authors, and the third illustrates three authors.

TABLE 8.1 ● APA Style References

Journal Articles

One Author:

Bem, D. J. (1995). Writing a review article for *Psychological Bulletin. Psychological Bulletin, 118*(2), 172–177. doi:10.1037/0033-2909.118.2.172

*Note that in the above example, *Psychological Bulletin* is capitalized in the article title because it is a journal name; otherwise, the article title is generally written in sentence case, with the first letter of the first word in the title capitalized.

Two Authors:

Dearnley, C., & Matthew, B. (2007). Factors that contribute to undergraduate success. *Teaching in Higher Education, 12*(3), 377–391. doi:10.1080/13562510701278740

Three Authors:

Cooley, E. L., Garcia, A. L., & Hughes, J. L. (2008). Undergraduate research in liberal arts colleges: Reflections on mutual benefits for faculty and students. *North American Journal of Psychology, 10*(3), 463–471.

Books

One Author:

Palladino Schulthesiss, D. E. (2008). *Psychology as a major: Is it right for me and what can I do with my degree?* Washington, DC: American Psychological Association.

Two Authors:

Landrum, R. E., & Davis, S. F. (2014). *The psychology major: Career options and strategies for success.* Upper Saddle River, NJ: Prentice Hall.

Three Authors:

Silvia, P. J., Delaney, P. F., & Marcovitch, S. (2009). *What psychology majors could (and should) be doing: An informal guide to research experience and professional skills.* Washington, DC: American Psychological Association.

Chapters in Edited Books

One Author:

Handlesman, M. M. (2001). Learning to become ethical. In S. Walfish & B. Tolan (Eds.), *Succeeding in graduate school: The career guide for psychology students* (pp. 189–202). Mahwah, NJ: Erlbaum.

Two Authors:

Campbell, C., & Anderson, T. L. (2010). Mentoring in professional psychology. In M. B. Kenkel & R. L. Peterson (Eds.), *Competency-based training for professional psychology* (pp. 237–247). Washington, DC: American Psychological Association.

(Continued)

TABLE 8.1 ● (Continued)

Three Authors:

Wasik, B. H., Song, S., & Knotek, S. (2009). Preparing for careers in school psychology. In S. F. Davis, P. J. Giordano, & C. A. Licht (Eds.), *Your career in psychology: Putting your graduate degree to work* (pp. 231–244). Hoboken, NJ: Wiley-Blackwell.

Internet

Lloyd, M. M. (2004). *Marky Lloyd's careers in psychology page.* Retrieved January 8, 2015 from https://www.psywww.com/careers/

List books as follows:

- Books are listed by the author's last name and first initial.

- The year of publication follows, in parentheses, with a period.

- Next comes the book title, which is italicized. Like the journal article title, only the first word of the book title is capitalized. If the book title contains a colon, the first word after the colon is capitalized as well.

- Finally, list the place of publication, followed by a colon, and the publisher.

- The first book example in Table 8.1 illustrates a book by one author, the second example illustrates two authors, and the third illustrates three authors.

List edited books as follows:

- List the chapter author's last name and first initial.

- The year of publication follows, in parentheses, with a period.

- The title of the chapter follows, with only the first word capitalized, ending with a period.

- Next indicate the editors and book title by writing "In" and listing the editors by first initial and last name, followed by "Ed." (or "Eds.") in parentheses, with a comma. Then list the title of the book, capitalizing only the first word.

- Provide the page numbers in parentheses (signified by "pp."). Note that this is the only time that "pp" is used in APA style.

- Finally, provide the place of publication, followed by a colon, and the publisher.

- Electronic books include a DOI, which should be listed after the period following the publisher, with "doi" in lowercase.

- The first example in Table 8.1 lists a sole-authored chapter in a book edited by two people. The second example illustrates two authors and two editors, and the third example lists three authors and three editors.

List Internet sources as follows:

- Cite Internet sources by the author's last name (if no author appears, then cite the organization; if there is no author or organization, the article title moves to the position of author).

- Indicate the year of publication (if listed) in parentheses. If the year of publication is not listed, then use "n.d." (to indicate no date) in parentheses.

- The title of the page appears next, in italics (with only the first word capitalized).

- Next, list the date that you retrieved the information and provide the Internet address (to note, don't use a period after the Internet address).

- Note that the *Publication Manual* includes different reference styles for blog posts, online forum/discussion group posts, and messages on electronic mailing lists. Learn more by perusing the *Publication Manual* or ask your instructor for assistance.

Complete Exercise 8.3 to practice preparing a reference list.

EXERCISE 8.3
PRACTICE PREPARING REFERENCE LISTS

1. Conduct a PsycINFO search on the topic of your choice. Identify five publications, including at least one article and one book chapter.

2. Construct a reference list.

3. Compare your reference list with another student's list. Do they differ in style? Together, review the guidelines for APA style and correct your reference lists.

4. Seek feedback from your professor.

5. APA style is challenging, and most beginning writers make errors. What kinds of errors did you make? Correct your reference list.

6. Locate three more publications and try again.

PRACTICAL TIP
VERIFY APA STYLE IN DOWNLOADED CITATIONS

Many students quickly realize that article entries in library databases such as PsycINFO are often accompanied by a link listing the article citation in various formats such as APA or MLA. Likewise, Google Scholar also includes a citation link for each article. These citations are valuable information for your records, but take care in using these citations. Do not trust them. Check automatically generated citations carefully, as they are often incorrect. Don't lose points on your paper to careless errors.

Writing an empirical paper entails using a highly structured, scientific style. The sample paper in the Appendix at the end of this chapter illustrates how to format your empirical paper and provides additional information about formatting. Use Table 8.2 to help you determine whether your paper meets the major guidelines set by APA style. At first the elements of an empirical paper—and the formal style of writing—may seem foreign. The sample APA-style paper at the end of this chapter illustrates the sections as well as describes the content of each section. With practice you will find that writing comes more easily and perhaps you will come to see the value in clear, concise scientific communication (Exercise 8.4). It likely will not be as easy as the other forms of writing you have undertaken to date, but the ability to write in a formal style and with precision will suit you well in your career.

EXERCISE 8.4
APA STYLE TEMPLATE

Choose an empirical article and create your own APA style template that summarizes the information in the article. Apply APA style to complete the following.

1. Prepare a title page for the article.

2. Prepare an abstract in which you briefly describe the study.

3. Prepare an introduction section in which you summarize the literature review and purpose within two to three paragraphs.

4. Prepare the methods section, including participants, method, and procedure. Summarize each.

5. Prepare the results section. Summarize their findings.

6. Prepare the discussion section. Describe the findings and implications in two paragraphs.

TABLE 8.2 ● APA Style Checklist

Page Formatting

☐ Have you used 1-inch margins?

☐ Have you used 12-point font?

☐ Have you double-spaced the document?

☐ Have you used a running head and page number on every page?

☐ Have you checked for typographical errors?

☐ Have you used five- to seven-space (or ½-inch) paragraph indents?

Title Page

☐ Is your title no longer than 12 words?

☐ Is the running head no longer than 50 characters and placed as a header at the top of each page?

☐ Did you include your name and affiliation below the title and centered on the page and line?

Abstract

☐ Does the abstract appear on a new page, without indentation, headed by the word "Abstract" centered?

☐ Is the abstract no longer than 120 to 150 words?

Introduction

☐ Does the introduction begin on a new page, headed by the paper's title?

☐ Have you included the names of all authors in the first in-text citation? (Note: For references with one or two authors, cite the names each time. For references with three to five authors, cite all authors the first time and then use the first author's name followed by "et al." for each subsequent citation. For references with six authors or more, cite the first author's name followed by "et al." for all citations.)

☐ Have you used "and" to link authors' names in text?

☐ Have you used "&" to link authors' names in parenthetical citations?

☐ Did you include the year in parenthetical citations?

Method

☐ Does the method section begin immediately after the introduction, with no page break?

☐ Does the method section begin on a new line, with "Method" centered and bolded?

(Continued)

TABLE 8.2 ● **(Continued)**

☐ Is the method section written in the past tense?

☐ Is the method section broken into participants, materials/apparatus, and procedure subsections?

Results

☐ Does the results section begin immediately after the introduction, with no page break?

☐ Does the results section begin on a new line, with "Results" centered and bolded?

☐ Is the results section written in the past tense?

☐ Have you reported the effect size?

☐ Have you organized the results into paragraphs and subsections?

☐ Did you italicize mathematical symbols, use numbers rather than words, and capitalize the names of independent variables?

☐ Did you report the values for nonsignificant results without interpreting them?

☐ Did you interpret all significant results?

☐ Did you explain interactions?

☐ Did you create tables to summarize all data?

☐ Did you create figures to illustrate interactions?

Discussion

☐ Does the discussion section begin immediately after the introduction, with no page break?

☐ Does the discussion section begin on a new line, with "Discussion" centered and bolded?

☐ Did you use the past tense to describe results and refer to prior findings?

☐ Did you use the present tense to discuss theories and conclusions?

References

☐ Did you begin the reference list on a new page, with the "References" heading centered and bolded?

☐ Are the references listed in alphabetical order?

☐ Is the first line of each reference flush with the left margin and are the subsequent lines tab-indented (i.e., is a ½-inch hanging indent used)?

☐ Have you cited only work that you have read?

REFLECTION EXERCISES

My Research Question

What's your research project? Don't use your notes or readings, but write as much as you can about your project. What is your research question? How did it evolve? Where did you get the idea? How is your study an improvement over prior studies? Why is your study important? How well can you remember your points? How can you immerse yourself more fully in your project?

My Research Findings

Tell a story about your research project. What did you set out to do, and what did you find? Try to explain what your statistical analyses tested. Pretend that you're explaining your project to a friend or a high school student. How would you explain your results in a way that a student could understand?

My Study's Implications

Answer the question "So what?" You don't have to have completed your research to consider this question. In fact, thinking about how your study matters (i.e., what it contributes) can help you refine your question. Be grandiose and try to think about far-reaching implications for laws, social policy, regulations, education, and so on.

If I Could Do It All Over

Pretend that you are going to revise your study and start from the beginning. What would you do differently? Why?

Appendix: Sample Paper

Running head: TEMPLATE PAPER   1

My Paper: A Template From Which to Work

Jane J. Smith

Your State University

TEMPLATE PAPER   2

Abstract

The abstract should be self-explanatory and self-contained and should not exceed 120 words. Describe the problem under investigation and include the major hypotheses, participants, materials, and procedure. Summarize the results and conclusions, indicating the implications or applications. A good abstract interests readers and convinces them that the study is worth reading. Remember that the entire paper, including cover page and abstract, is double spaced.

My Paper: A Template

Begin the introduction with a general statement about your topic area. Consider your readers and attempt to pique their interest. Use the funnel effect in the first paragraph of your introduction so that you begin with general statements, each one becoming more narrowly focused, until you end with a statement of the problem under study.

A second paragraph of the introduction might explain the importance of the research question. What is its theoretical or applied relevance?

After the problem is introduced, the next part of the introduction provides a literature review of what is known about the topic. What has prior research shown? What are limitations in prior research? How is your study an extension of prior research? As you write the literature review, cite only those studies that are most pertinent to your research question (and use appropriate documentation, as described in Chapter 7). The literature review is typically several pages long.

End the introductory section with a clear statement of the purpose and rationale of your study. Discuss hypotheses and set the stage for the Method section.

Method

The method section explains how the study was conducted. Provide enough detail so that a reader could replicate your research. Typically the method section contains several sections: participants, apparatus materials or measures, and procedure.

TEMPLATE PAPER   4

Three levels of headings are often used in this section. The first level ("Method") is centered, bolded, and written in uppercase and lowercase letters. The second level is written in uppercase and lowercase letters, flush left, and bolded. The third level is indented and italicized; only the first letter of the first word is capitalized, and the heading is followed by a period and run into the paragraph. Headings may be used to organize your introduction section. Review the *Publication Manual* to learn more about the use of headings.

Participants

The participants section describes the characteristics of the participants and explains how they were selected. Explain any demographic details that might affect your study, including age, sex, ethnicity, geographic location, and number of participants assigned to each treatment group. Report any inducements to participate (e.g., money, extra credit).

Apparatus/Measures

Depending on your study, this section might be entitled apparatus, materials, or measures. Briefly describe the equipment or instruments used in the study. If you developed materials or an apparatus for your study, describe them in enough detail so that a reader could reproduce them. If standardized tests or measures were used, describe them, their psychometric properties (e.g., reliability and validity) and how they were coded or scored.

First instrument. Describe the first instrument or piece of equipment. If it is a manufactured item, include information on the manufacturer and the model number.

Second instrument. List the second instrument or piece of equipment here. Continue subheadings for any additional instruments or equipment.

TEMPLATE PAPER   5

Procedure

Describe each step in conducting the study. Clearly describe what happened to participants from the time they walked into the lab until the time they left, from the beginning to the end of the study. Describe your methodology and any control features of the design, such as counterbalancing or the use of control groups. What instructions were provided to participants? How were participants debriefed at the end of the study?

Results

Begin your results section by explaining the main findings. Follow up by explaining the analyses in detail. Report all relevant results, even those that are counter to your hypothesis. As you report tests of statistical significance, include the name of the test, degrees of freedom, and significance level. Provide enough detail to justify the conclusions that you will make in the discussion section. Provide tables to display complex sets of data (e.g., means and standard deviations, the results of complex analyses). For information on how to construct tables, see the *Publication Manual*.

Discussion

Begin the discussion section by reiterating the purpose of the study. Provide a statement on the support of your original hypotheses. Next, examine your findings. Explain what the results mean, consider them in the context of the literature, and discuss their implications. Identify possible limitations of your study. Close with a discussion of avenues for future research.

TEMPLATE PAPER 6

References

Note that, unlike this sample paper, the reference section begins on a new page and includes only articles that were cited in your study. List the references in alphabetical order. Like other sections of your paper, the reference section is double spaced with no additional lines or spaces between references. See Table 8.1 for sample journal article, book, and Internet references. Further examples of references appear in the *Publication Manual*.

Finding a Job With Your Bachelor's Degree

185

(Continued)

Chapter Outline	

Summary of
  Qualifications
Education
Experience
Types of Résumés
Create a LinkedIn Profile
The Cover Letter
	*Exercise 9.6: Construct a LinkedIn
	  profile*

Interview
  Prepare
  What to Wear
  During the Interview
  Thank-You Note
The Job Offer
	*Exercise 9.7: Common Interview
	  Questions*
	*Exercise 9.8: Questions to Ask During
	  an Interview*

As the saying goes, "time flies when you're having fun." Before you know it, graduation will be here. If you've decided to seek employment with your bachelor's degree, start planning early and hone your job-seeking skills. This chapter discusses how to find a job with your bachelor's degree, including where to look, how to construct a résumé, the importance of cover letters, interviewing, and more.

Applying for Jobs

The first stop on your job search should be the career services office at your college, where you'll find skilled professionals who can help you with all aspects of the job search. Career services offices have a variety of resources for locating available positions, including books, databases, and lists of employers who have contacted them seeking to employ college students and recent graduates.

Where to Look

There are several places to look for job advertisements. Job ads are often posted in local newspapers; most maintain searchable online databases of job ads. Job search sites permit job hunters to comprehensively search the job market. Some examples of job search sites include the following:

- Careerbuilder.com

- Idealist.org (for nonprofit jobs and volunteer opportunities)

- Indeed.com

- Monster.com

- Simplyhired.com

- USAJobs.gov (for government jobs)

Contact the human resources department of major businesses, corporations, and agencies in your area to inquire about job openings. Many businesses and organizations advertise jobs on their webpages, typically linked from the human resources webpage (Exercise 9.1).

Use Your Network

Remember the most important job-hunting resource of all: You! Applicants commonly overlook their own personal networks when scouting for available positions. Through school, friends (and friends' parents), part-time jobs, and internships, you've already made many connections. Tap into these personal and professional connections. If you've completed an internship or practicum, you may already have a foot in the door and a potential employer has already had a peek at your work habits. Even if the organization where you did your internship is not hiring additional staff, your supervisor probably has outside contacts. Take advantage of your personal connections to locate job openings because most jobs are not advertised in newspapers or other ads. You can learn about these unadvertised positions only by word of mouth. Networking (establishing connections) will help you to become more knowledgeable about positions within the hidden job market.

Job Applications

As you apply for jobs you'll find that many employers require applicants to complete a job application form or even a large packet of forms. Take care in completing these forms because they reveal a great deal about you. In addition to detailing your experience, your job application tells potential employers about your work habits, your ability to follow instructions, your personality and character, and your potential to succeed. Neatness, spelling, and grammar count, regardless of the position to which you apply. A sloppy application tells employers that they can expect carelessness and sloppiness from you. Be honest and accurate, and remember to ask the people you plan to list as references beforehand (notify them each time they are listed; if you begin a second job search in the future, ask again). You may find that some applications include personality inventories and other kinds of psychological assessments. Be truthful. Finally, many job applications do not instruct applicants to include a résumé but you should always supplement your application with a copy of your résumé because it lists all of your relevant experiences and highlights your strengths.

EXERCISE 9.1
DECONSTRUCTING JOB ADS

Conduct a search on a job search website, such as those listed earlier this chapter (see "Where to Look"). Locate one or two job ads that appeal to you.

1. What is the job?
2. What are the demographic details, such as location?
3. What education or experience requirements are listed?
4. What skills are needed to succeed in the job? If the ad does not list them (and it likely will not), brainstorm what skills would be coveted by the employer.
5. Consider the assessments that you conducted throughout this book. What is your skill set? How does it compare with that needed for the job?
6. What skills might you improve to enhance your fit to the job?
7. How would you sell yourself to the employer?

Social Media and Your Job Hunt

The last decade has witnessed a major shift in how people interact with each other. Social media sites, such as Facebook, Twitter, Instagram, Snapchat, Pinterest, and Vine, have made it possible to instantly share experiences and thoughts with others with a text or status update. Social media make it possible to quickly connect with everyone you know and often people you don't know, such as potential employers. Your activities on social media can help you find and win jobs, but they can also cost you jobs.

Use LinkedIn to Expand Your Professional Network

It is never too early to work on developing a professional network. The Internet makes it easier than ever to create a professional persona and develop useful contacts that will influence your career. The largest and most popular social networking site for professionals is LinkedIn.com. A basic account is free and permits you to create a profile, essentially an online résumé. Do not create a profile until you have written an effective résumé (more on résumés later). Your LinkedIn account will permit you to access a great deal of information to aid your job hunt and professional development. You can search for companies, research employees in companies, make contact with and ask professionals relevant questions, and find communities of students and professionals who share your interests in psychology.

However, you're not taking full advantage of LinkedIn if all you do is post a profile and surf. The purpose of LinkedIn is to establish connections or links with others, especially people at companies where you want to work. When you view a profile, you can determine if you know any people in common or if you are connected through second-degree relationships (such as you share a friend of a friend in common). Make the most out of LinkedIn by joining groups or communities. There are more than 200,000 groups. Consider joining college and alumni groups and search for groups that are related to your major. For example, there are many psychology-related groups. Examples of psychology-related groups include the Psychology Network (141,000 members), the Psychology Students Network (41,000 members), and Psi Chi (8,200 members). More information about creating a LinkedIn profile is discussed later in this chapter.

Expect to Be Googled

Not all employers run Internet searches on potential employees, but you can never be sure. In one recent survey, nearly three-quarters of employers reported reviewing candidates' social media profiles (Salm, 2017). Why do employers Google applicants? Hiring an employee is a big deal. Employers invest money and time into the process and expect to hire an employee who is mature, responsible, and reliable. Applicants must be deemed trustworthy and capable of handling an employer's valuable business. In prior decades, employers relied only on interviews and references. Today applicants freely share much about themselves online that can influence an employer's hiring decision. A quick Internet search can reveal posts and photos on social media sites that can sway an employer against an applicant. Social media profiles and posts likely won't boost your application, but unprofessional profiles that suggest poor judgment can send an employer packing. Table 9.1 lists some turn-offs employers have reported.

TABLE 9.1 ● Social Media and Hiring Decisions: When Social Media Harms

Information on a social media profile that can prompt and employer to eliminate a candidate:

- Provocative or inappropriate photographs or information
- Information about drinking or drug use
- Posts bad-mouthing employers or colleagues
- Poor grammar, poor spelling, and texting/illiterate language
- Discriminatory comments related to race, gender, religion, and so forth
- Lies about qualifications
- Sharing of confidential information from previous employers
- Criminal behavior
- Unprofessional screen name

Source: Salm (2017).

EXERCISE 9.2
BECOME AWARE OF YOUR DIGITAL FOOTPRINT

It is in your best interest to review your online presence and determine if you are portrayed well.

1. Google yourself. Then use Bing and Yahoo. Enter your name. Try enclosing your name in quotation marks to search for your exact name. If your name is common, add your state or college.

2. How many results did you find? Do they refer to you?

3. Is the first page of results flattering? Is it the message that you want to send?

4. What, if anything, would you like to change? How might you go about changing the information (this may involve looking up information about how to influence search results)?

Scrub Your Social Media Accounts

Many people believe that setting social media accounts to private means that they don't have to worry about their profile's content because only friends or followers will see it. Unfortunately, there is no way to be absolutely certain that a post will stay private. Protect yourself by evaluating and curating your social media pages (Exercise 9.2). Untag or, preferably, remove drunken party photos and any other photos that portray you in a negative light. As you review photos, think about whether an employer would want you as an employee. Look at the content of your wall. Are there any particularly negative status updates? Do you trash any faculty or schools? Are there any saucy comments that are racist, sexist, or homophobic? Have you used profanity? Sarcastic comments and jokes that your friends know are flippant remarks likely won't be taken as such by employers.

Maintain an Appropriate Profile Photo

Even if you set your privacy settings high, your name and profile photo may still be visible. Make sure that your profile photo is what you want employers, professors, and admissions committees to see.

Filter Your Friends

It's not uncommon for individuals to have 1,000 or more "friends." Consider restricting your friends to people you actually know.

Restrict Public Search

Make it difficult for people to find your social media profile by going private and making your profiles visible to "friends only." Some candidates change their profile name (such as by using their middle name as last name). Others deactivate their accounts altogether. It's not necessary to deactivate your account as there is no need for paranoia, but restricting public search is a good idea. However, remember that setting a profile to private is not a guarantee. Students sometimes worry that employers will think that a candidate has something to hide when his or her Facebook or other profile is private. On the contrary, a private profile is a sign of maturity. It shows that you recognize a separation between your professional and private life. Moreover, be cautious about what you post online and recognize that even the tightest privacy settings can fail. Make sure that your online profiles reflect you as you'd like employers to see you (Exercise 9.3).

EXERCISE 9.3
ANALYZE YOUR SOCIAL MEDIA ACCOUNTS

Take a critical look at your Instagram profile from the perspective of an employer. Consider the following:

- Are there any photos that might be interpreted poorly?

- Are your posts grammatically correct?

- Is the content of your posts neutral or positive?

- Do you avoid commenting about drugs or alcohol?

- Do you know all of your friends?

- Are your privacy settings private? Can only friends view your material? Is your profile set to private? (Remember that nothing is every truly private on the Internet.)

- Discuss your observations. What changes will you make to improve your profile?

Now review each of your other social media accounts and respond to the following items:

1. Review your Twitter account. Discuss your results.

2. Review your Facebook account. Discuss your results.

3. Review your Pinterest account. Discuss your results.

4. Do you have other social media accounts? Try this exercise again and discuss your findings.

Prepare to Be Googled: Create Your Ideal Self

Rather than focus only on cleaning up your social media profiles, be proactive. Create the digital profile that depicts the ideal you—how you want to be portrayed. Use your social media presence to show your expertise in a given subject. Tailor your profile to demonstrate your passion. LinkedIn is particularly useful for self-promotion because it is essentially a social résumé. Unlike other social media, keep your LinkedIn profile visible to the public. If you use Twitter, post professional tweets about your interests. Do likewise for Instagram and Pinterest. Your profiles don't have to be limited to professorial interactions, as they're personal accounts; but before you post personal material, consider how a potential employer might interpret it.

Your online reputation follows you and is hard to erase. Control what you put online to ensure that your best most professional self is portrayed. You can never be sure whether an employer will review your digital reputation, but it is always a good idea to put your best foot forward.

Prepare Your Résumé

A résumé is a summary of your educational history, work experience, and career objectives. Employers always expect to see a résumé (even if it isn't stated in the advertisement). As you prepare yours, remember that your résumé often is the only impression that an employer has of you. It is a chance to present your strengths, to communicate that you have valuable skills, and to emphasize the aspects of your educational and employment background that make you unique. A résumé is your ticket through the door; its purpose is to convince an employer to interview you, but most employers glance at a résumé for only 20 to 30 seconds and sometimes as little as 6 seconds (Sanburn, 2012). If the initial scan of your résumé doesn't catch the employer's attention, the opportunity is lost. How do you make it past the 20-second test?

Consider the main question that employers ask themselves as they read a résumé: Why should I learn more about this applicant? Keep this question in mind as you prepare your résumé, answer it, and you'll have a unique résumé that will get you to the next stage of the job hunt. Before you write, re-evaluate your skills and abilities in light of employer preferences. Review the top qualities employers prefer in Chapter 3 as well as your responses to the self-assessments in Chapter 2. Outline your skills and abilities as well as your work experience and extracurricular activities to make it easier to prepare a thorough résumé. Highlight your strengths. Writing a résumé may seem overwhelming, but you'll soon see that it is a simple matter of showcasing your skills.

Parts of the Résumé

There are several ways of formatting résumés, but all include the same type of information: contact information, objective, summary of qualifications, education, and experiences (and related skills).

Heading/Contact Information

All of your contact information should go at the top of your résumé. Include your name, permanent address (this is particularly important if you live on campus and are moving home after graduation), phone number (with area code), and e-mail address. If you're graduating from college soon, think twice about using your university e-mail, as some graduates lose access to university e-mail soon after graduating. Use a professional e-mail address rather than a fun, personal e-mail address (silly usernames such as "Butterflygirl," "Temptress," or "JediMaster" are unprofessional and send the message that you are not ready for hiring). If possible, use your name as your e-mail address and choose a provider that will be around for years to come, such as Gmail or Outlook. Add your LinkedIn profile link. Include your website or blog only if the content reflects your professional ambitions.

Objective

This is the first component of the résumé, placed after the contact information. The objective is a simple statement of the position and industry in which you're prepared to work. You will likely tailor this to each position to which you apply.

Summary of Qualifications

Sometimes just referred to as a summary, this section is a newer addition to the résumé. Not all candidates use this section, but it can help an employer quickly zero in on your competencies. It appears at the top of your résumé and contains an overview of your major qualifications, or what you want the employer to remember about you. Place the most important and relevant information first.

Education

Report the name of the degree that you received or will receive, institution name and city/state, month and year of graduation, major, minor/concentration, grade point average (only if it is higher than 3.0), and academic honors, if applicable.

Experience

Discuss your work experience. List your most recent job first and work your way backward. For each job, indicate the position title, company or organization name, address, and dates of employment. Include all relevant employment experiences: part-time jobs, internships, cooperative education, or self-employment. Recruiters are interested in the skills that you've developed, not whether or how much you were paid. Experiences also include activities that are relevant to the objective stated on your résumé. Include activities and awards only if they are significant experiences that speak to your capacities as an employee (such as leadership experience). If you can draw a valid connection between your professional goal and the activity, keep it in. If not, take it out. For each position, briefly describe your duties and responsibilities as they relate to the position you are seeking and emphasize specific skills and achievements. Use active words to describe your duties and the results that you produced. Table 9.2 provides a list of action verbs to help you construct this section of your résumé.

TABLE 9.2 ● Action Verbs for Your Résumé

Analytical and Critical Thinking

analyzed	deciphered	formulated	questioned
ascertained	deliberated	integrated	rated
assessed	determined	investigated	recommended
compared	devised	justified	researched
computed	diagnosed	measured	studied
conceptualized	estimated	negotiated	substantiated
concluded	evaluated	prescribed	synthesized
confirmed	examined	prioritized	validated
critiqued	forecasted	projected	verified

Communication

addressed	composed	involved	represented
apprised	convinced	marketed	spoke
arbitrated	corresponded	mediated	summarized
authored	drafted	persuaded	welcomed
canvassed	edited	presented	wrote
clarified	elicited	promoted	
collaborated	explained	publicized	
communicated	informed	reported	

Quantitative and Research

analyzed	detected	fabricated	researched
appraised	dissected	formulated	reviewed
audited	envisioned	gathered	shaped
cited	estimated	illustrated	studied
classified	evaluated	inspected	summarized
collected	examined	investigated	surveyed
compiled	exhibited	measured	tested
computed	experimented	quantified	visualized
critiqued	explored	recorded	

Leadership and Management

administered	delegated	enhanced	moderated
advised	designated	facilitated	monitored
allocated	directed	fostered	motivated
allowed	educated	founded	recruited
appointed	elicited	guided	sanctioned
approved	employed	influenced	supervised
assigned	empowered	instructed	trained
authorized	enabled	interviewed	
chaired	encouraged	judged	
coached	endorsed	led	

Planning and Organization

arranged	classified	linked	purchased
assembled	collected	orchestrated	recorded
budgeted	compiled	organized	regulated
calculated	consolidated	oriented	scheduled
catalogued	correlated	planned	systematized
centralized	indexed	processed	tabulated

Problem Solving

adapted	developed	procured	restored
alleviated	elevated	produced	retrieved
ameliorated	foresaw	reconciled	revived
analyzed	formulated	rectified	solicited
brainstormed	fulfilled	reduced	solved
composed	generated	refined	streamlined
conceived	identified	reinforced	strengthened
conceptualized	invented	rejuvenated	supplemented
constructed	lightened	relieved	transformed
created	modeled	remedied	
debugged	modified	remodeled	
decided	performed	repaired	

Teamwork

accommodated	collaborated	helped
aided	contributed	mediated
assisted	cooperated	participated

Sources: Adapted from Michigan State University Career Services Network (n.d.) and Yale University Office of Career Strategy (n.d.).

Types of Résumés

There are at least two types of résumés. The *chronological résumé* is organized by position or job. All jobs are listed in reverse chronological order, starting with the most recent. Duties and skills are highlighted within each work experience (Exercise 9.4). Table 9.3 illustrates the chronological résumé. Chronological résumés are challenging when a job seeker has little experience. The *functional résumé* is a good option for recent graduates, as it is organized by skills and competencies regardless of when they were obtained. Each skill is listed and the work experience and duties are discussed within. The material that appears first in a résumé tends to get the most attention (Exercise 9.5). Consider that an employer may review a résumé for only about 30 seconds and a functional résumé makes sense. Table 9.4 illustrates a functional résumé.

EXERCISE 9.4
WRITE THE EXPERIENCE SECTION FOR YOUR CHRONOLOGICAL RÉSUMÉ

This exercise will walk you through the most challenging part of the résumé: writing the experience section.

1. List all of the jobs that you have had, along with the dates of employment.

2. What did each job entail? Free write about your activities, responsibilities, and everything you did. What were you particularly good at? Identify achievements.

3. Condense each description into one to two sentences.

4. Identify action words to describe each job and further condense each job description into one sentence.

5. Format the experience section of your résumé.

EXERCISE 9.5
WRITE THE SKILL SECTION FOR YOUR FUNCTIONAL RÉSUMÉ

A functional résumé is useful because it presents your skills in light of your experience. This exercise will help you to translate your experiences into skills.

Preparation

1. List the skills that employers value (see Chapter 7).

2. Gather the results of Exercise 9.4 (i.e., your list of jobs and duties).

Brainstorm

3. Brainstorm the skills that you used to complete the duties for each job. Also consider the exercises in Chapter 2 (especially Exercise 2.7: Assess Your Skills).

4. Link each skill to one or more trait the employers value (see Chapter 3, especially Table 3.1 on "Top 15 Attributes Employers Seek in Prospective Employees").

5. Choose a main skill to describe each job.

Write the Skills Section

6. Organize your skills by importance.

7. List each skill, then the place you developed it and your duties (how you developed and demonstrated it). Alternatively, describe your skills and list your prior jobs in a Work Experience section as shown in Table 9.4.

PRACTICAL TIP
CREATE A TEXT RÉSUMÉ

Sometimes an online application will require that you cut and paste your résumé into a form or e-mail rather than attach a file. Create an electronic copy of your résumé in plain text. Remove all formatting (i.e., bold, tabs, centering, and bullets). Include straight text that will not confuse the scanner. Use asterisks (*) instead of bullet points. Save your résumé as a plain text file (.txt) and cut and paste as needed.

Make your résumé as professional looking as possible. Be concise; a new graduate's résumé should be no more than one page in length. Carefully proofread your résumé, because typographical, spelling, and grammatical errors are unacceptable and will cost you an interview. Print your résumé on white or off-white paper, using a laser printer. Review Table 9.5 for more résumé tips. Also note that many employers request that applicants upload electronic résumés to their website or e-mail them to the human resources department. Convert your résumé to a pdf file so that the formatting is retained regardless of what computer system the employer uses. Appearances count, so proof your résumé pdf file for errors in formatting even if the copy in your word processing file is flawless.

TABLE 9.3 ● Chronological Résumé

JANE R. DAVIS
123 Gammon Street, Dunkin, Connecticut 12345
janedavis@gmail.com | 555-555-5555 | linkedin.com/jane-davis

OBJECTIVE

An entry-level position in human resources with opportunities to apply interpersonal and research skills

EDUCATION

University of Connecticut, Storrs
Bachelor of Arts in Psychology, Cum Laude, May 2021
GPA: 3.5/4.0

WORK EXPERIENCE

Waterbury Neuroscience, Storrs, CT   April 2020–Present
Administrative Assistant

- Entered data for psychiatric research team resulting in published articles
- Applied skills in SPSS, Microsoft Word, Excel, and spreadsheet development
- Interacted with patients in person and by phone
- Maintained weekly schedule of appointments for three psychiatrists

Macy's, Waterbury, CT   May 2019–March 2020
Sales Associate

- Greeted and helped customers, restocked merchandise, arranged displays
- Operated the register and accurately balanced the cash drawer

Olive Garden, Waterbury, CT   June 2019–August 2019
Server

- Interacted with customers, and took and served orders in a fast-paced environment

Takiki Summer Camp, Warren, CT   Summer 2017, 2018
Counselor

- Supervised and engaged 12 special needs and at-risk youth in activities for 7 hours each day
- Developed camp-wide crafts activities and games

HONORS AND AWARDS

- Connecticut Scholarship for Excellence in   2020
  Community Leadership Award
- Psi Chi   2019

ACTIVITIES

- Academic peer mentor for first-year students   2019–2020, 2020–2021
- Volunteer: Foundation for Families   Fall 2019
- Volunteer: Food for All   Spring 2020
- President, Psi Chi, University of Connecticut chapter   2020–2021

TABLE 9.4 ● Functional Résumé

JANE R. DAVIS
123 Gammon Street, Dunkin, Connecticut 12345
janedavis@gmail.com | 555-555-5555 | linkedin.com/jane-davis

OBJECTIVE

An entry-level position in human resources with opportunities to apply interpersonal and research skills

EDUCATION

University of Connecticut, Storrs
Bachelor of Arts in Psychology, Cum Laude, May 2021
GPA: 3.5/4.0

RELEVANT SKILLS

Research and Data Management

Supported a psychiatric research group with data entry in SPSS and participated in research discussions of a project that resulted in a publication.

Interpersonal Communication

Communicated with customers, patients, and at-risk youth, in a range of settings, including medicine, sales, and education.

Organization/Administration

Maintained medical office, insurance files, and weekly schedule of appointments for a team of psychiatrists.

Technical Skills

Proficient in Excel, spreadsheet development, PowerPoint, Microsoft Word, and SPSS

WORK EXPERIENCE

- Administrative Assistant, Waterbury Neuroscience, Storrs, CT — April 2020–Present
- Sales Associate, Macy's, Waterbury, CT — May 2019–March 2020
- Server, Olive Garden, Waterbury, CT — June–August 2019
- Counselor, Takiki Summer Camp, Warren, CT — Summer 2018, 2019

HONORS AND AWARDS

- Connecticut Scholarship for Excellence in Community Leadership Award — 2020
- Psi Chi — 2019

ACTIVITIES

- Academic peer mentor for first-year students — 2019–2020, 2020–2021
- Volunteer: Foundation for Families — Fall 2019
- Volunteer: Food for All — Spring 2020
- President, Psi Chi, University of Connecticut chapter — 2020–2021

TABLE 9.5 ● Résumé Checklist

❑ Clearly communicate your purpose and value.

❑ Communicate your strongest points first.

❑ Don't make statements that you can't document.

❑ Be direct, succinct, and expressive with language.

❑ Don't use lengthy sentences and descriptions; this is the only time that sentence fragments are acceptable, but use them judiciously.

❑ Don't use the passive voice.

❑ Don't change the tense of verbs throughout the résumé.

❑ Confine your information to one page.

❑ Use space to organize your résumé; it should not appear cramped.

❑ Aim for overall visual balance on the page.

❑ Use a font size of 10 to 14 point.

❑ Choose a simple typeface and stick to it (i.e., don't change fonts).

❑ Use spacing and bold for emphasis.

❑ Don't fold or staple your résumé.

❑ Check spelling, grammar, and punctuation.

❑ Proofread.

❑ Ask someone else to proofread your résumé for spelling, grammar, and formatting.

❑ Get outside help. Get feedback on the content of your résumé from two or three people, including someone who regularly evaluates résumés and hires employees.

❑ Do not include your reference information on your résumé (see sample).

❑ Before giving their names to a potential employer, ask your references if they are willing to serve as references.

Create a LinkedIn Profile

As discussed earlier, LinkedIn is the most commonly used social networking site for professionals. LinkedIn is a source of job information and career contacts. More importantly, employers use LinkedIn to learn about potential employees. Your LinkedIn profile can help employers quickly learn about your experience and qualifications. Use the information in your résumé to prepare your LinkedIn profile. Do not construct your LinkedIn profile until you have created a résumé. Complete Exercise 9.6 to convert your résumé into an effective LinkedIn profile.

EXERCISE 9.6
CONSTRUCT A LINKEDIN PROFILE

Use the information in your résumé to construct a LinkedIn profile. Specifically, create your profile on paper or offline first, in order to seek feedback and edit it prior to posting it. Compose text for each of the following sections.

1. Headline: Your headline is a short, memorable professional slogan.

2. Education: Include all your schools, major(s) and minor, courses, and study abroad or summer programs.

3. Experience: List the jobs you held, even if they were part-time, along with what you accomplished at each.

4. Organizations: List any clubs you've joined at school or outside of school. Describe what you did with each organization.

5. Skills and Expertise: List at least five key skills.

6. Volunteer Experience: Even if you weren't paid for a job, be sure to list it.

7. Honors and Awards: List them.

8. Courses: List the classes that show off the skills and interests you're most excited about.

9. Summary: Write a concise and confident statement about your qualifications and goals, as well as aspirations.

10. Recommendations: Brainstorm who you might ask to write a recommendation. Do not add recommendations to your profile without permission.

Unlike your résumé, a LinkedIn profile contains a headshot photo. Most people prefer to connect with a face, so a photo is an important addition to your profile. However, be sure that your photo is appropriate and professional.

PRACTICAL TIP
CHARACTERISTICS OF AN EFFECTIVE LINKEDIN PHOTO

Your LinkedIn photo is likely not the same photo you use in your Instagram profile. Instead it must convey professionalism. What makes for an effective LinkedIn photo?

(Continued)

(Continued)

- It should look like you.

- Avoid a distracting background.

- Your face should take up at least two-thirds of the frame. Crop your image to include only your head and the tops of your shoulders.

- Wear what you'd wear to work (e.g., a collared shirt or even a neat T-shirt, but not club attire).

- Appear approachable, look at the camera, and smile or hold a natural expression.

- Use photo editing apps or software sparingly (e.g., to remove a blemish, but not to contour your cheekbones).

After you have created your profile and proofed it carefully, seek input from an advisor at the career development center at your institution or another professional who can provide trusted feedback. Take great care in preparing your profile, as employers will see this before they see you. A poor profile can hurt your search more than a good profile can help. When you are ready for the world to see it, adjust your profile's privacy settings to "Public." Your profile will show up in search results.

The Cover Letter

The cover letter is an introduction to your résumé that enables you to tailor your application to the prospective employer. Your cover letter must be concise and explain what you can offer an employer. An employer might spend a few seconds scanning your cover letter; get your message out quickly and efficiently. In no more than three paragraphs explain your interest in the position and how you can contribute to the organization. Highlight the most important aspects of your background that are relevant to the position and/or organization. Finally, provide contact information (a phone number and e-mail address), thank the reader, and reiterate your interest in the position.

Remember that the cover letter is an introduction that should motivate the reader to examine your résumé. An effective cover letter is written with the needs of the audience (i.e., prospective employer) in mind. Before writing a cover letter, ask yourself, "What is the purpose of this letter? What are the needs of the reader? What benefits will an employer gain from me? How can I maintain the reader's interest? How can I end the letter persuasively, so that the reader will want to examine my résumé and contact me?" Be explicit and communicate what you can do for the employer, not what the job will do for you. Remember that this is a "free sample" of your work and indicates what the employer can expect of you. Table 9.6 provides tips for writing your cover

PRACTICAL TIP
TAILOR YOUR APPLICATION TO THE EMPLOYER

As you prepare a job application, do your homework to know exactly why you want to work for the employer. Employers want to hire people who are interested in them, not just those who want a job. Convey your interest and what you can contribute in your cover letter (and tailor the objective stated in your résumé to the position).

TABLE 9.6 ● Cover Letter Checklist

❑ Address the letter to an individual, using the person's name and title. If answering a blind advertisement, use the following address: "To Whom It May Concern."

❑ Indicate the position for which you are applying and explain why you are qualified to fill it.

❑ Include a phone number and e-mail where you can be reached.

❑ Ask someone to proofread your letter for spelling, grammar, and punctuation errors.

❑ Indicate how your education and work skills are transferable and relevant to the position for which you are applying.

❑ Keep a copy of each cover letter for your records; write notes from any phone conversations that might occur on your copy of the cover letter.

❑ Make a connection to the company through a person you know, some information you've researched, or a specific interest.

letter. If you are submitting your résumé by e-mail, shorten your cover letter to simply identify the position to which you are applying and why you are a good fit (in about two to three sentences).

Interview

Congratulations! If you have been asked to come for an interview, you have made it past the first round of reviews and have an opportunity to land the position. The interview is the most important criterion for hiring; it beats out grades, related work experience, and recommendations. Second, and even third, interviews often occur. The interview is your one chance to impress the prospective employer. How do you do it? Display good communication skills, clearly defined professional goals, and an honest upbeat demeanor. Interviews are stressful, but you can increase your confidence by being thoroughly prepared.

Prepare

Understand the purpose of the interview and keep the interviewer's objectives in mind. From your perspective, the purpose of the job interview is to get a second interview or job offer; for employers, the purpose of the job interview is to whittle down the list of applicants to one or two finalists. The interviewer is interested in answering several questions:

- Why does this person want to work for us?
- What position is this person suited for?
- What are his or her qualifications?
- Why should I hire him or her?
- Does this person meet my employment needs?
- Is he or she trustworthy?

Because many applicants apply for each position, the interviewer often looks for reasons why you should not be hired. Interviewers are interested in identifying your weaknesses. Your job is to communicate your strengths. This means that you must understand yourself, but you also must understand the company or organization to which you are applying to determine how to package your strengths in order to appeal to the interviewer.

Research the company. Learn as much as you can about the company and the people with whom you'll interview. What is the relative size and growth of the industry? What product lines or services are offered? Where is the headquarters? Identify the competition. Be familiar with any recent items in the news. Try to predict what will be asked during the interview and prepare answers. Expect to be asked to identify a challenge you faced and how you overcame it. It's a difficult, but predictable, question. Think about it now and you'll be better equipped to respond during your interview. Be ready to show that you are interested and enthusiastic in the company. Exercise 9.7 presents common questions asked during interviews. You also will be judged on the questions that you ask. Ask thoughtful and intelligent questions about the company and position. Exercise 9.8 provides sample questions that an applicant might ask on an interview.

EXERCISE 9.7
COMMON INTERVIEW QUESTIONS

What do you hope to be doing 5 or 10 years from now?

Why did you apply for this job?

Tell me about yourself.

What are your strengths and weaknesses?

What can you offer to us and what can we offer to you?

What are the two or three accomplishments in your life that have given you the greatest satisfaction?

Do you work well under pressure?

Have you ever held any supervisory or leadership roles?

What do you like to do in your spare time?

What other jobs are you applying for?

Is there anything else we should know about you?

Why do you feel that you will be successful in this position?

What courses did you like best? Least? Why?

What did you learn or gain from your part-time and summer job experience?

Why did you choose your major?

What can a psychology major do for this organization?

If you could do it all again, what would you change about your education?

Did you do the best you could in school? Why or why not?

Why did you leave your last employer?

What job did you like the most? The least? Why?

What did you like least about your last job?

Describe your best or worst boss.

Have you ever been fired?

Why do you want to join our organization?

(Continued)

(Continued)

Why should we hire you?

When will you be ready to work?

Do you have any actual work experience?

How would you describe your ideal job?

Are you a team player? Explain.

What motivates you?

Tell me about some of your recent goals and what you did to achieve them.

Have you ever had a conflict with a boss or professor? How did you resolve it?

If I were to ask one of your professors to describe you, what would he or she say?

Describe a situation when you made a mistake. How did you handle it?

Why did you choose to attend your college?

What qualities do you feel a successful manager should have?

What do you know about our company?

What kind of salary are you looking for?

What was the last book you read?

What questions do you have for me?

Prompt

1. Which of these questions do you find most challenging? Select three.

2. Why are they challenging?

3. Discuss how you might answer each of the questions you have identified.

Sources: Adapted from Greene and Martel (2014) and Johnston (2014).

EXERCISE 9.8
QUESTIONS TO ASK DURING AN INTERVIEW

Tell me about the duties and responsibilities of this job.

What is the career path for this position?

How long has this position been in the company?

What is the person who performed this job doing now?

What would be the ideal type of person for this position?

What kinds of skills or personality characteristics are ideal for this position?

For whom would I be working?

Are there training opportunities in this position?

Are there opportunities for professional growth in this position?

What are the most critical skills needed to perform this job?

What am I expected to accomplish during the first year?

What are the most critical challenges that I may encounter in the first year?

How will I be evaluated?

Are promotions and raises tied to performance criteria?

What is unique about working for this company?

Why did you choose to become a part of this organization?

What is the next step in this process?

Sources: Adapted from Greene and Martel (2014) and Johnston (2014).

Prompt

1. Which of these questions is most important to you?

2. Identify two other questions that you might ask potential employers.

3. Discuss why you have selected each question.

What to Wear

It may not be nice, but we are judged on our appearance. Dress appropriately for your interview because your appearance communicates messages about your level of seriousness and professionalism. During the first 5 minutes of an interview, interviewers make initial judgments or create expectations about your professionalism and "fit" for a position based on your appearance and demeanor. Use this to your advantage by dressing appropriately. Even if you are applying to a company with a casual dress code, dress better than you would for work. Dressing up conveys your enthusiasm and interest in the position.

Whether you're a man or a woman, you can't go wrong with a basic dark suit. Casual dress is more common in some fields than others but you can't go wrong with a simple suit and subtle accessories. Men should wear a white or blue oxford shirt with an understated tie. Women should wear a modest blouse, with understated hair and makeup. Keep jewelry to a minimum. Consider removing facial piercings. Err toward the side of conservative, as you want to be remembered for what you say and not what you're wearing. Also note that these are merely general rules. You might want to see how others in your field dress for appropriate cues. You can't go wrong if you dress for the position, wearing attire that you might wear to work, but dressier.

During the Interview

Be enthusiastic. Remember that your interviewer is committed to his or her position and the company and wants to hire someone who is similarly committed. Demonstrate your enthusiasm by discussing what you've learned from your research and preparation. Ask questions to fill in any gaps in your understanding. Convey a sense of long-term interest by asking about opportunities for further professional education and advancement.

Throughout the interview, be aware of your body language and keep fidgeting to a minimum. Lean very slightly toward the interviewer to communicate your interest in what he or she is saying. Maintain eye contact to convey interest and trustworthiness. Smile to convey your positive attitude. Don't forget that your tone of voice can indicate how interested you are in the interview and the organization. Here are some other helpful tips for acing interviews:

- Bring a copy of your résumé. It comes in handy if you have to fill in applications and provides initial information for your interviewer.

- Allow the interviewer to direct the conversation.

- Answer questions in a clear and positive manner.

- Never speak negatively about former employers or colleagues, no matter what.

- Let the interviewer lead the conversation toward salary and benefits. Try not to focus your interest on these issues (at least not during the initial interview).

- When discussing salary, be flexible.

- If the employer doesn't say when you'll hear about their decision, ask when you can call to follow up.

- Thank the employer for the interview.

Above all remember that employers anticipate applicants to be on their best behavior during an interview. They recognize that any perceived flaws, such as arrogance, impoliteness, or poor listening skills, will likely be more exaggerated when the applicant becomes an employee. Be self-aware because any negative interactions or ambivalent signals can stop your application in its tracks.

Thank-You Note

Immediately after your interview, e-mail a thank-you note and follow it up with a mailed note. Surprisingly few applicants do this, so you'll stand out as a professional (Greene & Martel, 2014). A mailed note signifies extra effort and is especially memorable. Express your appreciation for the opportunity to meet the employer and his or her time and consideration. Restate your interest, and highlight any noteworthy points made in your conversation. Be brief.

The Job Offer

Usually job offers are made over the phone or in person; however, an offer may also be delivered by e-mail. No matter how the offer is delivered, you're likely to be surprised. The most appropriate response to an offer in person or by phone is to ask any questions that come to mind, and then request time (a day or two) to think about the offer.

Before accepting an offer, be sure that you understand the conditions and elements of the job. In many cases, salaries for entry-level positions leave little room for negotiation. Take your lead from the employer as to whether the salary is negotiable. If the salary is lower than you hoped and it isn't negotiable, you must decide whether you're still willing to accept the position and what, if anything, would make it more attractive. As you think about whether to accept the job offer, consider the scope of the position, how it fits your career goals, opportunities for professional growth, and pragmatics (geographic location, benefits, salary, work hours, etc.). If you decide to accept the offer, be sure to inform any employers still actively considering you. Also contact your references to inform them of your new job as well as to thank them for their assistance.

If you decide not to accept the job, notify the employer by telephone as soon as possible. Timeliness is important because other applicants also are waiting for a response. Be polite, thank the employer for the offer, and wish him or her success. Follow up with a polite e-mail as well, which ensures that your reply is recorded.

REFLECTION PROMPTS

Think Ahead

Try to imagine your ideal life 5 years from now. What are you doing? Where do you live? How do you spend your days? What steps should you take now to get there?

What Are My Priorities?

What is important to you in a career and job? For example, is geography important to you? Are you willing to move anywhere a job will take you? What do you value (i.e., proximity to family and friends, time off, fascinating work)? What are the things that matter to you? How can these inform your job hunt?

Social Media

What role do social media play in your life? Pay attention to your social media use. How often do you find yourself checking your phone? How do you use social media in your everyday life? How might your use of social media influence your job search? How might you minimize negative effects and maximize opportunities?

10

What Can I Do With a Graduate Degree in Psychology?

Each year, about 117,000 bachelor's degrees are awarded in psychology (National Center for Education Statistics, 2017b). Armed with a blend of liberal arts and research skills, the majority of psychology majors successfully enter the workforce following graduation. About one-quarter of graduates, however, choose to pursue graduate study. In 2015–2016, nearly 28,000 master's and over 6,500 doctoral degrees were awarded in psychology (National Center for Education Statistics, 2017b). In this chapter we discuss some of the reasons psychology majors pursue graduate study and the opportunities that accompany graduate study.

Why Go to Graduate School?

There are a variety of reasons to consider attending graduate school. First and foremost is a deep-seated interest in understanding human behavior. Successful graduate students love to learn, and they have a thirst for knowledge and thrive on discovery. Some pursue graduate study to work closely with others in need and improve others' quality of life. Although graduate study isn't necessary to find a career in a helping field, it can open doors to additional opportunities to supervise, administrate, and conduct research. A graduate degree also affords opportunities for research careers in and out of academia.

Specialized Knowledge

During college, psychology majors are exposed to all subfields of psychology and obtain a broad knowledge of the field. Graduate study, in contrast, entails specializing in one subfield of psychology (such as experimental psychology, for example). Graduate students become experts in specific fields such as cognitive psychology, clinical psychology, or developmental psychology. All graduate students gain advanced knowledge. Doctoral students become psychologists.

Generalizable Skills

As you are aware, undergraduate training in psychology provides students with opportunities to learn many valuable skills. Graduate education further hones these skills and provides other opportunities for personal and professional development. Although the particular set of skills developed varies depending on the student, program, advisor, and experiences, generally speaking, graduate training in psychology gives students the opportunity to develop and master skills that are useful in any career setting (see Table 10.1).

Financial Opportunities and Considerations

Graduate study offers opportunities for personal enrichment as well as enables graduates to increase their salaries substantially. The median salary for bachelor's graduates age 25 to 29 in 2016 was $40,100 (National Center for Education Statistics, 2018). In 2018, the average salary for a master's degree

TABLE 10.1 ● Generalizable Skills Honed in Graduate School	
Problem finding, definition, and solving skills	Training in research design and methodology offers graduate students valuable experience in identifying, defining, and solving problems, honing their critical thinking skills. Given limited or ambiguous information, graduate degree holders learn to identify central issues and extrapolate the most important problems to be addressed. They learn that there is often more than one acceptable way to solve a problem.
Information acquisition, management, and synthesis	Some of the most highly valued skills obtained in graduate school include the ability to gather, summarize, synthesize, and draw conclusions from information. Graduate students develop cognitive tools needed to deal with inconsistent and uncertain information, extract key ideas from information rapidly, impose structure on ambiguous or messy data, and translate information into meaningful conclusions and recommendations.
Methodological and quantitative skills	Graduate students in psychology develop inferential skills, statistical reasoning, and analysis skills. Students become able to draw appropriate inferences from numerical data, and learn how to present data to a nontechnical audience. They learn to not only conceptualize phenomena based on cause and effect but also understand the limitations of conclusions given particular methodological approaches.
Planning and leadership skills	Conducting therapy and engaging in long-term research projects encourage graduate students to develop planning skills. Students learn how to identify the steps needed to complete a given project, from beginning to end, and gain expertise in identifying and anticipating problems.
Interpersonal and intrapersonal awareness and agility	Working closely with others in research contexts provides valuable opportunities for learning how to be a team player. Training in psychology offers an understanding and appreciation of the capabilities and limitations of people from cognitive, perceptual, physical, motivational, and developmental as well as other perspectives. Graduate students often learn how to become more self-observant and aware of their abilities and limitations, as well as develop an understanding of how to motivate themselves.
Reading, writing, and communication skills	Graduate students learn how to structure and evaluate written and oral arguments, as well as how to write concisely in a professional style. Research presentations and teaching assistantships give students opportunities to learn how to communicate research and theoretical concepts to professional and lay audiences.

(Continued)

TABLE 10.1 ● (Continued)	
Application	Graduate education provides opportunities to learn how to apply research-based knowledge to solve real-life problems, and to use psychological principles and methods to change behaviors and mental processes in clinical and organizational settings. These are important skills that place advanced degree holders at an advantage in a variety of career settings.
Adaptability	Graduate education trains students to think flexibly and accept some ambiguity. Students learn to become action oriented and develop the ability to work on and consider several problems at once.

holder in psychology was about $60,000, according to Payscale.com. Salaries vary dramatically by setting, with workers in education and human services often earning less than those in business and industry. For example, in 2015, doctoral trained psychologists earned a median salary of $85,000, but psychologists earned a median salary of $62,000 in teaching positions, $95,000 in research positions, and $110,000 in management positions (Lin et al., 2017b). Practicing psychologists in government positions earned a median salary of $86,000, and those who were self-employed earned a median salary of $120,000. Salaries vary by geographic location, field, and experience. Your salary will increase as you accumulate experience. However, the increase in salary that typically accompanies a graduate degree comes at a price: Graduate degrees are expensive. The 2015–2016 median annual graduate school tuition was about $18,000 ($11,000 for public institutions and $24,000 for private institutions) (National Center for Education Statistics, 2017a). Note that these numbers do not include books, equipment, room and board, or additional living expenses. The financial considerations of graduate study are important, as the loss of income and potential increase in debt can have life-long consequences.

PRACTICAL TIP
CONSIDER THE FINANCIAL SIDE OF GRADUATE STUDY

As you consider graduate study, keep in mind that the costs are greater than just tuition. Consider the years in which you will not earn a salary and the benefits that you might miss, such as health insurance and retirement savings. What will it mean to enter the work world several years later than your friends? What might this late entry coupled with possibly hefty education loans mean for your ability to buy a house or start a family? Keep these in mind. Lots of people go to graduate school without thinking about the future beyond having a shiny new degree. Make an informed decision.

Graduate Degrees

There are two types of graduate degrees: master's and doctoral. Both offer specialized training in psychology but they differ in the quantity of training, length of study, and specific requirements. Let's consider the more popular of the two degrees: the master's degree.

What Can You Do With a Master's Degree?

Master's degrees comprise the vast majority of graduate degrees awarded each year. Depending on the program and curriculum, a master's degree enables graduates to (a) teach psychology in high school (other certification may be needed); (b) become more competitive for management, leadership, and consulting positions in government and industry; (c) practice counseling (credentials vary by state); and (d) obtain data management and analysis positions in government, industry (e.g., insurance, pharmaceutical, and manufacturing companies), and nonprofit organizations. Individuals who wish to practice school psychology earn a specialist degree, which requires an additional year of study beyond the master's degree.

Master's-level professionals in psychology are employed in a variety of settings, all of which also employ doctoral-level psychologists. The following are some examples (Singleton, Tate, & Kohout, 2003):

- Educational settings: elementary or secondary school, school system district offices, special education, and vocational or adult education.

- Human services settings: counseling and guidance centers, student counseling centers, nursing homes, substance abuse facilities, mental retardation facilities, developmental disability facilities, head injury facilities, and other community social services agencies.

- Business and government: consulting firms, private research organizations, government research, corporations, small business, criminal justice system, military, government agencies, and nonprofit organizations.

- Hospitals and clinics: outpatient mental health clinics, community mental health centers, and HMO and other managed care settings.

Master's degrees offer several advantages over doctoral degrees, as discussed in the following sections.

Earning a master's degree typically requires 2 years compared with the 5 to 8 years entailed by a doctoral degree. Length of time to degree is an important consideration for all students but especially those with families. Consider how the length of graduate study will affect your family. Doctoral programs place students under great economic and personal stress for an extended period of time. Students with families may not be able or willing to place long-term stress on their families.

Master's degrees are less expensive than doctoral degrees. Although master's degrees are a less expensive option, they aren't cheap once you factor in tuition as well as any salary lost while attending school. But because master's degrees typically take about 2 years of study, they will nearly always be less expensive than doctoral degrees.

Master's programs are more readily available and flexible. Many more colleges offer master's programs than doctoral programs. A doctoral program may not be available in a given geographical location, and students may not be able or willing to relocate to attend graduate school. Master's programs are more likely to offer part-time study, which allows time for employment and family responsibilities. In addition, most doctoral programs allow for entry only in the fall semester, whereas master's programs often allow spring admissions.

Master's programs have lower admissions requirements. Some students choose a master's degree as a stepping stone to a doctoral degree. Students whose credentials do not permit them immediate entry to graduate school often consider this route.

Master's programs provide sufficient training and credentials for a variety of careers. A master's degree will not permit you to use the term *psychologist* because this term is regulated by state licensing boards and requires a doctoral degree, supervised experience, and passing an exam. However, master's-level professionals may conduct individual counseling and therapy by obtaining certification appropriate to their level of education and experience. Specifically, master's-level professionals in psychology can be licensed in all states as marriage and family therapists and/or licensed professional counselors and sometimes as clinical social workers. They provide assessment and intervention services in community-based programs, public and private institutions, and programs dealing with special problems such as substance abuse, spouse abuse, crisis intervention, and vocational rehabilitation. In institutional settings, master's degree holders may work as behavior change specialists who design and implement programs to serve special populations. States differ in regulations and requirements, so learn about the requirements in your state to ensure that you obtain any needed experiences while in school. A variety of related fields permit graduates to work in a helping capacity with people. Consider the careers in Table 10.2.

If you choose a master's degree in psychology, expect to complete 2 years of full-time graduate study. Requirements for service-oriented subfields such as clinical, counseling, and school psychology usually include experience in an applied setting. Research-oriented subfields such as experimental or developmental psychology usually require a master's thesis based on an empirical research project. Some programs require students to pass a comprehensive exam that evaluates students' knowledge and reasoning.

TABLE 10.2 ● Master's Degrees in Other Helping Fields		
	Activities	**Education**
Social work	As a profession, social work is dedicated to helping people to adapt and function as best they can in their environment. Social workers provide direct services or therapy, serving individuals, families, and communities. They work in hospitals, clinics, schools, correction facilities, specialized programs, and private practice. Social workers assist clients in identifying problems, issues, and concerns, help them to consider and implement effective solutions, and guide them in locating reliable resources.	The master of social work (MSW) enables degree holders to practice therapy independently, because they are eligible for licensure in all states. The MSW requires 2 to 3 years of study, depending on the program and when the supervised internship (of 900 hours for licensure) is scheduled.
Counseling	There are many different types of counselors, but all help people who are experiencing personal, family, or mental health problems. Counselors also help people make educational and career decisions. Counselors work in schools, colleges, health care facilities, job training, career development centers, social agencies, correctional institutions, residential care centers, drug and alcohol rehabilitation programs, state and government agencies, group practice, and private practice.	Typically, a master's degree in counseling requires 2 years of coursework, including 600 hours of supervised clinical experience. Master's degree holders in counseling may conduct therapy independently and may seek licensure or certification.
Occupational therapy	Occupational therapists work with clients who are experiencing disabilities (emotional, mental, physical, and developmental) that influence their occupational performance or well-being.	All 50 states in the United States regulate occupational therapy, meaning that graduates must obtain licensure. The minimum educational requirement for entry into this field is a

(Continued)

TABLE 10.2 ● (Continued)

	Activities	Education
	Occupational therapists assess physical, mental, and emotional deficiencies and counsel patients to help them improve their ability to function in their daily environments. For example, an occupational therapist might help a client to improve basic motor functions or reasoning abilities, as well as help him or her to compensate for permanent losses of function. Occupational therapists obtain positions in hospitals, offices and clinics of occupational therapists and other health practitioners, school systems, home health agencies, nursing homes, community mental health centers, adult day care programs, job training services, and residential care facilities.	master's degree in occupational therapy with at least 6 months of supervised practice.
Speech pathology	Speech pathologists assess, diagnose, and treat communication disabilities such as stuttering or impaired language. They work with clients who have difficulty understanding and producing language, including clients with cognitive communication impairments such as attention and memory disorders. Speech pathologists help clients to develop and regain language (e.g., assist with making speech sounds). Their work also involves counseling clients and families to help them to better understand the disorder and treatment. Speech pathologists provide direct clinical services in schools, nursing homes, mental health centers, private practices, and medical settings, often as part of a team of allied health professionals.	A master's degree in speech pathology (approximately 2 years of coursework) is required for entry into the profession. Nearly all states require speech pathologists to be licensed, with 300 to 375 hours of supervised clinical experience required for licensure (varying by state).

What Can You Do With a Doctoral Degree?

A master's degree may allow you to work directly with people, but if you're planning on conducting independent research or teaching at the college level, a doctoral degree is essential. A doctoral degree provides a greater range of flexibility and autonomy, but it requires a great commitment of time and expense. Most students earn doctoral degrees after 5 and as much as 8 years of study. In clinical or counseling psychology, the requirement for the doctoral degree generally includes a year or more of internship or supervised experience.

Why do students seek doctoral degrees? Generally students pursue doctoral degrees for any of the following reasons: (a) to teach at a college, (b) to conduct research in a university or private organization in industry or business, (c) to be licensed as a psychologist and practice psychology independently, or (d) to engage in a variety of consulting roles allowing autonomy. Many psychologists engage in more than one of these roles. For example, a college professor might consult to a pharmaceutical company, or a practicing psychologist might also teach a few college courses. Among clinicians, PhD degrees offer the flexibility of research careers and practice careers, whereas the PsyD offers opportunities for practice and administration.

Graduate-Level Careers in Psychology

Graduate education opens the door to many opportunities. What follows are a sampling of careers, but note that no one program will prepare you for all of these careers. Before you decide on a graduate degree and program, it's important to consider all the types of careers that you might enjoy and choose a degree and program that will not limit your options.

Teaching Careers

Many students seek a graduate degree in order to teach at a high school or 2-year or 4-year college. Master's degree holders may teach psychology in a high school (although additional certification may be necessary, depending on the state) or 2-year community college setting. In recent years, faculty positions at community colleges have become more competitive; many are held by doctoral degree holders. Similarly, although master's degree holders may be hired to teach at 4-year colleges on a part-time basis, they are unlikely to be hired for full-time positions.

If your goal is to teach at the college level, it's in your best interest to pursue a doctoral degree, which will provide you with the most opportunities for employment, mobility, and advancement as a faculty member. Graduates with doctoral degrees may teach undergraduate, master's, and doctoral students in a variety of educational settings, including universities, professional schools, and medical schools. When you consider a career as a professor, recognize that there is more to the professorate than lecturing and teaching in class each day. Time in the classroom is only the most obvious thing a professor does.

A professor's career entails many roles, usually including research and service to the campus and community (advising, committee work, administrative work). During a typical week, a professor may give lectures, spend time writing an article or book, conduct statistical analyses and continue with his or her research, conduct literature searches, sit in on faculty meetings, advise students, write letters of recommendation, spend time grading papers, give a talk at a professional meeting, engage in consulting work, serve as an advisor for community agencies, and much more.

Research Careers

A graduate degree in psychology is excellent preparation for a career in research. Many research positions are available to master's degree holders, especially in business and private organizations. Master's degree recipients in research-oriented fields such as quantitative psychology, developmental psychology, general psychology, and experimental psychology have developed useful methodological and quantitative skills. They are often employed in research positions in university research centers as well as in government, business, and private organizations.

Particularly in academic settings, the doctoral degree offers more flexibility, opportunities for advancement, and opportunities to serve as the primary investigator of federal grants. Research psychologists conduct basic and applied studies of human behavior and may participate in research programs sponsored by universities, government agencies, and private organizations. For example, a psychologist working in a university or hospital-based clinic might study smoking cessation; another working in a traumatic brain injury center might study the effects of particular kinds of brain injuries on behavior as well as resilience to brain injury and rehabilitation strategies. Psychologists who work in military research programs might examine the effects of exposure to trauma, whereas others might work as research and development officers at pharmaceutical companies and businesses. Medical schools are emerging as an important employment setting for research psychologists because medical research increasingly relies on contributions of multiple related fields such as anatomy, biochemistry, physiology, pharmacology, microbiology, and psychology. Interdisciplinary study is playing an increasingly important role in university life and is leading to more research and teaching opportunities for psychologists outside of psychology departments.

Service Delivery (Practice)

Graduate degree holders have a variety of opportunities to engage in service delivery. Mental health professionals with graduate degrees, including clinical and counseling psychologists, engage in a variety of practice activities including, but often not limited to, (a) conducting psychotherapy with persons with psychological disorders, crises, or problems of living; (b) administering and interpreting psychological tests of personality, intellect, and vocational aptitude; (c) facilitating psychoeducational and psychotherapy groups; (d) giving talks or workshops on specialty areas; (e) directing and administrating mental health programs; (f) supervising the clinical work of other therapists; and (g) responding to crises or emergency situations.

In order to be licensed as a psychologist, the applicant must have completed a doctoral program, obtained 4,000 hours of supervised practice (half prior to obtaining the degree and half post-degree), and pass a national and, often, state exam. All states permit several forms of licensure for master's-trained individuals, usually as counselors, which provides a great deal of autonomy. If you're considering a master's with the intention of setting up an independent practice, carefully research your options beforehand to ensure that the program you choose provides the experiences needed to be licensed or accredited in your state. Pay attention to specific coursework and especially the number of hours of supervised practice, two factors that licensing and accreditation boards require. The American Counseling Association includes links to licensure boards in all 50 states (https://www.counseling.org/knowledge-center/licensure-requirements/state-professional-counselor-licensure-boards).

Finally, if you are considering a career in school psychology, recognize that the field has very specific requirements for practice. The minimum level of education needed to practice school psychology is a specialist's degree, which falls between a master's and doctoral degree with regard to the amount of time and study. A specialist degree is composed of 60 credits and 1,500 supervised hours of practice and entails about 3 years of study. There are many service-delivery options for students interested in earning a graduate degree in psychology. Consider your desired career and look into state certification and licensure requirements as you apply to graduate school to ensure that the degree you earn offers adequate preparation (Exercises 10.1 and 10.2).

●

EXERCISE 10.1
PRACTICING WITH A MASTER'S DEGREE

1. Opportunities to practice therapy with a master's degree vary by state. Research the requirements of your state. Under what conditions may an individual with a master's in psychology practice? What types of credentialing or licensure are necessary?

2. What other types of master's degrees offer practice opportunities in your state?

3. If you were to pursue a master's degree with the intent of practicing, which degree would you choose and why?

4. Based on your research, with how much independence can an individual with a master's degree practice in your state?

EXERCISE 10.2
PRIVATE PRACTICE

Consider some of the realities of working as a therapist or psychologist in private practice. Search the Internet for articles that relay the experiences of therapists. Personal websites and blogs as well as forums might provide useful information. Use your judgment in evaluating the credibility of the information that you find.

1. What sites did you find? Include a brief description of each.

2. What did you learn about private practice? Discuss at least one advantage and one disadvantage.

3. What challenges do practitioners face?

4. How might this apply to you and your career plans?

Other Careers

Research and service-delivery skills come in handy for a variety of careers outside of research and practice settings. Graduate degree holders are found in all of the career settings mentioned in Chapter 3. Below are some additional examples of careers settings for individuals with a graduate degree in psychology.

Administration

Graduate degree holders in psychology and related fields work as managers and administrators in hospitals, mental health clinics, government agencies, schools, universities, businesses, and nonprofit organizations, where they may administrate research and applied activities. The ability to effectively administrate in each of these settings is enhanced by the research skills obtained in graduate school. Research skills are essential for evaluating programs and making decisions based on evaluations. Many administrative positions can be obtained with a master's degree and some experience, especially in smaller institutions and organizations. As in other applied careers, additional opportunities are often available to doctoral-level administrators.

Consulting

Graduate degree holders in psychology often are hired by organizations to provide consultative services on issues in their area of expertise. Consultative services can include designing a marketing survey, organizing outpatient mental health services, conducting individual assessments, providing expert testimony to a court, and designing webpages, as well as many other activities.

Health psychologists, for example, may be hired as consultants to design and implement programs to help people become healthier, stop smoking, lose weight, or manage stress. Some consultants work in policy: They conduct, interpret, and disseminate research to help national planners and policy makers reach decisions. Trial consultants work in several areas: They may help with jury selection, work with witnesses, or develop effective trial strategy in order to shape juror perceptions. Those trained in forensic or clinical psychology may conduct clinical work in corrections settings, serve as consultants for trial lawyers or as expert witnesses in jury trials, and conduct assessments that are used in trials. As in the other areas that we've discussed, some opportunities are available to master's degree holders, and additional opportunities for advancement are open to doctoral holders.

Business and Human Resources

Many graduate degree holders find a home in business, where they select and train employees, engage in human resources development, and develop employee assistance programs. Typical activities include designing and validating assessment instruments; determining the fairness of assessment and vocational tests, particularly for minority applicants; and creating work environments in public and private settings that maximize employee satisfaction.

The research skills honed in graduate school are applicable and valued in a corporate setting, such as market research. Like other research psychologists, market researchers design studies, construct questionnaires and other research instruments, analyze data, draw conclusions, and write reports. However, instead of conducting and publishing research to advance theory, a market researcher conducts applied research in an effort to help clients become more productive, competitive, and profitable. Business holds a variety of opportunities for master's degree holders because, unlike many other applied careers, doctoral degrees do not necessarily offer much of an advantage over master's degrees. For both master's and doctoral degree holders, advancement becomes possible with additional work experience (Exercise 10.3).

EXERCISE 10.3
EXPLORING PSYCHOLOGY SPECIALIZATIONS

1.   Identify an area of specialization in psychology that interests you. Why does this area interest you? What are typical topics of study within this area?

2.   What kinds of jobs do individuals with master's degrees in this area hold? Include information about typical settings, salary, and more.

3.   What kinds of jobs do individuals with doctoral degrees in this area hold? Include information about typical settings, salary, and more.

4.   How has what you have learned about this specialization influenced your views about graduate study in this area? Is a graduate degree a good career option? Which degree offers more opportunities? Conduct a cost-analysis of the pros and cons of seeking a master's degree verses a doctoral degree in this specialization.

Media and Publishing

Publishing (books, online, and other forms of media) offers opportunities for advanced degree holders in psychology. Some psychologists pursue careers as book acquisitions editors. An acquisitions editor works for a publishing company and engages in a variety of tasks, including reading book proposals, interpreting reviews of proposals, deciding whether to offer book contracts to authors, approaching potential authors with book ideas, discussing works in progress with authors, negotiating journal-publishing agreements with professional societies, and working on practical issues in publishing such as the design of book covers. Others work for media and Internet companies, writing and managing content and content providers. They might solicit, edit, and post articles to websites. Positions in publishing offer opportunities for master's degree holders with interests in writing and the ability to think critically and solve problems effectively. More advanced positions in publishing are held by doctoral degree holders and master's degree recipients with experience in the field (Exercise 10.4).

EXERCISE 10.4
INTERESTING CAREERS IN PSYCHOLOGICAL SCIENCE

The American Psychological Association has amassed a collection of articles by psychologists who describe their careers in a wide range of settings. Visit the APA page "Interesting Careers in Psychological Science" (http://www.apa.org/science/resources/careers/) and choose a specific career.

1. Describe the psychologist's position. What is his or her job? What duties does the job entail?

2. What experience and education led the author to enter this career?

3. What advice do you glean from the article?

In summary, there are many career opportunities for graduate degree holders in psychology. Graduate-level careers span a range of career settings, not simply practice settings. Graduate education translates into more advanced supervisory and leadership roles in business, health care, academic, and other settings, as well as higher salaries. The master's degree provides specific advantages in terms of cost, time to degree, and availability compared with the doctoral degree. Master's-level professionals engage in many of the same activities and are employed in the same places as doctoral-level professionals. The doctoral degree, however, offers distinct advantages in academic settings and the ability to use the term *psychologist*. Which degree is right for you depends on your career goals. Consider the careers in this chapter as a starting point for your research, and take an active role in pursuing the information you need to make responsible decisions that will meet your specific needs and desires. Remember, however, that the most successful graduates are those who take the reins on their professional development, are open to change, and are not afraid to explore new and nontraditional avenues.

REFLECTION PROMPTS

What Education Do You Require?

Look through your entries written to date. Considering all that you've learned about yourself, what type of career would make you happy? Now consider the information in this chapter. Will a graduate degree help you to achieve your goals? Be honest with yourself.

Comparing Jobs Across Degrees

Choose an area of psychology that interests you and brainstorm two to three jobs that fall within that content area. Identify jobs for bachelor's, master's, and doctoral degree recipients. How do the jobs and types of tasks change with the level of education? What do you think about each of these options?

Other Applications

Imagine that you went to graduate school and earned a doctoral degree in psychology, but you will not practice therapy. What would you do? What activities appeal to you, aside from therapy?

Considering Fields

Choose two or three psychology subfields. What is most interesting about the subfield? What are the drawbacks? Identify two career options for each. How well do these careers fit your interests and skills? Can you see yourself working in each? Why or why not?

11

Applying to Graduate School in Psychology

(Continued)

Chapter Outline	

Choose a Psychology Subfield
Gather Information on
    Graduate Programs
Evaluate Graduate Programs
    Department Emphasis
    and Program
    Philosophy
    Program Quality
    Accreditation	

The Application
    Graduate Record Exam:
      General Test
    GRE Psychology Test
    Admissions Essay
      Essay Topics
      Content: What to
        Include in Your Essay
      Writing as Process
    Curriculum Vitae
    Letters of Recommendation
      Who Should You Ask?
      Help Your Referees
      Confidentiality
    What Do Graduate Admissions
    Committees Look For?
	*Exercise 11.3: Your Personal Timeline
	for Applying to Graduate School*
	Exercise 11.4: Admissions Essay Prep
	Exercise 11.5: Create Your CV

The Interview
    Interview Prep
    Skype Interviews
Application Outcomes
    Wait-list
    Acceptance
    Dealing With Rejection	

Most graduates find that the bachelor's degree in psychology is the foundation for building a successful career. Some students, however, seek to enroll in graduate study in order to pursue the careers discussed in Chapter 10. If you think graduate school may be in your future, plan ahead because graduate admissions are very competitive. About 50% of applicants gain admission to master's programs and only about 13% to doctoral programs in psychology (Michalski, Cope, & Fowler, 2017). In this chapter we discuss the nature of graduate school, the application process, and how to compile a successful application to graduate school.

What Is Graduate School Like?

So what exactly do you do in graduate school? Do you know what to expect? Most new graduate students find that grad school is strikingly different from undergrad because coursework is only one way in which they spend their time. Moreover, classes themselves are different. They are smaller and instruction tends to be student-centered, emphasizing student-generated discussion about primary source readings. Expect fewer tests, many more papers, and a heavy reading load. The reading lists for some classes may seem impossibly long. Classes are a large component of master's programs and the first couple of years of doctoral programs. But graduate school entails more than completing a series of classes. The purpose of graduate school is to develop a professional understanding of your discipline through independent reading and study; classes do not fit that bill.

Most of what you learn in graduate school will not come from classes, but from other activities such as doing research and, in practice-oriented fields, clinical activities. In fact, in grad school, class grades and your grade point average (GPA) are much less important than your research. You'll work closely with a faculty member on his or her research. As an apprentice, you'll learn how to define research problems, design and carry out research projects to test your hypotheses, and disseminate your results. At the doctoral level, the end goal is to become an independent scholar and design your own research program. The extent to which students engage in research varies by field, degree, and program.

Graduate programs in applied fields, such as clinical, counseling, and school psychology, include training in the clinical skills that will permit graduates to practice psychology. Coursework emphasizes theory and assessment techniques. Students learn how to practice psychology through a series of clinical experiences that begin with observing an experienced therapist. Through supervised experiences, graduate students begin to deliver therapy and assessments to individuals and groups. Students are supervised by licensed psychologists (often faculty), are videotaped, and may be observed behind a two-way mirror. The amount of clinical training students obtain depends on the program and degree. Students in PsyD programs and others that emphasize practice will receive more supervision and training in clinical skills than will students in research-oriented PhD programs (see Chapter 1 and later in this chapter for more on PhD and PsyD degrees). Graduate students in the applied fields of clinical, counseling, and school psychology acquire hundreds of hours of supervised experience.

Some graduate students, especially those in programs that prepare students for academic careers, obtain experience teaching college classes. Teaching experience usually first comes in the form of teaching assistantships, in which graduate students assist an instructor by leading discussion sections, holding tutoring sessions, participating in grading, and presenting some lectures. More experienced graduate students may be instructors responsible for an entire course. Some graduate students have the opportunity to take a course or workshop that provides training in teaching skills. Others, unfortunately, learn "on the job." Not all students obtain teaching experience in graduate school.

Advancing through graduate school typically requires completing one or more comprehensive exams that test students' mastery of the field. Master's students may complete comprehensive exams in order to graduate, although exams are not required in every program. Doctoral students will complete at least one set of comprehensive exams in order to continue their studies. In some programs, students take a set of comprehensive exams at the end of the first year to receive a master's degree and then another set after completing all coursework (such as at the end of the third year) to progress to doctoral candidate status. Doctoral candidates have completed all of the academic requirements to earn a doctoral degree, except for the dissertation.

Once a graduate student earns doctoral candidate status, he or she may formally begin the dissertation. A dissertation represents the culmination of doctoral study in which a student constructs a project that will contribute new knowledge to the field, demonstrating significant independent scholarship that advances the field. Students must select a dissertation committee, typically four or five faculty who will advise and judge the dissertation. They select a topic and work closely with a mentor who provides guidance and feedback. The student constructs a proposal that must be presented to the dissertation committee and defended. Once the proposal is accepted by the dissertation committee, students are free to begin their research study. Graduate students then spend months or even years collecting, analyzing, interpreting, and writing about their data. The dissertation culminates in a defense, in which students present their research to their dissertation committee, answer questions, and support the validity of their work. If all goes well, students walk away from the meeting with a new title (Doctor) and letters behind their name (PhD or PsyD). Master's students usually complete a similar process and write a thesis. The thesis must be a significant project that demonstrates mastery and application of the material, but it typically is not required to make original contributions to the field, entails fewer requirements, and takes less time.

It's easy to see that graduate study entails much more than coursework, and all of these activities take time. The most successful students treat graduate school as a full-time job, one that doesn't fit the typical 9-to-5 schedule. Many students find that their work spills over into evenings and weekends, especially when they face a deadline. This is because graduate study is not just a matter of taking classes; it's about becoming a professional. In graduate school you will be socialized into your profession. In other words, you will learn the norms and values of your subfield of psychology and will learn to think like a scientist, educator, practitioner, or all of these roles.

Should You Go to Graduate School?

Graduate study isn't the right choice for everyone. Is it right for you? Only you can answer that question. Review Chapter 2 and reflect on your interests, goals, dreams, and abilities. Then consider the following questions in Exercise 11.1.

EXERCISE 11.1
IS GRADUATE SCHOOL FOR YOU?

Answer the following questions *honestly* (that's the hard part!).

1. Are you tired of studying?
2. Do you like to write papers?
3. Do you hope to never take another statistics course?
4. Are you comfortable with uncertainty?
5. Do you dislike library and database research?
6. Do you like to read psychology books or articles even if they are not assigned?
7. Do you put off studying for tests or writing papers?
8. Are you able to earn very little income for the next 2 to 7 years?
9. Are you sick of school?
10. Do you enjoy reading and studying?
11. Do you prefer group projects rather than individual papers?
12. Will you give up a social opportunity (like a party) to study for a test or to finish a paper?
13. Are your grades mainly Bs or lower?
14. Do you keep up with current research in psychology?
15. Are you unsure of what you can do with your undergraduate degree in psychology?
16. Are you driven to learn more about human behavior?
17. Do you like to keep up with your friends who have the latest technology or go to the best restaurants, clubs, and concerts?
18. Can you concentrate and study for hours at a time?
19. Are there other careers aside from psychology that you'd like to explore?
20. Did you earn a high grade in statistics?
21. Do you frequently hand assignments in late or forget to do them?
22. Do you enjoy conducting research?

Scoring: Assign 1 point for each even item to which you answered yes and 1 point for each odd item to which you answered no. Sum the points to obtain a total score. Higher scores indicate a greater potential for graduate study.

Sources: Adapted from Appleby (1997), Fretz (1976), and Keith-Spiegel and Wiederman (2000).

Prompt

How did you score? Given your score, how well do you think your characteristics and habits match those of successful graduate students? Is graduate study a realistic match to your characteristics? Why or why not?

At some point during college, most undergraduate students at least briefly consider attending graduate school, but it isn't the right choice for everyone. As we have discussed, most people with bachelor's degrees in psychology enter the workforce immediately after graduation. Only about 20% to 25% of new bachelor's degree recipients enter graduate school, but that figure rises to 43% over the course of their careers (Doran, Kraha, Marks, Ameen, & El-Ghoroury, 2016).

Is Graduate Study Needed?

Do you know why you want to go to grad school? What are your career goals? What are your reasons for choosing a master's or doctoral degree? If you've chosen a master's degree, why did you choose it over a doctoral degree? Why a doctoral degree over a master's? Think ahead to a few years after having earned your degree. What are you doing? Will you enjoy your career after graduation?

Do you need to attend graduate school to achieve your goals? Some people attend graduate school for the love of learning, and others seek career advancement. Can you fulfill your goals with your bachelor's degree? Or is a master's degree needed? Are there alternative ways of achieving your goals? Be honest with yourself. As we've discussed in prior chapters, if you would like to work with people, there are lots of alternatives to a doctoral degree in psychology (and some are preferable for reasons of time and expense). If you decide to attend graduate school, choose the level of education, whether master's or doctoral degree, that offers the training and coursework to prepare you for the career to which you aspire.

Are you considering grad school for the right reasons? Some students decide to apply to graduate school to avoid job hunting in a challenging market. Some students focus on status or the desire to be called "Doctor." Others believe that a graduate degree equates to a high salary (as we discussed in Chapter 10, salaries vary dramatically). These reasons are not likely to sustain you through the years it takes to earn a degree and, if you complete the degree, may lead to disappointment.

Can You Afford Graduate School?

Without a doubt, higher education is expensive, and most people find that graduate study typically is more expensive than their undergraduate degrees. As we discussed in Chapter 10, the 2015–2016 median annual graduate school tuition was about $18,000 ($11,000 for public institutions and $24,000 for private institutions) (National Center for Education Statistics, 2017a). Room and board, books, supplies, and fees are additional expenditures.

One of the costs that many students don't consider is the loss of income from full-time employment. Many graduate programs frown on outside employment. Doctoral programs in particular often forbid it. Even if holding a job is permitted, most full-time graduate students find that employment is more than they can handle. Part-time students, on the other hand, often can find some time to work, but full-time employment will likely pose great stress to their studies and personal lives. Dealing with the loss of income, or delay of earning an income, is often easier for students who attend graduate school right out of college, but this is an expense related to graduate study that you should consider. For example, a student who chooses a 4-year graduate program over a full-time job with a salary of $40,000 per year forfeits $160,000 of earned income to attend graduate school.

How do students fund graduate school? Funding varies with type of degree and program. Doctoral students are much more likely to obtain department funding for graduate study, typically in the form of research and teaching assistantships, which usually pay for tuition and a small stipend. Most students who earn a stipend will still have to adjust their standard of living and likely borrow money to cover living expenses. Research assistants are hired by a professor to work alongside him or her and advance research. Research assistants are usually funded by a professor's grant. Therefore, research assistantships are more common in graduate programs where faculty win grants to conduct research. Doctoral programs that emphasize professional, applied training for practitioners are less likely to offer funding. Teaching assistants are hired to help professors teach their classes. They are more common in universities that have large classes, and the funding usually comes from the department or university. Research and teaching assistantships are less common in master's programs.

The majority of students carry some debt after graduation. Given that research assistantships and grant funding are more common in research-oriented graduate programs, it should not be surprising that doctoral recipients in the practice subfields are more likely to report debt after graduation than are those in the research subfields. A recent study of early career psychologists revealed that PsyD recipients are most likely to carry debt (91%), compared with 77% of PhD recipients in the practice fields and 63% of PhD recipients in research fields (Doran et al., 2016). PsyD recipients carried the most debt ($146,000, on average), followed by PhD practitioners ($80,000) and PhD academics and researchers ($63,000). Despite these differences in debt, this sample of about 600 early career psychologists earned similar starting salaries ($62,000 for PsyD practitioners, $65,000 for PhD practitioners, and $63,000 for PhD researchers). These findings are in line with prior work showing that among 2009 doctoral recipients in psychology, the median level of debt for those in the practice subfields was more than double that for those in the research subfields, with PsyD recipients owing nearly twice as much as PhD clinicians (Michalski, Kohout, Wicherski, & Hart, 2011). Whether to pursue graduate study is a decision with lifelong financial repercussions.

Are You Prepared for the Academic Demands of Graduate Study?

Do you have good grades? A high GPA is one of the prerequisites for admission to graduate school, but academic expectations remain high in graduate school. Generally, it is expected that students will maintain at least a 3.0 average during graduate school. Many programs deny funding to students with less than a 3.33 average.

Do you like to write? Do you enjoy writing term papers? How do you feel about conducting library research? Regardless of the program, you will spend a lot of your time reading and will write many papers. Expect instructors to list a maximum length for papers rather than the minimum often assigned in undergraduate courses.

Do you have good academic habits? Can you juggle multiple tasks, projects, and papers? Can you manage time effectively? Look back over your responses to the assessments in Chapter 2. What did they reveal about your academic habits? Are your habits suited for graduate study? Do you enjoy studying and the school environment? Expect your academic work to be a full-time job. You'll study for several hours at a time, multiple times per week. The information that you learn will build on itself and be retained for years.

Are you interested in psychology? At first this may seem like a silly question. Of course you're interested. It's your major, right? Do you enjoy reading psychology books and journals outside of class? Do you read studies that aren't required? Are you committed to studying psychology, or do other fields remain career possibilities? Graduate study immerses you in psychology research. You likely won't have time or energy to study other fields.

Are you prepared to take graduate-level statistics courses? How well did you perform in your undergraduate statistics course? If you are weak in math, you may not be able to complete the basic statistical requirements for psychology. If you like math and statistics and performed well in these courses (for example, with grades of B or higher), then you will be better able to handle graduate-level statistics. Before you rule out graduate school based on the statistics requirements, do a little soul-searching. Are your abilities in math and statistics truly weak, or do you just think so? Remember from Chapter 5 that our beliefs about our abilities are powerful influences on our performance. Perhaps if you adjust your studying strategies or devote more time to statistics, you'll find that you're better at statistics than you think.

Do you enjoy conducting research? All graduate programs involve at least some research. Research-oriented programs, especially PhD programs, require extensive research, including preparing literature reviews, designing studies, and collecting, analyzing, and interpreting data and then writing papers to disseminate the results. Students can expect to juggle several projects as they work on their advisor's research as well as design their own research studies.

Are You Prepared for the Personal Demands of Graduate Study?

Are you willing to take on a heavy workload for many years to earn the degree? Are you willing to put much of your personal life on hold? Incur debt? This is a personal decision. Consider the following questions.

Are you motivated? Do you have a strong desire to learn? Are you a self-starter? Graduate school entails a greater personal commitment than undergrad. Gone are the days of skipping classes, waiting until the last minute to write papers, and late-night partying. Excelling in college may have come easily but you likely will find graduate school to be quite different. You'll be surrounded by students who performed just as well and even better than you did in college. The bar is set much higher, and you'll work harder and more consistently than ever before. Successful graduate students are self-reliant, disciplined, committed, and intellectually curious.

Can you tolerate ambiguity? Can you manage uncertainty? The nature of knowledge is often uncertain. Research uncovers new information that can challenge existing views. Sometimes the results of research are not clear. Often psychologists must make treatment decisions with incomplete information. Can you live with ambiguity? Can you progress through several years of education without knowing your ultimate career?

Do you have strong interpersonal skills? Practicing psychologists must have good communication and interpersonal skills. Researchers also need the skills to interact with many people. Graduate students will interact with others, professors, staff, and students. Can you receive and respond appropriately to critical feedback? Can you give constructive criticism? Graduate students may supervise other students in conducting research. The ability to work with others is essential to your success. Successful graduate students are socially skilled, are able to work well with others, and are good at managing their own emotions.

Do you have good self-management skills? Are you organized? Can you concentrate your attention at will? Do you manage your time well? Can you delay gratification, such as put off socializing until after a paper is complete?

Speak with professors and graduate students to get a better idea of what's involved in graduate study. Most first-year graduate students are overwhelmed and remark that they had no idea of what they were getting into. Consider this first-year student's perspective:

> As an undergraduate, I wish I had spoken with someone about what graduate school is really like. Grad school requires a higher level of dedication, time, professionalism, and maturity. I'm working nonstop. Successful grad students study or work on research, 8 hours per day 6 to 7 days per week. Professors just expect you to read it and get it. Reading lists are long and you're expected to understand and discuss it intelligently. It's a whole other world from the innocence of undergraduate work. It's a ton of work and I feel like I'm in over my head a lot of the time, but I'm glad I'm here.

Does all of this sound overwhelming? Nearly everyone feels that way at some point. This information is not meant to dissuade you or change your mind; rather, it aims to provide a more realistic picture of what attending graduate school really entails. Going to graduate school affects the rest of your life. There are both pros and cons to continuing your education. Seek information from multiple sources, such as this book, the career counseling center, graduate students, professors, and your family. Take your time with the decision. More importantly, trust your judgment and have faith that you'll make the choice that's best for you.

Selecting Graduate Programs

Deciding to pursue graduate study in psychology is the first of many decisions that you'll make. You'll confront decisions about the type of degree, training models, and then among programs.

Decide Among Training Models and Degrees

Graduate programs in psychology follow one of three basic models of training. Choose a program whose model best fits with your interests, because most psychologists engage in the same type of activities that they experienced in their graduate program of study.

Research–Scientist Model (PhD)

Programs that follow a research-scientist model focus on molding students into scholars who will make new discoveries and advance the knowledge in their field. From a historical perspective, this was the first training model to emerge because it characterizes the emphasis of the PhD, or doctor of philosophy degree. Most of your college professors hold this degree; it is conferred in nearly all academic fields. The PhD in psychology provides training in experimental methods, methodological skill, and a background in a particular specialty area (such as cognitive or social psychology). Individuals trained in the research-scientist model conduct original research, teach, and write about their research findings, typically in the core academic areas of psychology such as experimental, social and personality, quantitative, physiological, and developmental psychology. PhD recipients tend to be employed as researchers or college and university professors and some work as consultants or conduct research for the government or corporations.

Scientist–Practitioner Model (PhD)

Programs adopting the scientist-practitioner model seek to train scholars who integrate their research training with human service. Graduates engage in practice activities and conduct basic and applied research. This model is commonly found in PhD programs in clinical, counseling, school, and industrial-organizational psychology. Similar to the research-scientist model, students trained in the scientist-practitioner model receive training in research and methodology, but they take more courses in applied areas and complete more internships and practica than do students trained in the research-scientist model. Graduates trained in the scientist-practitioner model may practice in hospitals, clinics, mental health centers, and private practices; they may teach in colleges and universities; and they may work in industry and government settings. The extent to which a particular psychologist engages in practice and research depends on his or her job setting and commitment to research; many practicing clinicians do little to no research.

Professional Psychologist–Practitioner Model (PsyD)

Graduate programs that adopt the professional psychologist-practitioner model train students to provide psychological services and award the PsyD, a practitioner degree that emphasizes clinical training or the practitioner model of training. The PsyD and the practitioner model of training place greater emphasis on clinical practice than that in the scientist-practitioner model, and much less emphasis on research. PsyD programs train students to be consumers of research rather than producers of it.

PsyD programs tend to be larger than PhD programs and accept more students, so your chances of acceptance are much higher. For example, acceptance rates for PhD programs in clinical psychology fall somewhere between 9% and 13% compared with about 30% of PsyD programs (Kohout & Wicherski, 2010; Michalski et al., 2017). The PsyD degree often is offered at private or professional schools and is generally more expensive than a PhD. Most funding for PhD students comes from faculty research grants. Because little research is conducted in PsyD programs, there are fewer opportunities for funding. PsyD students earn their degrees a little quicker yet they usually graduate with more debt than do PhD students.

Practice-oriented students often find the curricula of professional programs to be better aligned with their own interests and career aspirations than those of traditional scientist-practitioner programs. Some psychologists are skeptical about the PsyD because acceptance rates are high, quality varies, students may have difficulty obtaining American Psychological Association (APA)–accredited internships (more on APA accreditation later in this chapter), and PsyD students graduate with substantially more debt (on average, 80% more) than PhD students (McFall, 2006). If you're interested in practicing psychology and do not want to teach in a university setting or conduct research, the PsyD might be for you. However, a master's degree in a helping field can prepare you to engage in many of the same activities—in fewer years and, usually, with less debt. Graduates from professional schools are at a disadvantage when they apply for positions in research or academic settings. Understand your interests, abilities, and professional goals in order to choose a training model and degree that will prepare you for the career you desire.

Choose a Psychology Subfield

What will you specialize in? This is a crucial question. Unlike college in which you might major in psychology (a general degree), graduate school entails specializing in a particular area of psychology. Carefully consider your area of specialization (e.g., clinical, experimental, developmental, school, and others) because that will determine the schools and programs to which you'll apply as well as your likelihood of gaining admission to a program.

How do you choose? Examine your responses to the assessments in this book as well as your reflective writing. Consider your interests. Do you want to work with people? Work in a laboratory? Teach college? Conduct research? What were your favorite classes in college? On what topics have you written term papers? Seek advice from professors in your department, especially from those in the areas in which you wish to specialize. Chapter 1 notes the major specialty areas of psychology. Before you can apply to graduate school, you must choose an area in which to specialize. Take your time in making this decision because it will shape your education and career.

Gather Information on Graduate Programs

Once you have a specialty area(s) in mind, it's time to gather program information. How do you get information about programs? Google searches are a good start but you should use a variety of resources. For decades students relied on a heavy set of educational guidebooks, known as the *Peterson's Guide*, which listed graduate programs in every field, organized alphabetically by university. It was available in the reference section of the library and required strength to lift, good eyesight to read the tiny print, and stamina to leaf through and record the information in one or two library sessions. Fortunately, the days of relying on a printed copy of the *Peterson's Guide* are gone, as it's available online (http://www.petersons.com/graduate-schools.aspx). You can search by school or subject area. Each graduate program listing includes a great deal of information, such as an overview of the program, degrees awarded, number of full- and part-time students, admissions statistics, acceptance rate, tuition and fees, and more.

One of the best sources of information about graduate programs is the APA *Graduate Study in Psychology*. Updated annually, this book includes information on every psychology graduate program in the United States and Canada. Organized alphabetically by state and by school, this guide provides the following information: criteria for admission, program emphasis, number of faculty, enrollments, and additional admissions information, including the average GPA and Graduate Record Exam (GRE) scores for each school. The online version is searchable and contains the most up-to-date information about programs. A 3-month subscription to the database costs about $20. (Visit http://www.apa.org/pubs/databases/gradstudy/ for more information.)

Once you have a list of programs, your next step is to gather more detailed information. Visit the school's website to review the program, degrees, coursework, research and applied opportunities, and faculty. Most graduate programs include admissions statistics such as the acceptance rate and average GRE scores. Before you spend a great deal of time gathering information about graduate programs, reflect on your priorities (Exercise 11.2). What field are you interested in? Are you interested more in research or practice? Are there geographic restrictions on where you live?

EXERCISE 11.2
LEARNING ABOUT GRADUATE PROGRAMS

This exercise will help you begin to consider graduate programs.

1. Identify your priorities with regard to graduate study. Identify a field, degree, and, if relevant, a geographic location.

2. Search for graduate programs in your chosen field. List the program, department and university, specialization, degree, and URL for 10 to 12 graduate programs.

3. Brainstorm the factors that you will consider in making selections among graduate programs. How will you make choices?

4. Review the websites for the graduate programs that you have selected. Categorize them into programs that are a good fit to your criteria, those that match some criteria, and those that match few criteria.

5. Share your observations about this process.

Evaluate Graduate Programs

All too often, students state that they want to go to graduate school "anywhere I'm accepted." You're worth more than this. It's understandable that you'd like to get into graduate school, but it's also important to be an educated consumer and look for a program that *you* want, not just one that accepts you. The admissions committee evaluates you as a potential student, but you should evaluate the program to see whether it fits your needs. Is it someplace where you can spend the next few years? Take the time to carefully review and evaluate each graduate program. As you read the information about programs, you'll notice that there are differences among departments in goals, program philosophies, theoretical orientations, facilities, and resources. What are you looking for as you peruse the volumes of information obtained through your research? Basically you're looking to see how well each program matches your goals and aspirations—the "fit" between you and the graduate program. How do you determine fit? As you examine a graduate program, consider the areas listed in the following sections.

Department Emphasis and Program Philosophy

What are the program goals? Do they fit with your own? Is the department heavily research oriented, or is it more theoretical or applied? What's the program's theoretical orientation (e.g., cognitive-behavioral, psychoanalytic)?

Is the program oriented toward producing researchers? Is it heavily oriented toward theory? Are theory and practice united? Where does the program fall on the scientist-practitioner continuum? Consider the following:

1. **Faculty research interests and publications.** Do you share interests with any of the faculty? Do the faculty publish often and in refereed journals? Google faculty members to view their webpages. Use Google Scholar or PsycINFO to find their publications.

2. **Information about students and graduates.** Where do graduates go? Do they find jobs in academia, practice, or the "real world"? Do students present at conferences or publish in journals?

3. **Course offerings.** Look over the program course book and requirements to get a feel of what courses you'll take and what you'll learn. This gives you a chance to see some of the program's inner workings, so that you're not surprised once you're admitted.

4. **Teaching goals and style.** Can you find any information about how classes are run? Look at the website. Do faculty have their own webpages? Do any of them describe classes or provide resources for students? Try to find out what it's like to be a student in the program. Does it appear to be a student-oriented program?

Program Quality

Program quality is difficult to access because some factors are somewhat subjective. Here are some considerations in evaluating program quality.

1. **Attrition.** What is the attrition, or dropout, rate? Some programs select only a handful of the top students and lose a few of them; other programs take in more students than they can effectively manage and lose many of them. Some programs use comprehensive exams to weed out students.

2. **Time to completion.** What is the average time to completion of the degree? In psychology, 5 to 7 years is a normal range. If a program's average time to completion is close to 7 years or beyond, you should examine it more closely to determine why.

3. **Logistical resources.** Are there adequate computer facilities, library resources, money for travel to conferences, and other forms of support?

4. **Financial support.** Are research and teaching assistantships used to fund students? Does it appear to be a quality program? To help you evaluate the overall quality of the program, Table 11.1 presents some characteristics of quality PhD programs.

TABLE 11.1 ● Checklist: Characteristics of a Quality PhD Program

❑ Program faculty work closely with students

❑ Faculty regularly publish in their field and make presentations at conferences at the regional, state, national, and international levels

❑ Faculty publish with students and graduates

❑ Program is accredited by APA (if clinical, counseling, or school)

❑ Program emphasizes research productivity

❑ Program faculty are tenured or tenure track

❑ Department is large enough to have faculty who represent the major areas in psychology

❑ Program is able to support or partially support students through assistantships and other means

❑ Program has adequate facilities for research and practica

Sources: Buskist and Sherburne (1996) and Keith-Spiegel and Wiederman (2000).

In addition to program quality, consider the prestige of the department. How much does prestige matter? That depends on what you hope to do with your degree. In academia there generally is a correlation between departmental stature and job quality. Doctoral recipients from prestigious departments are more likely to land prestigious jobs (e.g., at research institutions) than are those from less distinguished institutions. Advisors and mentors in prestigious graduate departments often have excellent reputations and important connections that can help you advance in your career. Powerful mentors can write persuasive letters of recommendation, lend authority to student papers, and pull strings because their old classmates, friends, and former students often hold prestigious positions. However, you should also note that powerful mentors often are very busy, so you may have little direct contact with them.

Accreditation

Many clinical, counseling, and school psychology programs advertise that they are APA accredited. What does that mean? Recall that the APA is a national association of psychologists. One of APA's many activities is to evaluate practice-oriented psychology programs to ensure that the educational criteria meet the public's needs. APA accredits doctoral programs in the practice areas of clinical, school, counseling, and combined professional-scientific psychology (for example, some programs in applied developmental psychology seek accreditation).

In order to be accredited, a program must meet the minimum standards for clinical training established by APA. The criteria include faculty credentials, specific coursework, eligibility for state licensure, adequate research and clinical opportunities, and internships for clinical and counseling students. A site visit confirms that these requirements are met, and they must be maintained over time. If you are applying to clinical, counseling, or school programs, it is in your best interest to be sure that they are accredited because a degree from an APA-approved program carries more weight; students from accredited programs are more successful in competing for clinical internships and jobs. In fact, many states *require* applicants to have earned doctoral degrees from APA programs in order to apply for licensure. Accredited programs are stringent and meet the requirements for state licensure, and students in accredited programs are more likely to obtain an internship (which is needed for licensure) and obtain employment more easily than those who enroll in programs that are not accredited.

PRACTICAL TIP
RESEARCH-BASED PROGRAMS

The American Psychological Association accredits programs that train students to be *practitioners*. Programs in research (nonpractice) areas, such as experimental and social psychology, are *not* part of the APA accreditation program. Accreditation applies *only* to programs that train students to be practicing psychologists. If you're applying to a research program, *do not* look for APA accreditation.

The Application

Once you have narrowed your choice of programs, you're ready to begin the application. Apply to enough programs to have a reasonable chance of being accepted, given your credentials. There is a great deal of competition for entry into doctoral programs in psychology. Plan on applying to 6 to 10 programs and possibly more if you're applying to particularly selective programs (especially in clinical psychology). This can quickly become expensive; application fees are over $50 for most programs. In addition to investing money, plan on investing a significant amount of time on each application.

Most graduate programs use online applications. The process varies but usually you will create a login on the school's website. The online application will include forms for entering your personal information as well as information for all of the components described in the following section. Table 11.2 provides a timetable for applying to graduate school, and Exercise 11.3 shows you how to construct your personal timeline. Now, let's examine the typical components of a graduate application.

TABLE 11.2 ● Timeline for Preparing for Graduate School

First Year

❑ Complete your general education mathematics requirements.

❑ Begin taking the required methodology and statistics courses in psychology.

❑ Take a class in writing.

❑ Take several lower-level psychology classes to learn about the field.

❑ Get to know at least one professor outside of class.

❑ Participate in department activities (e.g., attend speaker presentations, participate in the psychology club).

Second Year

❑ Take a least one more math and science course beyond the general requirements.

❑ Learn about the research interests of the faculty and identify potential mentors.

❑ Ask a faculty member if you can help with his or her research.

❑ Attend a regional psychology conference.

❑ If you are interested in the clinical, counseling, or school areas of psychology, seek volunteer experiences.

❑ Join Psi Chi and get involved.

❑ Get to know at least one other professor outside of class.

❑ Ask professors for their opinions on what courses and other experiences you should obtain to prepare for graduate school.

Third Year

❑ Participate in an independent research project with a faculty member.

❑ If you are interested in the clinical or counseling areas of psychology, seek an internship.

❑ Attend a psychology conference.

❑ Get to know at least one other professor outside of class.

❑ Study for the Graduate Record Exam (GRE).

❑ Explore graduate programs.

❑ Study for the Psychology GRE. Take it either in April of your third year or October of your fourth year.

Summer Prior to Fourth Year

❑ Take the GRE.

❑ If you have not yet taken it, study for the Psychology GRE.

(Continued)

TABLE 11.2 ● (Continued)

❑ Draft your curriculum vitae (CV).

❑ Review your transcript for errors.

❑ Narrow your list of graduate programs.

❑ Begin drafting your admissions essay.

Fourth Year: September

❑ Share your list of graduate programs with faculty, ask for input, and ask them if they will write recommendation letters when the time comes (bring your CV).

❑ Prepare your admissions essay and get feedback.

❑ Finalize your list of graduate programs.

❑ Begin online applications.

❑ Take the GRE Psychology Test, if you have not already.

Fourth Year: October

❑ Take the GRE Psychology Test, if you have not already.

❑ Formally request recommendation letters from faculty.

❑ Complete online applications.

Fourth Year: November

❑ Finalize your applications (pay attention to deadlines, as they may come as early as November and as late as March).

❑ Check back with professors and thank them for writing your recommendations.

EXERCISE 11.3
YOUR PERSONAL TIMELINE FOR APPLYING TO GRADUATE SCHOOL

Construct your personal timeline for applying to graduate school. Table 11.2 provides a generalized timeline. Consider your own situation.

1. How much time do you have to prepare? Are you a sophomore, junior, or senior?

2. How far along are you in completing required coursework, especially methodology and statistics requirements? What additional coursework do you need to become competitive?

3. Map out your plan for coursework for each semester over the next 2 years. What will you take in the fall? What will you take in the spring?

4. What out-of-class practical experiences do you need? Will you seek an internship? If so, where does it fall in your 2-year plan? Planning ahead is especially important if internships are awarded competitively so that you can be prepared.

5. What is your plan for obtaining research experience? Have you gotten to know professors? Have you worked with them on their research? Determine how to obtain these experiences and how to eventually conduct independent research with a professor.

6. Flesh out your 2-year plan. When do you plan to apply to graduate school? Will you carry out your plan in time to apply? If you have extra time, how will you spend it? (I suggest on more research!)

Graduate Record Exam: General Test

The GRE is a standardized test that all applicants to graduate programs must complete. The GRE General Test is an aptitude test that is administered by computer and measures a variety of skills, acquired over the high school and college years, that are thought to predict success in graduate school. The GRE is only one of several criteria that graduate schools use to evaluate your application, but it is one of the most important. This is particularly true if your college GPA is not as high as you'd like. Exceptional GRE scores can open up new opportunities for grad school. Low GRE scores can remove your application from the admissions pool.

The GRE General Test yields three scores: verbal ability, quantitative ability, and analytical ability. As shown in Table 11.3, the verbal section assesses your ability to understand and analyze written material. The quantitative section tests basic math skills and your ability to understand and apply quantitative skills to solve problems. The analytical writing section examines critical thinking and analytical writing skills. It examines your ability to explain and support complex ideas, and engage in focused and coherent discussion and analysis of arguments. The GRE General Test takes nearly 4 hours to complete, plus time for breaks and reading instructions.

The GRE General Test is administered by computer year-round. Plan to take the GRE well in advance of application due dates. Generally you should take it in the spring or summer before you apply to grad school. Remember that it may take a few weeks for scores to be reported to schools. If you take the GRE too late in the fall, the scores may not arrive in time for your application to be considered. Also, you will want to have enough time to retake it if necessary. You can always retake the GRE, but remember that you're allowed to take it only once every 21 days per calendar month, up to five times in 12 months.

TABLE 11.3 ● Overview of the Graduate Record Exam

GRE Verbal Section

Overview	You will be asked to read passages and analyze information obtained from your reading, analyze sentences and the relationships among component parts of sentences, as well as recognize relationships between words and concepts within written material. This section measures your ability to analyze and evaluate written material and synthesize information obtained from it, analyze relationships among component parts of sentences and recognize relationships among words and concepts.
Types of questions	**Reading comprehension** questions measure your ability to read analytically, identify the main idea, identify explicitly stated information, identify implied ideas, apply the author's ideas to other situations, identify the author's logic or persuasive techniques, and identify the attitudinal tone of the passage.
	Text completion questions omit crucial words from short passages and ask the test taker to use the remaining information in the passage to select words or phrases to fill in the blanks and create a coherent, meaningful whole.
	Sentence equivalence questions consist of a single sentence with just one blank, and they ask you to find two choices that lead to a complete, coherent sentence while producing sentences that mean the same thing.

GRE Quantitative Section

Overview	The quantitative section does not require mathematic skills beyond the high school level. It measures problem-solving ability, focusing on basic concepts of arithmetic, algebra, geometry, and data analysis.
Types of questions	**Problem-solving** questions are word problems that assess your understanding of, and ability to apply, arithmetic, algebra, and geometry.
	Quantitative comparison questions ask you to compare two quantities, one in column a and one in column b. Your task is to determine if they are equal, if one is larger than the other, or if not enough information is presented to make the determination.
	Data analysis questions require use of basic descriptive statistics, the ability to interpret data in graphs and tables, and elementary probability. Questions emphasize the "ability to synthesize information, select appropriate data for answering a question, and to determine whether or not the data provided are sufficient to answer a given question" (GRE Bulletin, p. 8).
	Numeric entry questions. Rather than multiple choice, questions of this type ask you to enter the answer either as an integer or a decimal in an answer box.

GRE Analytical Writing Section	
Overview	The analytical writing section examines your ability to communicate complex ideas clearly and effectively, support your ideas, examine claims and supporting evidence, sustain a focused and coherent discussion, and effectively use the elements of standard written English.
Subsections	**Analyze an issue:** This task assesses your ability to think critically about a topic of general interest and to clearly express your thoughts about it in writing. Each issue statement makes a claim that you can discuss from various perspectives and apply to many different situations or conditions. The issue statement is followed by a set of specific instructions.
	Analyze an argument: This 30-minute task presents you with an argument. Your task is to critique the argument, assess its claims, and conclude whether it is reasoned.

If you retake the GRE, you have the option of sending all scores to graduate schools or scores only from a particular test date.

What score should you strive for? The verbal and quantitative subtests yield scores ranging from 130 to 170, in 1-point increments. Most graduate schools consider the verbal and quantitative sections to be particularly important in making decisions about applicants. The analytical writing section yields a score ranging from 0 to 6, in half-point increments. Among all test-takers from 2014 to 2017, the average GRE scores were 150 for Verbal, 153 for Quantitative, and 3.5 for Analytical Writing (Educational Testing Service, 2018). To note, students who score at the 60th percentile or below are not likely to gain admission to graduate school. The average GRE scores for incoming students are often listed on program webpages in addition to the APA *Guide to Graduate Study in Psychology*.

GRE Psychology Test

Many but not all doctoral programs require that applicants take the Psychology Test. The GRE Psychology Test consists of 205 questions that tap information from the core psychology courses required in most undergraduate programs. The questions are drawn from commonly offered courses at the undergraduate level and are designed to measure what an undergraduate psychology major who plans to attend graduate school should know about the field of psychology. Until recently, the Psychology Test yielded three scores: (1) a general score, (2) an experimental subscore, and (3) a social subscore.

In September 2017, the GRE Psychology Test was revised to yield a general score and the following six subscores (Educational Testing Service, 2017):

1. Biological (17% to 21% of the questions): sensation and perception, attention, physiological function, and cognitive and behavioral neuroscience.

2. Cognitive (17% to 24%): learning, conditioning, language, communication, memory, thinking, decision-making, and intelligence.

3. Social (12% to 14%): social cognition, attribution, beliefs, attitudes and behavior, conformity, persuasion, group processes, and cultural and gender issues.

4. Developmental (12% to 14%): physical and motor development, perception, cognition, language, learning, and social and emotional development.

5. Clinical (15% to 19%): personality and behavior, stress, conflict, coping, diagnostic systems, health psychology, neurophysiological factors, and the causes, development, and treatment of disorders.

6. Measurement/methodology/other (15% to 19%): history, industrial-organizational, educational, psychometrics, test construction, research designs, statistical procedures, scientific method, ethics and legal issues, and analysis and interpretation of findings.

The GRE Psychology Test is designed to sample a broad overview of topics in psychology. The best way to prepare is by studying an upper-level introductory psychology textbook. Ask a faculty member for guidance in selecting an appropriate textbook to use.

Unlike the General Test, the GRE Psychology Test is administered only by pencil and paper three times a year, typically in September, October, and April. Ideally, you should take the GRE Psychology Test in April so that you have time to retake it if needed. Scores are sent several weeks after the test date. If you are taking it as a senior, take it in September to allow enough time for scores to be reported. However, you will not receive your test scores early enough to retake it.

Although the GRE scores are an important part of your application, remember that graduate admissions committees consider many other factors. Many programs will accept students with lower GRE scores if they have strengths in other areas, such as research. How do you communicate your strengths to graduate admissions committees? Admissions essays and personal statements offer you an opportunity to speak directly to the committee.

Admissions Essay

The admissions essay, also known as a letter of intent or personal statement, is often the most difficult part of the application because the task is often ambiguous yet it is very important. Many programs simply ask applicants to describe their interests and career objectives. How do you address such a vague question? Don't get overwhelmed. The essay is your chance to present yourself as you would like to be viewed. The most important determinant of success is the degree to which you match the faculty and program. Faculty look for applicants who are interested in the program, share their research interests, and are prepared to engage in collaborative research or scholarship. Your essay is your chance to show your enthusiasm for the program but especially to highlight how your interests fit with particular faculty members. No matter the question, your job is to show that you're a good fit to the faculty and program. Know as much as you can about the program and faculty, and target your essay to one or two faculty with whom you'd like to work.

Essay Topics

Often programs give applicants a question or two to answer, or a specific topic on which to write. Keith-Spiegel and Wiederman (2000) have noted that there is a remarkable similarity among essay topics requested by graduate programs. Most questions posed by graduate programs fall into one of several categories:

- **Career plans.** What are your long-term career goals? Where do you see yourself 10 years from now?

- **General interest areas.** What academic or professional areas interest you?

- **Research experiences.** Discuss areas in which you might like to do research, research experiences you have had, or both. Describe your research interests.

- **Academic objectives.** Why are you undertaking graduate study? Describe how graduate training is necessary for your goals.

- **Clinical or other field experience.** Describe your clinical experience. How have your field experiences shaped your career goals?

- **Academic background and achievements.** Discuss your academic background.

- **Personal.** Is there anything in your background that you think would be relevant in our evaluation of applicants? Describe your life up to now: family, friends, home, school, work, and particularly those experiences most relevant to your interests in psychology and you. Write an autobiographical sketch.

- **Personal and professional development.** Describe your values and your approach to life.

Although there are many similarities among essay topics, you should not write a generic essay. Tailor your essay to the specific question and the program. Be sure to save each version of your essay. Many essays ask the applicant to discuss how the program or faculty matches his or her individual needs. This means that you must demonstrate that you have researched the program and are familiar with its faculty and curriculum. Explain how the specific program will prepare you for the career you desire, offering clear examples. While writing your essay, remember that your goal is to come across as someone with an interest in the specific program and the potential to succeed.

Content: What to Include in Your Essay

The admissions essay is sometimes called a personal statement, but don't take that term literally. Do not get *too personal*. The essay is a professional essay, not a place to discuss your own mental health, experiences with therapy, or heartaches. Instead explain the experiences that have prepared you for graduate school and have led to your decision to apply to graduate school. Use concrete examples whenever possible. Your essay should include at least these four components: your previous research experience, research interests, relevant experience, and career goals (Bottoms & Nysse, 1999).

Discuss the details of your involvement with research. Who supervised the work? Was the research part of a course requirement, for class credit, or as an independent study? Discuss the purpose of the research, including the theory, method, and results. Explain your role. Rather than merely explaining that you entered data for Dr. Smith's research study, for example, show that you have worked to understand the purpose of the research. If the research resulted in class papers, conference presentations, or publications, mention that. If you were an author on a conference presentation or publication, include a copy in your application packet. Discuss how your attitude about research has changed as a result of the experience.

Discuss the areas of psychology that most interest you now. You've already chosen graduate programs to which you'll apply based on the fit between your and the faculty's research interests. For each program, identify faculty whose research interests you and tailor your personal statement so that it will entice faculty with whom you'd like to work. This entails doing your homework first. Read the faculty members' webpages and locate articles they have published. Explain what interests you about the professor's work. State your preferred research interests but also that you are open to studying related areas (if that is true). You are more likely to be accepted at a particular program if you discuss the research interests of several faculty (because not all professors look for new students each year).

Discuss any other relevant experiences. Your statement should also include other relevant experience that pertains to your decision to go to graduate school or makes you qualified for graduate school. Internship experiences and volunteer experiences are included here. Avoid personal emotional self-disclosures. That is, it's not a good idea to explain, for example, that your interest in psychology arose from your own experiences in therapy.

Discuss your goals. Explain what you would like to do after graduation. What kind of career do you envision after receiving your degree? Illustrate how the specific program will prepare you for the career that you desire. Personal details that you include about yourself should be relevant to your ability to be a successful graduate student and reflect maturity, adaptability, and motivation.

Writing as Process

Writing your admissions essay is a process, not a discrete event. The first step involves preparation: gather the information needed to compose the essay that sets you apart from the rest. Exercise 11.4 helps you prepare by examining your personal history. Use the self-assessment and writing techniques that we have discussed throughout this book. Leave yourself plenty of time. Look back over reflective writing, especially your responses to the exercises in Chapter 2. Then sit down and write. Don't censor yourself in any way. Simply write what comes to mind. Begin taking notes on what drives you. Describe your hopes, dreams, and aspirations. What do you hope to gain from graduate study? Given the importance of carefully sharing (and often censoring) information that is *too* personal, much of this writing may not make it into the essay, but your goal at this point is to brainstorm.

EXERCISE 11.4
ADMISSIONS ESSAY PREP

Prepare to write your admissions essay by examining your personal history. Identify as much of your personal history as possible so that you can carefully sift through and sort out events and personal items that will strengthen your essay. Consider the following:

- Hobbies
- Projects you've completed
- Jobs you've held
- Responsibilities
- Personal and academic accomplishments
- Challenges and hurdles that you've overcome
- Life events that motivate your education
- People who have influenced you or motivated you
- Traits, work habits, and attitudes that will ensure your success

After you've considered the above, respond to the following items:

1. Choose three topics that you feel are most appropriate to include in an essay. What would you tell an admissions committee regarding these three? How would it bolster your application?

2. Specifically consider a challenge that you have overcome. Do you think the topic is appropriate for your essay? What story would it tell the admissions committee about you?

3. Can you identify a life event that has motivated your education or a person who has influenced you? Choose one and explain whether you think it is appropriate for your essay. What story would it tell the admissions committee about you? Would it be helpful?

Carefully consider your academic record and personal accomplishments. How do the attitudes, values, and personal qualities that you've listed correspond to these experiences? Try to pair them up. For example, your curiosity and thirst for knowledge may have led you to conduct independent research with a professor. Consider how each pair of attitudes, personal qualities, and experiences shows that you're prepared to excel in graduate school.

Once you have a master list, examine the information. Remember that the information you choose to present can portray you as a positive and upbeat person or as a tired and discouraged student. Think about the image you want to portray, and revise your master list accordingly. Use the revised list as a basis for all of your admissions essays. Remember to be forthcoming about your weaknesses. If your early academic record is weak, explain why. Bright people will be evaluating your application, and they'll spot weaknesses. Don't force them to make assumptions about you. Instead, explain how you've overcome weaknesses. Don't dwell or provide too much backstory. Instead focus on how you've improved.

There's still more information to consider for your admissions essays. Tailor your essay to each program. Show that you're interested and that you've taken the time to learn about each program. If you're truly interested in the graduate programs to which you're applying, take the time to tailor your essay to each program. One size clearly does not fit all.

As you write your essay, occasionally stop to make sure that you're answering the question posed by the admissions committee. Think about the question, the central theme asked, and how it corresponds to your master list of experiences and personal qualities. Some applications offer a string of questions. Pay attention to your responses, and try to avoid being redundant. Remember that this is your chance to present your strengths and really shine. Take advantage of it. Discuss your accomplishments, describe valuable experiences, and emphasize the positive. Show that you're motivated. The committee is composed of professionals who have read hundreds, even thousands, of such statements over the years. Make yours stand out.

Curriculum Vitae

Not all graduate programs request a curriculum vitae, or CV, but it's always a good idea to provide one. A CV is an academic résumé that summarizes and highlights your scholarly experiences, accomplishments, and interests. Unlike a résumé, which is one page in length, a CV contains more information and grows in length throughout your academic career. The goal is to construct and depict your identity as a scholar.

What goes into a CV? The contents of a CV differ across disciplines and expand as one progresses through graduate school. Your CV probably will not have all of these sections yet, and that is to be expected.

- **Contact information.** Include your name, address, phone number, and e-mail addresses for home and office, if applicable. The same rules for professionalism apply (no silly e-mail addresses).

- **Education.** Indicate your college major, type of degree, and the date each degree was (or is expected to be) awarded for each postsecondary school attended. Do not list your high school degree.

- **Academic achievements.** List each award, describe it, and note the granting institution and the date awarded. If you have completed a thesis, list the title and your advisor. If you have only one award (e.g., graduation honors), consider incorporating this information within the education section.

- **Research experience.** List assistantships, practica, and other research experience you have had working under a faculty member. List the institutions at which the research was conducted, the dates during which it was conducted, the topics researched, and any resulting papers or publications.

- **Teaching experience.** If you have teaching experience as a teaching assistant or tutor hired by the university, list it. Most students will not include this section.

- **Professional experience.** List your employment history. List the name of the employer, location, position you held, dates of employment, and a brief description of your duties and responsibilities. The description does not need to be extensive unless it is related to your field of study.

- **Relevant coursework and technical skills.** List statistical and computer programs and data analysis techniques with which you're competent. Consider listing specialized courses. This section is especially relevant for research-oriented doctoral programs. What skills can you "sell" faculty?

- **Grants awarded.** It's unusual for undergraduate students to have been awarded grants, so don't worry if you don't have anything for this section. If you do, include the title of the granting agency, projects for which funds were awarded, and dollar amounts.

- **Publications.** If you have a publication, list it here in APA style. Most students begin writing this section during graduate school. Eventually you'll separate publications into sections for articles, chapters, reports, and other documents.

- **Conference presentations.** List any poster presentations that you've given at conferences. It is unusual for a college student to have presented a paper (talk) at a conference, but if you have, list it here. Similar to the section on publications, separate this category into sections for posters and papers.

- **Research interests.** Briefly summarize your research interests with four to six key descriptors. Admissions committees pay attention to your research interests: Are they consistent with what you say in your essay? How well do they fit faculty interests?

- **Professional affiliations.** List any professional societies with which you're affiliated (for example, Psi Chi, or student affiliation with the American Psychological Association or Association for Psychological Science).

- **References.** Provide names, phone numbers, addresses, and e-mail addresses for your referees. Usually this is left off of CVs but given that you've already requested recommendation letters, include your referees here.

Your CV probably will not include all of these sections. As you organize your CV, remember that the education section typically goes first. Order the other items in your CV as you see fit. Keep in mind that the items toward the beginning receive more attention than those later on. Highlight your most important information first. Table 11.4 illustrates a sample CV, and Exercise 11.5 encourages you to create your own.

EXERCISE 11.5
CREATE YOUR CV

Convert your résumé into a curriculum vitae. Choose the areas that apply to your experiences and convert your résumé into a CV that is two pages or longer.

Letters of Recommendation

Every graduate program requires applicants to submit three letters of recommendation. What is a letter of recommendation? It's a letter, written by a faculty member, that discusses the personal qualities, accomplishments, and experiences that make you unique and perfect for the programs to which you've applied. Don't underestimate the importance of these letters. While your transcript, standardized test scores, and admissions essay are vital components of your application, an excellent letter of recommendation can bolster a weak application. The letter of recommendation gives admissions committees information that isn't found elsewhere in the application.

TABLE 11.4 ● Sample Curriculum Vitae

Doug Smith
123 Appletree Lane
Washington, DC
(555) 555-8978
dougsmith@gmail.com

EDUCATION

BA, Psychology   Expected 2020
New University, Peartown, IL
GPA: 3.78

HONORS THESIS

Title: College Students' Exposure to Community Violence
Mentor: Martha Jones, PhD
      Examined cognitive and psychosocial correlates of college students'
      self-reports of exposure to violence in their neighborhoods and communities.

CONFERENCE PRESENTATIONS

Smith, D., & Jones, M. (2019, August). *College students' exposure to community
      violence.* Poster session presented at the meeting of the American Psychological
      Association, Orlando, FL.

Teach, C., & Smith, D. (2018, March). *Integrating ethics into the introductory psychology
      curriculum.* Poster session presented at the meeting of the Midwestern
      Psychological Association, Indianapolis, IN.

MANUSCRIPT UNDER REVIEW

Teach, C., Grad, S., & Smith, D. (2019). *Teaching psychology students to be ethical.*
      Manuscript submitted to *Teaching of Psychology.*

MANUSCRIPT IN PREPARATION

Smith, D., & Teach, C. (2019). *Psychosocial correlates of exposure to community
      violence.*

RESEARCH EXPERIENCE

Research Assistant   2018–2019

New University, Peartown, IL

Supervisor: Carla Teach, PhD

Project: Integrating Ethics Into the Introductory Psychology Curriculum
      Assisted Dr. Teach in conducting her NSF-sponsored research studying
      ways of teaching ethics in the introductory psychology course. Duties
      included conducting focus groups with introductory psychology students,
      administering surveys, and entering the data into SPSS.

(Continued)

TABLE 11.4 ● (Continued)

Research Assistant   Spring 2017

New University, Peartown, IL

Supervisor: Martha Jones, PhD

Project: Classical Conditioning in College

> Assisted Dr. Jones in conducting a study that compared college students and rats with regard to the number of trials to classically condition college students. Responsibilities included maintaining the animal lab, recording observational data, and entering the data into SPSS.

INTERNSHIPS AND PROFESSIONAL EXPERIENCE

Intern, Center for Violence   2018–2019

Peartree, IL

Supervisor: Dawn Yoke, PhD

> Participated in group sessions with women exposed to domestic violence. Maintained treatment and attendance records.

Peer Tutor, Statistics for the Behavioral Sciences   2017–2018

Department of Psychology

New University, Peartown, IL

Supervisor: Beau Stats, PhD

> Tutored students in statistics. Helped them format SPSS files and choose appropriate analyses.

HONORS AND AWARDS

Willerman Award for Excellence in Psychology   2019

College of Arts and Sciences Dean's List (Fall and   2017–2019
Spring Semester)

Undergraduate Research Travel Award ($200)   2019

Psi Chi   2018

New Psychology Student Award   2017

RESEARCH INTERESTS

Relationship between community violence and adolescent risk taking

Development of interventions to help people exposed to violence

Decision-making in college students

RELEVANT COURSEWORK AND SKILLS

Research Methods

Statistics

Advanced Statistics

Ethics in Animal Research

Ethics in Research With Human Participants

Honors in Developmental Psychology

Advanced Issues in Moral Development

Experience With SPSS

OTHER WORK EXPERIENCE
Assistant Child Care Provider, ChildrenRUs   2018–2019

Hometown, IN

Supervisor: Kitty Richards

> Provided care for children ages 2 to 5. Responsibilities included curriculum planning and communication with parents.

PROFESSIONAL AFFILIATIONS
American Psychological Association, Student Affiliate

Association for Psychological Science, Student Member

REFERENCES
Martha Jones, PhD
Department of Psychology
New University
Peartown, IL
(555) 555-1234
Jones@NewU.edu

Carla Teach, PhD
Department of Psychology
New University
Peartown, IL
(555) 555-5678
Teach@newu.edu

Dawn Yoke, PhD
Center for Violence
Peartown, IL
(555) 555-9101
YokeD@viocenter.org

Nearly all graduate programs accept electronic recommendation letters. Typically after an applicant completes an online application and lists faculty contacts, the listed faculty get an e-mail with a link to a form to submit.

Who Should You Ask?

Deciding who will write your recommendation letters often is difficult. Consider faculty members, administrators, internship or co-operative education supervisors, and employers. But remember that it's faculty who will be reading the recommendation letters (and they've been through graduate school), so faculty tend to write the most credible recommendation letters.

Appleby, Keenan, and Mauer (1999) examined recommendation forms from the application packages of 143 graduate programs in clinical, experimental, and industrial-organizational psychology. The applicant characteristics that faculty were requested to discuss and rank were identified and categorized.

About 40% of the 802 characteristics referred to personal characteristics; about one third referred to acquired skills, and about one quarter referred to intellectual abilities or knowledge. The top characteristics that recommendation forms asked faculty to discuss are listed in Table 11.5. As you can see, grad programs are interested in more than your academic abilities.

The persons you ask to write your letters should meet some of the following criteria:

- Know you well

- Have known you long enough to write with authority

- Know your work

- Describe your work positively

- Have a high opinion of you

- Know where you are applying

- Know your educational and career goals

- Be able to favorably compare you with your peers

- Be well known

- Be able to write a good letter

Keep in mind that no one faculty member will satisfy all of these criteria. Aim for a set of letters covering the range of your skills. Letters should include

TABLE 11.5 ● Top Characteristics Assessed by Recommendation Forms
Motivation
Intellectual/scholarly ability
Research skills
Emotional stability and maturity
Writing skills
Speaking skills
Teaching skills or potential
Ability to work with others
Creativity
Knowledge of area of study

Source: Appleby et al. (1999).

your academic and scholastic skills, research abilities and experiences, and applied experiences (e.g., co-operative education, internships, and related work experience).

When you approach potential recommenders (in person), ask if they know you well enough to write a meaningful letter. Pay attention to their demeanor. If you sense reluctance, thank them and ask someone else. Remember that it is best to ask early in the semester. As the end of the semester approaches, faculty may hesitate because of time constraints.

Help Your Referees

The best thing you can do to ensure that your letters cover all the bases is to provide your referees (those who will write your letters of recommendation) with all the necessary information. Start from scratch, pretending that you have just met them and that they know nothing about you. Give them the info you'd like included. Frame the material, highlighting what you think is most important. Make an appointment to speak with each of your referees. Give them plenty of time, preferably a month at minimum. Ask each professor about his or her preference for receiving material in hard or electronic copy. If he or she chooses a hard copy, provide one folder with all of your background information neatly arranged. If your professor requests an electronic copy, offer it by e-mail or a cloud service such as DropBox. Organize the material into one folder and clearly label each file. Don't make your referee open multiple files to find what he or she needs. What do you include?

- Transcript
- CV
- GRE scores
- Courses you've taken with them and grades that you've earned
- An excellent paper from their class
- Thesis or other capstone paper
- List of research experiences and explanation of each
- Internship and other applied experiences
- Honor societies to which you belong
- Awards you've won
- Relevant work experience
- Professional goals
- Due date for the application
- Copy of the application recommendation forms

Confidentiality

The recommendation forms supplied by graduate programs require you to decide whether to waive or retain your rights to see the recommendations. As you decide whether to retain your rights, remember that confidential letters tend to carry more weight with admissions committees. In addition, many faculty members will not write a recommendation letter unless it is confidential. Other faculty may provide you with a copy of each letter, even if it is confidential. If you are unsure of your decision, discuss it with your referees.

What Do Graduate Admissions Committees Look For?

As you think about what's important to you in a graduate program and how to compile your application, consider the flip side: What do graduate admissions committees look for in applicants? The most important criterion is goodness of fit. Do your interests and abilities match the training opportunities provided by the program? Faculty are interested in the students who will benefit most from their program. In addition, faculty search for students who fit their own research needs and who are interested in their work and will be competent research assistants. Research experience is another important criterion for success in gaining admission to graduate school.

What else matters? GPA, GRE scores, admissions essay, and letters of recommendation factor in, but their relative importance varies, often in ways that surprise students (Table 11.6). GPA and standardized test scores are important to your application but less so and in different ways than students typically believe. Typically the question with regard to grades and test scores is if they are good enough: Do they make the cut? Frequently grades and test scores are used as cutoff criteria to weed applicants out. This is particularly true in graduate programs that receive a large numbers of applicants, such as clinical programs that typically receive hundreds of applications for a handful of slots. The files of applicants who do not make the cut don't make it to the admissions committee and are never viewed. Your GRE scores provide information about how you rank among your peers (that's why it's important to do your best!).

Admissions essays or personal statements are critical to your application because this is your opportunity to speak directly to faculty. Your essay introduces you and your intentions for graduate study. Does your intent match the training the program provides? Do your interests match a faculty member's work? Applicants with excellent qualifications are weeded out if they don't match the program or faculty. In this case, an applicant who is less qualified but shows a good fit to the program can gain admittance.

Letters of recommendation provide an outside perspective on your ability and interests. Your letter writers should have something significant to say about you, your potential to succeed in graduate school, and your match to the program and field. Who you choose matters. Generally speaking, letters

TABLE 11.6 ●	**Important Criteria for Evaluating Applicants (as Rated by Faculty Members)**

1. The fit or match between the applicant's interests and skills and the program's goals

2. Research experience (especially research resulting in publication in a scholarly journal or a paper presented at a professional conference)

3. Interest expressed by one or more members of the selection committee in working with a particular applicant

4. The clarity, focus, and content of the applicant's admission essays

5. Experience as a research assistant

6. Writing skills

7. Knowledge about, and interest in, the program

8. Number of statistics, research methodology, and hard science courses taken

9. Prestige and status of faculty in undergraduate department, especially of those who are writing letters of recommendation

10. Potential for success as judged by interview

11. Honors and merit scholarships

Source: Adapted from "Applicant characteristics valued by graduate programs in psychology," by D. Appleby, J. Keenan, and B. Mauer, *Eye on Psi Chi, 3*(3) p. 39. Copyright 1999 by Psi Chi, the International Honor Society in Psychology.

written by professors known to committee members tend to carry more weight than those written by "unknowns." Letters written by well-known people in the field, if they signify that they know you well and think highly of you, can be very helpful in moving your application toward the top of the list. But a letter that is written by someone who knows you and provides clear examples of your ability and potential is more important.

The Interview

Some programs conduct phone or Skype interviews, some conduct onsite interviews, and some don't interview at all. What happens if you're invited to interview? How do you prepare? What are admission committees looking for? The interview gives admission committees an opportunity to meet candidates and see the people behind the GPAs and GRE scores. It's a chance for them to meet you, to see how you react under pressure, and to assess your verbal and nonverbal communication skills. The interview might range from half an hour with one or two faculty to a full day or more filled with meetings with students and faculty. Activities might range from small group discussions to larger group interviews and even social hours or parties.

Interview Prep

How do you prepare for the interview? Learn as much about the program as possible. Review the program description, department webpage, and faculty webpages. Understand the program's emphasis, and be aware of the faculty's research interests. Consider how you will answer common interview questions, such as the following:

- Why are you interested in our program?

- What do you know about our program?

- What are your career goals?

- Why did you choose a career in psychology?

- What are your research interests? Describe your research experience. Regarding research, what are your strengths and weaknesses?

- What are your academic strengths? What was your favorite course, and why?

- What do you like best about yourself?

- Who would you like to work with? Why?

- Describe the accomplishment you're most proud of.

- If you were to begin a research project now, what would be the topic?

- Describe your theoretical orientation.

- Discuss your experiences in clinical settings. Evaluate your clinical abilities.

- What are your strengths and weaknesses?

- Tell us about yourself.

Consider how you might answer each of these questions, but don't memorize answers. Instead, be prepared to speak extemporaneously so that you're ready for interview curveballs. To gain confidence, practice with family, friends, or in front of the mirror.

Don't forget that this is your opportunity to ask questions too. In fact, admissions committees expect you to ask questions, so prepare some thoughtful questions about the program, faculty, and students. Use this opportunity to learn about the program and whether it meets your needs. During your visit, try to get a sense of the department's emotional climate. What do graduate students call professors (e.g., "doctor" or first name)? Are students competitive with one another? Try to get a sense of whether the atmosphere matches your personality. Is it excessively formal? Would you be happy there?

PRACTICAL TIP
QUICK PRIMER ON WHAT TO WEAR

Neatness is the rule. A suit in a dark color is the easiest and safest way to approach the what-to-wear dilemma. Err on the side of overdressing than underdressing, but don't worry if you don't have a suit. Men can wear slacks, a button-down shirt, and one or more of the following: tie, pullover sweater, or blazer. Women can wear slacks or a skirt with a modest top or a conservative dress. Practical comfortable shoes are the rule for both men and women. Stay away from trends. Minimize accessories. Sometimes applicants who look too pulled together may be perceived as more interested in their appearance than their career. This is unfair, I know; but you want to be remembered for your ideas, not your fashion sense. Also, be sure that your clothes fit and that you don't show unnecessary skin. Finally, pass the smell test. Don't wear perfume, cologne, or stinky products that might distract your interviewers. Some people are sensitive to smells and heavy perfume might unconsciously sway them against you.

Skype Interviews

Many graduate programs are moving toward conducting interviews by video conferencing via platforms like Skype. Skype interviews permit graduate programs to interview students cheaply and efficiently, and perhaps even squeeze more applicant interviews in than they would in real life. An interview for admission to graduate study, regardless of whether it's on campus or by Skype, means that the admissions committee is interested in you and is your opportunity to demonstrate your fit to the faculty and graduate program. Treat a Skype interview like a campus interview: Dress up. Also do a practice run with a friend so that he or she can give you feedback on what you look and sound like (and what's in the background). Skype interviews pose special challenges. Overcome them by considering the following steps.

Be prepared. Plug in your laptop. Do not rely on its battery. Also, have the phone number for the admissions chair at hand in case tech problems arise. Log out of messaging programs, Facebook, and other apps with sound notifications. Mute notifications in Skype. Make sure that you will not be interrupted by any sounds on your computer. Whatever you hear, your interviewers hear.

Attend to visuals. What will the committee see behind you? Pay attention to your background. Posters, signs, photos, and art can detract from your professional demeanor. Don't give professors an opportunity to judge you on anything other than your words and persona. Choose a well-lit space.

Make eye contact. Sit at a desk. The camera should be level with your face. Sit far enough away that your interviewer can see your shoulders. Look into the camera, not at the image on the screen and certainly not at yourself. If you look at the image of your interviewers, you'll appear to be looking away. Challenging as it may seem, try to look at the camera to simulate eye contact.

Be heard. Be sure that the interviewers can hear you. Know where the microphone is located and direct your speech toward it. Speak slowly and pause after the interviewer finishes speaking. Sometimes video lag can interfere with communication, making it harder for interviewers to understand you or making it appear as if you are interrupting them. Eliminate any potential sources of background noise, such as barking dogs, crying children, or insensitive roommates.

Skype interviews share the same purpose as old-fashioned in-person interviews: this is an opportunity for the graduate admissions committee to get to know you. Preparing for the technological aspects of video interviews can sometimes overshadow the basic interview preparation that will help you learn about the program and put your best foot forward. As you prep, don't forget to focus on the content of the interview.

Application Outcomes

When can you expect to hear from programs? Every program has a different method and style of handling admissions. Some programs review applications and make decisions early, and others wait. How quickly applications are reviewed depends on a variety of factors, including the number of applications received, how many people are on the committee, academic demands, conferences, holidays, how well the members of the committee work together, and so on. Programs inform applicants of their status by mid-April, but you might hear from programs earlier.

Wait-List

Applicants who are wait-listed meet the criteria for acceptance but are not first choice. Graduate programs have a limited number of seats. Admissions committees have notified their top choices and have yet to hear if they accept admittance. Applicants who are on the wait-list literally wait to hear if a slot becomes available. If you're on a wait-list, there is a very good chance that you may be admitted.

Acceptance

You've received good news. Congratulations! Most programs inform applicants of their acceptance from March through early April. In most cases, your decision on whether to accept an offer is due by April 15. Once you decline an offer, it can be passed along to someone else who is waiting, so do not hold on to offers that you don't plan on accepting. As soon as you have two offers, decide which to decline. Each time you receive a new offer, decline your least preferred offer so that you're not holding on to offers that you don't intend to accept. How do you decide which to decline? Consider your priorities. Know what you are accepting. Ask about financial aid, housing, and assistantships. Compare acceptance packages to decide among programs. Don't be afraid to do some negotiating, because they've decided that they want you. Help them make it possible for you to accept by explaining any financial limitations that might impede accepting their offer. How do you decline a graduate program? E-mail a letter explaining that you appreciate their interest but will not be accepting their offer. Mail a hard copy of the letter as well.

Dealing With Rejection

What if you're not accepted? It is difficult to be told that you are not among a program's top choices. From a statistical standpoint, you have lots of company; rejection rates are as high as 91% in clinical psychology programs. Most graduate programs must split hairs in making decisions, as there are many highly qualified applicants. As we discussed, it usually comes down to fit, or how well an applicant fits a particular faculty member's needs. Regardless, a rejection letter is difficult, especially if you were invited for an interview. Yet programs often interview two or three times as many students as they can enroll.

Why are students rejected? Most simply, because there aren't enough slots; graduate programs in psychology receive far more applications from qualified candidates than they can accept. Why were you eliminated by a particular program? There is no sure way to tell but in many cases, applicants are rejected because they didn't fit the program. For example, an applicant to a research-scientist program who didn't read the program materials carefully might be rejected for indicating an interest in practicing therapy.

You might find it difficult to inform family, friends, and professors of the bad news, but it is essential that you seek social support. Allow yourself to feel upset and acknowledge your feelings, and then move forward. If you are rejected by every program you've applied to, reassess your goals but don't necessarily give up.

- Did you select schools carefully, paying attention to fit?
- Did you apply to enough programs?
- Did you complete all parts of each application?
- Did you spend enough time on your essays?
- Do you have research experience?
- Do you have field experience?
- Did you know your referees well, and did they have something to write about?
- Were most of your applications to highly competitive programs?

Your answers to these questions may help you determine whether to reapply to a greater range of programs next year or to apply to a master's program instead, as either a first step toward the doctoral degree or an end in itself. Or you may want to choose another career path. If you are firmly committed to attending graduate school in psychology, consider reapplying next year; but don't send out the same application. Use the next few months to improve your academic record, seek research experience, and get to know professors. Apply to a wider range of schools (including "safety" schools), select programs more carefully, and thoroughly research each program.

REFLECTION PROMPTS

Why Graduate School?

Where does graduate education fit into your life? What goals will it help to accomplish? What are the costs of graduate school? It is sometimes said that as one door of opportunity closes, another opens. What door will close when you enter graduate school? What will you miss out on in your years of graduate study?

Where Do I Stand and What Must I Do?

Imagine that you are to apply to graduate school. What steps are entailed? What preparation is needed? Do you have the necessary academic, research, and/or applied experiences? What are your strengths as an applicant? What are your weaknesses? Everyone can improve in some area. Consider ways of addressing the weaknesses in your application.

Recommendation Letters

If I were to ask for letters of recommendation right now, who would I choose? How would I make this choice? Who would be able to speak about my competencies? What can I do to strengthen these relationships? What if I can't identify three faculty? What specific things can I do to establish working relationships with faculty?

• References •

American Psychological Association. (2010). *Publication manual of the American Psychological Association* (6th ed.). Washington, DC: Author.

American Psychological Association. (2013). *APA guidelines for the undergraduate psychology major: Version 2.0.* Washington, DC: Author.

Appleby, D. (1997). *The handbook of psychology.* New York, NY: Longman.

Appleby, D. (1999). Choosing a mentor. *Eye on Psi Chi, 3*(3), 38–39.

Appleby, D. (2001). The covert curriculum: The lifelong learning skills you can learn in college. *Eye on Psi Chi, 5*(3), 28.

Appleby, D. C. (2016). *An online career-exploration resource for psychology majors.* Society for the Teaching of Psychology Office of Teaching Resources in Psychology. Retrieved from http://teachpsych.org/page-1603066

Atkins, D. C., & Christensen, A. (2001). Is professional training worth the bother? A review of the impact of psychotherapy training on client outcome. *Australian Psychologist, 36*(2), 122–130. doi:10.1080/00050060108259644

Appleby, D. C., Keenan, J., & Mauer, B. (1999). Applicant characteristics valued by graduate programs in psychology. *Eye on Psi Chi, 3*(3).

Baumeister, R. F., Campbell, J. D., Krueger, J. I., & Vohs, K. D. (2003). Does high self-esteem cause better performance, interpersonal success, happiness, or healthier lifestyles? *Psychological Science in the Public Interest, 4*(1), 1–44. doi:10.1111/1529-1006.01431

Bottoms, B. L., & Nysse, K. L. (1999). Applying to graduate school: Writing a compelling personal statement. *Eye on Psi Chi, 4*(1), 20–22.

Buskist, W., & Sherburne, T. R. (1996). *Preparing for graduate study in psychology: 101 questions and answers.* Needham Heights, MA: Allyn & Bacon.

Carrier, L. M., Rosen, L. D., Cheever, N. A., & Lim, A. F. (2015). Causes, effects, and practicalities of everyday multitasking. *Developmental Review, 35*, 64–78. doi:10.1016/J.DR.2014.12.005

Corballis, M. C., Lalueza-Fox, C., Orlando, L., Enard, W., & Green, R. (2014). Left brain, right brain: Facts and fantasies. *PLoS Biology, 12*(1), e1001767. doi:10.1371/journal.pbio.1001767

Cranney, J., Botwood, L., & Morris, S. (2012). *National standards for psychological literacy and global citizenship: Outcomes of undergraduate psychology education.*

Retrieved from https://groups.psychology.org.au/Assets/Files/Cranney_NTF_Final_Report_231112_Final_pdf.pdf

Doran, J. M., Kraha, A., Marks, L. R., Ameen, E. J., & El-Ghoroury, N. H. (2016). Graduate debt in psychology: A quantitative analysis. *Training and Education in Professional Psychology, 10*(1), 3–13. doi:10.1037/tep0000112

Dweck, C. S. (2017). The journey to children's mindsets—and beyond. *Child Development Perspectives, 11*(2), 139–144. doi:10.1111/cdep.12225

Dweck, C. S., Walton, G. M., & Cohen, G. L. (2011). *Academic tenacity: Mindsets and skills that promote long-term learning.* Retrieved from https://ed.stanford.edu/sites/default/files/manual/dweck-walton-cohen-2014.pdf

Educational Testing Service. (2017). *GRE Psychology subject test (for test takers).* Retrieved from https://www.ets.org/gre/subject/about/content/psychology

Educational Testing Service. (2018). *GRE Graduate Record Examinations guide to the use of scores: Communicating with the GRE program.* Retrieved from https://www.ets.org/s/gre/pdf/gre_guide.pdf

Fretz, B. R. (1976). Finding careers with a bachelor's degree in psychology. *Psi Chi Newsletter, 2,* 5–9.

Gazzaniga, M. S. (1998). The split brain revisited. *Scientific American, 279*(1), 50–55.

Golding, J. M., Lippert, A. M., & Malik, S. E. (2018). Using the Internet to facilitate career choices in psychology-related fields. *Teaching of Psychology, 45*(1), 60–66. doi:10.1177/0098628317745450

Goldstein, R. (2010). Major developments in undergraduate psychology. *Observer, 23*(3).

Greene, S., & Martel, M. C. L. (2014). *The ultimate job hunter's guidebook.* Stamford, CT: Cengage.

Grover, S. F. (2006). Undergraduate research: Getting involved and getting into graduate school (a student's perspective). *Eye on Psi Chi, 11*(1), 18–20.

Hirshkowitz, M., Whiton, K., Albert, S. M., Alessi, C., Bruni, O., DonCarlos, L., . . . Adams Hillard, P. J. (2015). National Sleep Foundation's sleep time duration recommendations: Methodology and results summary. *Sleep Health, 1*(1), 40–43. doi:10.1016/J.SLEH.2014.12.010

Holland, J. L. (1959). A theory of vocational choice. *Journal of Counseling Psychology, 6,* 35–45.

Holland, J. L. (1966). A psychological classification scheme for vocations and major fields. *Journal of Counseling Psychology, 13*(3), 278–288. doi:10.1037/h0023725

Holland, J. L. (1997). *Making vocational choices: A theory of vocational personalities and work environments* (3rd ed.). Odessa, FL: Psychological Assessment Resources.

Johnston, S. M. (2014). *The career adventure: Your guide to personal assessment, career exploration, and decision making* (5th ed.). Upper Saddle River, NJ: Pearson College Division.

Julian, T. (2012). *Work-life earnings by field of degree and occupation for people with a bachelor's degree: 2011*. American Community Survey Brief ACSBR/11-04. Washington, DC: U.S. Census Bureau.

Keith-Spiegel, P., & Wiederman, M. W. (2000). *The complete guide to graduate school admission: Psychology, counseling, and related professions*. Mahwah, NJ: Erlbaum.

Kohout, J., & Wicherski, M. (2010). *2011 graduate study in psychology*. Washington, DC: American Psychological Association.

Landmann, N., Kuhn, M., Maier, J.-G., Spiegelhalder, K., Baglioni, C., Frase, L., . . . Nissen, C. (2015). REM sleep and memory reorganization: Potential relevance for psychiatry and psychotherapy. *Neurobiology of Learning and Memory, 122*, 28–40. doi:10.1016/J.NLM.2015.01.004

Landrum, E. (2008). Evaluating the undergraduate research assistantship experience. *Eye on Psi Chi, 12*(3).

Landrum, E., & Davis, S. (2014). *The psychology major: Career options and strategies for success*. Upper Saddle River, NJ: Prentice Hall.

Landrum, R. E. (2009). *Finding jobs with a psychology bachelor's degree: Expert advice for launching your career*. Washington, DC: American Psychological Association.

Lewis, P., & Rivkin, D. (1999). *O*NET Interest Profiler: Reliability, validity, and self-scoring*. Raleigh, NC: O*NET Resource Center.

Lin, L., Christidis, P., & Stamm, K. (2017a). *2013 salaries in psychology*. Washington, DC: American Psychological Association Center for Workforce Studies. Retrieved from http://www.apa.org/workforce/publications/2013-salaries/index.aspx

Lin, L., Christidis, P., & Stamm, K. (2017b). *2015 salaries in psychology*. Washington, DC: American Psychological Association Center for Workforce Studies. Retrieved from http://www.apa.org/workforce/publications/2015-salaries/index.aspx

McFall, R. M. (2006). Doctoral training in clinical psychology. *Annual Review of Clinical Psychology, 2*(1), 21–49. doi:10.1146/annurev.clinpsy.2.022305.095245

McGovern, T. V., Corey, L., Cranney, J., Dixon, W. E., Holmes, J. D., Kuebli, J. E., . . . Walker, S. J. (2010). Psychologically literate citizens. In D. F. Halpern (Ed.), *Undergraduate education in psychology: A blueprint for the future of the discipline.* (pp. 9–27). Washington, DC: American Psychological Association. doi:10.1037/12063-001

McGovern, T. V., Furumoto, L., Halpern, D. F., Kimble, G. A., & McKeachie, W. J. (1991). Liberal education, study in depth, and the arts and sciences major: Psychology. *American Psychologist, 46*(6), 598–605.

Michalski, D. S., Cope, C., & Fowler, G. A. (2017). *Summary report, graduate study in psychology 2018: Admissions, applications and acceptances*. Washington, DC: American Psychological Association.

Michalski, D. S., Kohout, J., Wicherski, M., & Hart, B. (2011). *2009 doctorate employment survey*. Washington, DC: American Psychological Association Center for Workforce Studies.

Michigan State University Career Services Network. (n.d.). *Action verbs*. Retrieved from http://careernetwork.msu.edu/resources-tools/resumes/action-verbs.html

Monsell, S. (2003). Task switching. *Trends in Cognitive Sciences, 7*(3), 134–140. doi:10.1016/S1364-6613(03)00028-7

Mueller, P. A., & Oppenheimer, D. M. (2014). The pen is mightier than the keyboard: Advantages of longhand over laptop note taking. *Psychological Science, 25*(6), 1159–1168. doi:10.1177/0956797614524581

Myers, I. B., McCaulley, M. H., Quenk, N. L., & Hammer, A. L. (1998). *MBTI manual: A guide to the development and use of the Myers-Briggs type indicator* (3rd ed.). Palo Alto, CA: Consulting Psychologists Press.

National Association of Colleges and Employers. (2017). *Average starting salary for class of 2016 held steady*. Retrieved from https://www.naceweb.org/job-market/compensation/average-starting-salary-for-class-of-2016-held-steady/

National Association of Colleges and Employers. (2018). *Job outlook 2018*. Washington, DC: Author.

National Center for Education Statistics. (2017a). Average graduate tuition and required fees in degree-granting postsecondary institutions, by control of institution and percentile of charges: 1989-90 through 2015-16. *Digest of Education Statistics*. Retrieved from https://nces.ed.gov/programs/digest/d16/tables/dt16_330.50.asp?current=yes

National Center for Education Statistics. (2017b). *Digest of Education Statistics, 2017*. Retrieved from https://nces.ed.gov/programs/digest/2017menu_tables.asp

National Center for Education Statistics. (2017c). *Undergraduate retention and graduation rates: Indicator April (2017)*. Retrieved from https://nces.ed.gov/programs/coe/indicator_ctr.asp

National Center for Education Statistics. (2018). *Employment outcomes of bachelor's degree recipients: The condition of education 2018*. Retrieved from https://nces.ed.gov/pubsearch/pubsinfo.asp?pubid=2018144

Patterson, M. C. (2017). A naturalistic investigation of media multitasking while studying and the effects on exam performance. *Teaching of Psychology, 44*(1), 51–57. doi:10.1177/0098628316677913

Pittenger, D. J. (2005). Cautionary comments regarding the Myers-Briggs type indicator. *Consulting Psychology Journal: Practice and Research, 57*(3), 210–221. doi:10.1037/1065-9293.57.3.210

Powell, J. L. (2000). Creative outlets for student research or what do I do now that my study is completed? *Eye on Psi Chi, 4*(2), 28–29.

Richardson, M., Abraham, C., & Bond, R. (2012). Psychological correlates of university students' academic performance: A systematic review and meta-analysis. *Psychological Bulletin, 138*(2), 353–387. doi:10.1037/a0026838

Robinson, F. (1970). *Effective study* (4th ed.). New York, NY: Harper & Row.

Roche, M. W. (2010). *Why choose the liberal arts?* Notre Dame, IN: University of Notre Dame Press.

Rotter, J. B. (1990). Internal versus external control of reinforcement: A case history of a variable. *American Psychologist, 45*(4), 489–493. doi:10.1037/0003-066X.45.4.489

Ruff, E. A., Reardon, R. C., & Bertoch, S. C. (2007). *Technical Report 47: Creating a research database on Holland's theory and practical tools.* Tallahassee, FL: Florida State University Center for the Study of Technology in Counseling and Career Development. Retrieved from https://career.fsu.edu/sites/g/files/upcbnu746/files/files/tech-center/technical-reports/TechRept_47_200711.pdf

Ryan, R., & Deci, E. (2000). Intrinsic and extrinsic motivations: Classic definitions and new directions. *Contemporary Educational Psychology, 25*(1), 54–67. doi:10.1006/ceps.1999.1020

Salm, L. (2017). *70% of employers are snooping candidates' social media profiles.* Retrieved from https://www.careerbuilder.com/advice/social-media-survey-2017

Sana, F., Weston, T., & Cepeda, N. J. (2013). Laptop multitasking hinders classroom learning for both users and nearby peers. *Computers & Education, 62*, 24–31. doi:10.1016/J.COMPEDU.2012.10.003

Sanburn, J. (2012). How to make your resume last longer than 6 seconds. *Time.* Retrieved from http://business.time.com/2012/04/13/how-to-make-your-resume-last-longer-than-6-seconds/

Scott, J. M., Koch, R. E., Scott, G. M., & Garrison, S. M. (1999). *The psychology student writer's manual.* Upper Saddle River, NJ: Prentice Hall.

Seligman, M. E. (1995). The effectiveness of psychotherapy: The *Consumer Reports* study. *American Psychologist, 50*(12), 965–974. doi:10.1037/0003-066X.50.12.965

Singleton, D., Tate, A. C., & Kohout, J. L. (2003). *2002 master's, specialist's, and related degrees employment summary.* Washington, DC: American Psychological Association Center for Workforce Studies.

Sternberg, R. J., & Sternberg, K. (2017). *The psychologist's companion for undergraduates: A guide to success for college students.* Cambridge, UK: Cambridge University Press.

Strong, E. K., Jr., Donnay, D. A. C., Morris, M. L., Schaubhut, N. A., & Thompson, R. (2004). *Strong Interest Inventory* (Rev. ed.). Mountain View, CA: Consulting Psychologists Press.

Taylor, G., Jungert, T., Mageau, G. A., Schattke, K., Dedic, H., Rosenfield, S., & Koestner, R. (2014). A self-determination theory approach to predicting school achievement over time: The unique role of intrinsic motivation. *Contemporary Educational Psychology, 39*(4), 342–358. doi:10.1016/J.CEDPSYCH.2014.08.002

Uncapher, M. R., Lin, L., Rosen, L. D., Kirkorian, H. L., Baron, N. S., Bailey, K., . . . Wagner, A. D. (2017). Media multitasking and cognitive, psychological, neural, and learning differences. *Pediatrics, 140*(Suppl 2), S62–S66. doi:10.1542/peds.2016-1758D

Walfish, S., & Moreira, J. C. (2005). Relative weighting of admission variables in marriage and family therapy graduate programs. *American Journal of Family Therapy, 33*(5), 395–402. doi:10.1080/01926180500274542

Wong, L. (2015). *Essential study skills*. Stamford, CT: Cengage.

Yale University Office of Career Strategy. (n.d.). *Resume action verbs*. Retrieved from https://ocs.yale.edu/sites/default/files/files/2016_Resume_Action_Verbs.pdf

Zureick, A. H., Burk-Rafel, J., Purkiss, J. A., & Hortsch, M. (2018). The interrupted learner: How distractions during live and video lectures influence learning outcomes. *Anatomical Sciences Education, 11*(4), 366–376. doi:10.1002/ase.1754

• Index •